# Contemporary Post-Production



*Contemporary Post-Production* is an engaging and insightful guide through the often fraught and stressful phase of post-production. It brings the art and craft of editing to life, describes contemporary workflows, and demonstrates how to break the post-production process into manageable phases. It also explores editing approaches used by five award-winning filmmakers across fiction films, documentaries, and interactive works.

This text addresses key questions about the editor's role in shaping a story, the roles of various members of the post-production team, when and how to delegate to specialists, and how to engage in the most efficient and constructive conversations with them. Another key focus is on career pathways, with each featured filmmaker sharing how they broke into the editing field and offering advice on building a lasting career.

The featured filmmakers reflect a diversity of life experiences and work, and their interviews shed light on the people behind the process. They provide guidance on cutting-edge tools, such as the most essential software to know, how they incorporate GenAI into their work, and how they utilize remote workflows. A brief look at the past offers valuable context for understanding the future, including a section on key innovators in film history. Examples include Alice Guy-Blaché's pioneering use of sync sound and Oscar Micheaux's re-editing techniques to navigate censorship – stories that illustrate past innovations and continue to inspire today's filmmakers to push creative and technical boundaries.

Each technical chapter includes class activities and exercises to help readers practice specific skills. Additional resources provide ample opportunities for continued learning.

This book serves as an invaluable resource for students in post-production courses and anyone looking to enter the industry or refine their skills.

**Melanie La Rosa** is an award-winning filmmaker, film professor, and advocate for diversity in media. A 2022 Public Voices Fellow on the Climate Crisis with the OpEd Project and Yale Program on Climate Change Communication, her films have screened internationally and broadcast on PBS. Her work has won funding from NYSCA, Queens Council on the Arts, Brooklyn Arts Council, and Solutions Journalism Network. Her films include "How To Power A City," "The Poetry Deal: a Film with Diane DiPrima," and "Sir: Just A Normal Guy." Her articles appear in *World War Zero, The Progressive*, and *Gateway Journalism Review*, among other publications.

# Contemporary Post-Production

## Create, Cut, Collaborate, Color, Deliver

**Melanie La Rosa**

Routledge
Taylor & Francis Group
NEW YORK AND LONDON

Designed cover image credit: Getty Images

First published 2025
by Routledge
605 Third Avenue, New York, NY 10158

and by Routledge
4 Park Square, Milton Park, Abingdon, Oxon, OX14 4RN

*Routledge is an imprint of the Taylor & Francis Group, an informa business*



ISBN: 978-1-032-75270-9 (hbk)
ISBN: 978-1-032-64003-7 (pbk)
ISBN: 978-1-003-47315-2 (ebk)

DOI: 10.4324/9781003473152

Typeset in Times New Roman
by SPi Technologies India Pvt Ltd (Straive)

Access the Support Material: www.melanielarosa.com/contemporarypost and www.routledge.com/9781032640037

# Contents

**Full Interviews (on the Associated Website as Audio Stories with Transcripts)**



Associated website: www.melanielarosa.com/contemporarypost; and on the publisher's website: www.routledge.com/9781032640037

# Acknowledgments

I would like to express deep appreciation to everyone who helped bring this book to life. With a design built on the candid and thoughtful sharing of experiences by many editors and post-production teams, I am grateful to the filmmakers who generously gave their time and energy for interviews: Aashish Kumar, Allie Sultan, Carla Gutiérrez, Ryan Rehnborg, and Zeb Achonu. These thoughtful and talented storytellers are exemplary in how they use film and media to share, connect, excite, inform, and inspire. Their immediate responses to my invitation to participate show a deep commitment to helping others find a way to their own careers in film.

I would like to extend my sincere gratitude to:

Everyone who provided photographs to bring the interviews to life, thank you for sharing your work and the behind-the-scenes moments: Aashish Kumar, Adrián Gutiérrez, Alexa Ramirez, Allie Sultan, Carla Gutiérrez, Doc Hearts, Katia Maguire, Laura Pilloni, Paula Ospina, Renata Galindo, Ryan Rehnborg, Together Films, Víctor Hernández Stumpfhauser, Zeb Achonu, and the team of the "Incognita" series and their wonderful Instagram account.

The *Women Film Pioneers Project*, where I first learned about Alice Guy-Blaché and hundreds of other women filmmakers, and realized that the film history I had been taught had massive gaps in it. This wonderful digital archive inspired me to create something of my own to help set the record just a bit more straight.

The filmmaking and post-production team at Routledge/Taylor & Francis, and especially to commissioning editor Daniel Kershaw, who has collaborated with me from the initial concept I shared with him at a film professor's conference in Savannah, Georgia, through the proposal process and numerous revisions, all the way to the completion of the final manuscript. And also to Danielle Zarfati and the team skillfully assembling a collection of chapters into a fully realized book.

Former and current students at Pace University, including graduate student Kathryn Capobianco for providing student-perspective feedback on a draft of the manuscript and undergraduate student Chase Johnson, who are part of the team ensuring that this book reaches its audience.

The peer reviewers whose insight and feedback helped shape the directions of this book at early stages and at the full manuscript stage.

The Pace University Office of the Provost for their generous support of my sabbatical, which made the writing of this book possible, and to the Kenan Scholarly Research Fund for their financial assistance with related costs.

And to every reader who picks up this book, I'm grateful for your curiosity, attention, and desire to be part of the wonderful process of making films.

# 1 Introduction

Do you love stories? If you are reading this book, and in a film class, the answer is probably yes. Who doesn't love stories, after all? They take us on adventures, show us fantastical worlds, and imbue us with the sights, sounds, and energy of superheroes and super-heroines. They take us on romantic escapes, show us phenomenal worlds, and even (safely) take us to dark and dangerous places.

And now, you, you lucky filmmaker, are going to be part of that world.

Thank you for picking up this book and for your desire to help share the world's stories through film. Since people drew pictures on the walls of caves, stories have been central to culture. While technology, types of stories, actors starring in films, and nearly every other aspect of filmmaking has changed, one thing is eternal: stories draw people together. We enjoy watching movies together because it is a common shared experience. They provide a way to experience adventures and joys together, or to feel fear and chills that wrap themselves up by the end. (Or not – and we can bond over still being freaked out on Monday by a weekend of horror movie binging!) Our love of stories binds us together. Movies give us a way to talk about things we did not even know we wanted to talk about. They give shape to emotions we did not even know we were feeling. Stories are mirrors we hold up to our families, our friends, our selves. To see our challenges, successes, and desires. *As movies evolve and we find new ways to tell stories, new aesthetics and new technology also enable more people to share their perspectives, and [...we can learn...]* we can learn more about each other and about ourselves.

Your desire to be a storyteller is important. Without new generations of storytellers to push the evolution of how films and culture intertwine, we will lose that magic of discovery.

I am a film professor, documentary filmmaker, and author. Editing and directing are my main roles in filmmaking, although I have also done freelance camerawork, been a producer, and am a DaVinci Resolve certified color correction educator. I have taught college undergraduate and graduate courses on all aspects of filmmaking, primarily editing, since 2002.

DOI: 10.4324/9781003473152-1

I cut my first student films on reel-to-reel editing systems, and once even cut a film on Super8 celluloid, sticking it together with glue and hoping it would work. Trust me, using software is much better. When desktop computers hit the market, way back in 1998, I was interning for an Emmy-award-winning director in Cupertino. She had hired an editor to teach me and the other intern how to use this new software called Final Cut Pro, which was in its beta stage. The editor taught us, and it was literally a life-changing experience for me. We received a free version of this amazing new product. I was off and running. I also happened to be editing my first documentary, and with these new technological resources, I was able to do it myself at home. I finished a 52-minute film, sent it out to film festivals, and two years later it had been screened around the world, won awards, found distribution, and I found my way to a graduate film program.

I wanted to write this book for people like you, who want to have that same experience. Ask anyone in film who is older than 30 about how fast technology, especially software, changes. It is non-stop technological innovation from the earliest days of filmmaking. My very first film classes, as an undergraduate, were using a reel-to-reel system and filming on VHS cameras. Now, I teach students using 4K and 6K cameras, and we edit on the three most common editing software programs. New tools like remote editing and artificial intelligence (AI) are becoming more common in filmmaking. Even with all the complications and legal and ethical uncertainties of AI, it is quickly finding a home to perform certain parts of filmmaking. In this book, you will explore a wide range of contemporary tools and classic approaches. Consider this a buffet of film tools and techniques and can learn their pros and cons. Very few productions or editors will need to use every tool on every film, and yet each one is perfect for something.

This book also looks back into film history, to explore the filmmakers in the very first days of cinema. In the earliest days of filmmaking, there was a freedom that can only be compared to the earliest days of YouTube and other social media. No one really knew exactly how they wanted to use this exciting new invention of the cinematic camera, but they kept trying and found ways to engage with audiences. Perhaps more important than what was created is who created it. The earliest filmmakers include all sorts of people, most notably a woman who is widely recognized as being the first narrative director, and an African-American filmmaker who challenged racist tropes in other mainstream films. Contemporary filmmaking is only just starting to collect their works and restore a more complete history. These are enormous stories, and I could only offer some small highlights in this text. But, these highlights are meant to help you find out more about what has always worked in storytelling, even when everything else has changed, and who figured out how to do it.

In your other classes and professional or creative roles, you no doubt learned how to get a film "in the can." Now, this book will help you navigate the footage out of the can, into your computer, and all the way through to delivery. It discusses how you cut your footage, create a soundscape, shape footage into scenes, and scenes into a powerful film, color it, mix it, and get it onto the screen(s) of your choice.

Something like this would have been a beacon of guidance, insight, and optimism for me when I was starting out. I hope that it serves that purpose for you.

### What Each Section Covers

- **Part 1** is about the daily practices, contemporary procedures, and skill-sets for contemporary post teams and editors. It also covers the massive area of "workflow," which is deceptively simple. As its name indicates, it is the process by which the work flows. The order of tasks, how you create a strong foundation before taking on the sometimes-chaotic story edit, and what you do when you have achieved picture lock But workflow is anything but simple. All experienced professionals know that it is the make-or-break crux of an excellent film. "Workflow" means everything from which specialist(s) need to be in the budget to how the audio and video files are captured and logged, when the editor receives dailies, and the time allocated for producers to provide creative input and the post-production team to make revisions. Workflow encompasses every aspect of filmmaking.
- Workflow now also extends to remote filmmaking, which has been possible for years but was clunky and error-prone; however, in recent years it has become enormously smoother. Tools for remote workflows will only improve, and as they do the film industry will likely see huge shifts in who works on post-production teams. If people do not need to be in one place to edit, what does that mean for traditional film hub cities like New York, Los Angeles, Toronto, Vancouver, Sydney, and London, which have very high costs of living that are hard to keep up with when film budgets are shrinking? What does it mean for cities like Mumbai, Sofia, Warsaw, Mexico City, and other cities with strong film industries, lower costs of living, and excellent film schools and studios? Will remote productions foster new international collaborations? Will people who want to work in production be able to live wherever they want and still work for the biggest media and film names in the world? While this book certainly does not attempt to predict the future, it does briefly look at how contemporary film practices have evolved and poses these questions, so that readers can understand the direction of current trends in the industry.
- **Part 2** is about creative aesthetics in several types of films and media products. It includes interviews with four editors and directors, each

working in a different part of the film industry, and takes a deep look at a signature project for each.

- **Part 3** is about the industry. Who today's editors are, who yesterday's editors were, and how techniques that we take as commonplace today were begun. Why include a look at the past in a book called *Contemporary Post-Production*? Because we learn from the past, and the facts of the past indicate directions to take in the future. And because the first people to do anything – film, music, sports, business – become role models and case studies for all practitioners. If filmmaking's past is inaccurately portrayed and full of enormous gaps in its founding members, what kind of future can we expect? One that is also full of gaps?
- Film students deserve to learn from the real founders of filmmaking, and while there is much more that needs to be done to teach a full film history, this section attempts to include key people as a way to scratch the surface. It is not everything, but it is something. Looking back we can see, by comparison, the massive shifts in our technology, process, timeframes, and abilities and filmmakers. We can also see what has never changed: the drive, motivation, and self-confidence that are required to find a sustainable career in film. Very few industries evolve as rapidly as media and film, and neither do other industries evolve as deeply, with their technologies, basic form, and leadership all regularly refreshing and changing. Yet at its core, film has never changed. Since its earliest days it has been about two things. The first, telling stories that connect people across time, cultures, and wide geographies. The second, applying new image and sound technologies to enliven these collective stories, and immerse audiences in the experience of a story. There is a third through-line to filmmaking: who was allowed to tell stories – or allowed themselves to make films – and which stories they chose to share, with which audiences. All of these are still the forces that govern the film industry today.
- **Part 4** consists of class exercises, charts, tables, guides, and worksheets that can guide you through your own edit. These are also available for download on the websites associated with this book.

Off you go!

# 2 The Who, What, and Why for This Book

*Contemporary Post-Production* is inclusive and written for everyone. It uses interviews with four professional editors as contemporary case study and reflects the current realities of working on a film, television show, or online channel. It is designed to be a beneficial guide for everyone from film students learning overall methods to film directors learning new editing techniques and professionals upgrading their skills.

There is a strong need for a post-production text that focuses on time-tested, universal editing techniques that can be done in any type of software, and also a text that looks at how the work in a project flows from one person to another. Often, new editors are part of a team and in the hurry and pressure of an editing schedule they are instructed to do one task, such as name and organize files, create selects reels, or edit the dialog. In these situations, there is little time to learn an overview of the editing process.

You will find many stories of creative, passionate visions coming to life in these chapters, and I hope that they inspire you to find your own creative, passionate voice and express it in film. You will also find an equal amount of guidance on planning and management, as those are other core themes in this book. Try not to skip the planning and management sections and only read the creative story sections, as the heart of any creative activity lies in being able to access the material you need to make the vision come to life. Think of a painter carefully laying out their paints before working on their canvas, or a band setting up the stage before a performance. If the paints are not in the right place or easy to access, the painter cannot work as fast. If the band's setup is messy or someone forgot to plug an instrument in, they might trip over each other, the music will not be balanced, and some instruments might not work. Filmmaking and media production are the same: you need to have your materials arranged carefully so that you can hit a creative flow and edit your film with a painter's elegance and a band's harmony.

Elegance and harmony in editing? The post-production phase is notorious for being stressful, full of deadlines, managing lost files or corrupted media assets, and just plain time-consuming and laborious. But, there are also

DOI: 10.4324/9781003473152-2

moments of pure magic in editing, like when everything lines up and the story just clicks together. There are also more tools than ever to help with your edit and simply more ways to be an editor or work in post-production. Filmmaking is both highly collaborative and highly individualistic at the same time. By design, we work with many other people, but by occupation many editors and post professionals work alone. The more that the people entering this field start to understand the process, and make informed choices about how they want their editing or post phase to go, the better the phase will become. Managing and planning your post-production phase is a large part of that. Many editors hit snags at the near-final point of their project, and realize that if they had done some aspect of their organization differently from the beginning, they would have not hit this snag. Had they planned, they would have saved time, headaches, and money. The snags can be as simple as how the files are organized or named to as complex as how an entire project timeline is organized or how feedback and notes are incorporated into the process. And those are just the technical and practical aspects.

Snags also emerge in structuring the story and from differences in creative opinions. A particularly thorny snag is the discouragement and disappointment that comes from the final cut seemingly not matching up to the picture in the mind of the producer, director, editor, or others on the post-production team. Filmmaking is an emotional field and all of those creative and passionate stories are fueled by emotion. So it is natural and a bit expected for emotions to come up during editing phases, which can include disappointment along with many other emotions like delight and surprise. The fact often is that the post-production team may have made an excellent film. You, as the editor, may have made an excellent film. Creative disappointments should be understood as the hidden snags that can affect the entire post-production team, probably more than other phases of filmmaking as the post team is the one shepherding the film into life. By ensuring your film is designed as the best possible, planning your post process, understanding and using the widest array of tools possible, including how and when to collaborate, you can navigate the editing team to a sense of accomplishment about having created a unique new story.

This book also aims to bring to light some people whose contributions to the film industry deserve more attention. Many people are told that groups they might identify with – women, people of color, immigrants, LGBTQI folks, and many other demographics – do not have a history of success in film. This is completely untrue, and film historians are starting to pull the evidence out of dusty archives and show that the world's first filmmakers were from all of these groups. It is dangerous to perpetuate the myths that there were no Black filmmakers until Spike Lee or John Singleton came along, or no women leading films until Kathryn Bigelow won an Oscar. It devalues the entire field. Archives have compiled the work of early filmmakers – women, people of color, LGBTQI, and immigrants – from the

US and around the world. Their films were not always preserved but their stories are now more available, and today's filmmakers need to learn about their place as leaders of this industry. These are relatively new developments, and sorely needed in an industry that prides itself on being a bearer of culture, and a place where stories both innovate the way we see ourselves and preserve the values of our cultures.

While the section in this book only looks at filmmaking history in the US, there also needs to be similar initiatives in other countries to ensure that today's filmmakers learn from all the original filmmakers. In post-production women have not only been editors, they have created some of the tools and techniques we still use today. As filmmaking technologies expand, we also need to expand our understanding of its origins and add the right people to textbooks and other written materials.

Even if you do not identify with one of these groups, why would anyone not want to learn about who really created the field in its earliest days? That is how we will start to see the magic come alive, and why this art, based on a combination of illusion, identification, and reality, is so powerful. That is how we will continue to evolve the field. Looking at history gives us all more precedents and role models than ever before. While the space in this text for history is somewhat limited, it is a start. There are also several additional resources listed in the appendixes for those who would like to continue learning who the early filmmakers were. I offer a small handful of examples in the pages of this book, and there are many, many more out there. Perhaps reading these chapters will inspire you to do your own research and add to the knowledge of the entire field.

## The Industry

This book was conceived as a way to fill a gap in the resources for how to learn filmmaking. There are hundreds of excellent books about filmmaking: from post-production, which is what this book covers, to specialized texts on cinematography, producing, writing, visual effects, casting, and many other specialities, as well as books that cover introductions to filmmaking, field production, and careers in the film and media industry. This volume was created to fill a perceived gap in this literature: there are no books that look at workflow and contemporary editing, and serve as a software-agnostic guides to the challenging process of editing a film.

After teaching editing and filmmaking for over 20 years, I realized that students generally neither purchase nor read technical books, despite having assignments based on them; making free copies available to classes, using the book during class and linking it to lessons, students simply would not pick up a technical manual. But that did not mean they were not learning, nor did it mean they were not reading. It simply means that watching an online video about a technical skill is much easier than reading a book. And that for learning editing software, online videos are far superior to books. Software changes constantly. Upgrades and new tools are impossible to keep up with in a publishing timeframe. And learning the tools of editing software is best done by watching someone else do it. Ask anyone who learned to use editing software with a printed manual and then through an online video – there is no comparison. So, why write another book about software?

In planning this guide, I asked myself what I saw students really learning when they learned post-production. What was the most important thing, because if it really was just software they would not need to be in a class. I realized they were learning a process. It seemed that a guide to that process would be a valuable addition to the already-existing body of resources on post-production, as would a guide that shared stories of exceptional filmmakers who are working in contemporary filmmaking.

Technical skills are only one aspect of editing, and while technical skills clearly are crucial, if that is all that was required then everyone would finish their films ahead of deadline, they would all be magnificently paced and timed, and the entire post-production crew would feel like a million dollars at the end of an edit session. Sadly, that is not the case. Routinely, in both my teaching and professional life, I have found that the main challenges to learning editing (or filmmaking in general) are not technical but are much broader and have to do with goals, a place in the industry, confidence, and getting good experience. A particular challenge is knowing how to navigate through the steps of a project, and finish on time and as planned. In the industry this is called "workflow." Another challenge is confidence: believing that you will learn the skills, develop your talents, and that by practicing your skills you will constantly improve and find a way to a great career. Knowing how to get a first job is important, and how to build a network from that job, so it can lead to another job, then another. Everything else: technical skill development, creativity, time management, and knowing many different types of software, are all extremely important. But without an underlying confidence and sense of purpose, those are disconnected and a bit fragmented.

This book is based on 20 years of teaching students editing. And, in all of those 20 years, seeing only two or three students who simply could not, would not, or just did not learn to edit. At the beginning of my semesters and workshops, I make a point to ask for a show of hands on experience level. "Who has editing experience of any kind, even using the most rudimentary phone and computer apps?" "Who has experience with the professional software we learn in class?" "Who has never touched an editing system of any kind, not even once?" Always, the first category has the most hands. The second category – having used professional software – used to have only one or two per semester but it grows every semester and now as many as half the students raise their hands. The third category – never having touched any type of editing software at all – used to be sizable but every year it shrinks a bit. No matter what experience level they start with, all these students learn to become at least proficient editors. Computers and software are easier than ever to learn. Many students arrive in college classes having learned Avid or Adobe in high school. Some participated in high school broadcasting programs or film clubs. Others just like software and learned on their own. It has become clear that teaching software is only one aspect of teaching editing and post-production, but there is so much more to this process. My courses, and this book, also cover workflow, project management, collaboration, new tools, understanding the field of editing, and learning about the day-to-day lives of contemporary editors, leading to students seeing the whole forest and learning to navigate their own paths.

This book is also for people in professional film roles who have had a chance to learn a bit and want to expand their skills. Maybe they came to their role through a different route than film school, and never had a chance to step back and learn from a broader perspective. Maybe they have been in their role for quite some time, and want to refresh their knowledge. Maybe they want to learn about the careers of contemporary editors. In the appendixes, there are many resources – other books, podcasts, technical resources – for those who seek to develop a robust professional career and want to continue learning.

In the last few years, two highly influential and external forces on filmmaking were the social movements #MeToo and #OscarsSoWhite. The first highlighted the meaningful inclusion of women in the film world, and their right to come to a workplace free from sexual harassment. The second highlighted the lack of diversity and BIPOC filmmakers, particularly at the highest ranks and on the largest budgeted productions. These social movements have driven a degree of much-needed change. They also elevated the need to create structures to continue to make this wonderful, creative industry that so many love more open, welcoming, and diverse. And to acknowledge the talents and rigor of far more people throughout history whose contributions have, so far, gone unrecognized.

That is not all – there have been countless internal influences causing filmmaking industries to change, from technical advances to the coronavirus pandemic. Changes like remote productions have accelerated. Remote filmmaking was a technical possibility before the pandemic, and during the lockdowns and work-from-home period it became common. Now, it is quite routine. While in the first days of remote workflows, each team had to figure out how to do this on their own, and now those workflows are starting to become more refined and supported by better tools, so emerging filmmakers do not need to reinvent that wheel.

Remote work has led to another change that is both internal and external – filmmaking and post-production are moving around the world from the traditional centers like Los Angeles, New York, Toronto, London, Vancouver, and other cities in North America and Western Europe. Film production has always moved, finding ideal locations and ever-more-affordable sound stages. But post-production was often done on site in these major production hubs. With remote workflows, this no longer is the case, and post-production has followed the way of field production, moving to other cities in varied places around the world and forming new production hubs in other places with strong film industries. While traditional production hubs have by no means disappeared, they now must compete to maintain their role in film production.

It also means that it is easier than ever, technically, to make a fiction film or documentary. Yet, with more films, it is also harder than ever for those films to reach audiences. For people focusing on a passion project, making their first big film, or creating a signature piece for their portfolio, the tools are more affordable and accessible than ever. So accessible, in fact, that there are so many films that no one can watch them all. So how do today's filmmakers find ways for their work to reach audiences? And how do they know who that audience is? To help find one's way along this path, there are interviews with four contemporary editors, each with a unique and distinct path to their career. They generously shared their experience as a way to help others. Each editor's unique career provides insight for those trying to get started or to advance to the next professional level.

**Learning from the First Filmmakers**

A section on the film industry also offers glimpses of two historically significant filmmakers, among the world's first, whose work was left out of so many film history books that it is senseless at best and scandalous at worst. Over the last decade or so, the works of Alice Guy-Blaché and Oscar Micheaux, two originators of filmmaking in France and the US, have been slowly brought out of archives and into classrooms and festivals. When possible, their films are being restored and made available to audiences, although some of their work was unfortunately lost forever. Still, many articles and books about both Micheaux and Guy-Blaché are starting to show up in publications devoted to film history, in mainstream media, and in films and documentaries. While they do not yet have the type of name recognition as do their contemporaries like D.W. Griffith and George Méliès, that is changing. There were many other early filmmakers whose work contributed to editing and post-production, although my choice to focus on Micheaux and Guy-Blaché was because of their truly unparalleled contributions. Each carved out their own particular niche in the film world, including founding film studios. Guy-Blaché was a pioneer who created new technology and story forms. Micheaux was instrumental in establishing films made for Black audiences; he created complex stories, possessed a respected business acumen that included making deals with theaters, and navigated state censor boards.

# Part 1

# Practical Skills

# 3 Create

Creativity in editing is the best part, right? We are all creative people, as filmmakers, and we are attracted to this profession and art form because we want to express ourselves. We want to make something beautiful, or to say something. Creativity is about making something within a structure and having a specific and focused story, not an endless stream of information or opinion. Good films put scenes in a particular order, reveal story elements, and create drama. Consider creativity in editing as synonymous with structure.

As a post-production professional, understanding the relationship between structures and the creation of your film is one of your most important conceptual frameworks. It is crucial to set up structures from the beginning of a project, and follow them while being able to make changes when necessary. Otherwise, enormous amounts of time can be wasted, resulting in messy projects (at best) and frustrations, lost materials, lost creative opportunities, and emotional and physical burnout at worst.

## Structure Is the Core of a Great Film

Film and video production has grown exponentially since the start of the internet and online media. That doesn't mean there is just more content – it means there are more content forms. As streaming and social media continue to expand, all film and media production will also continue expanding, because most forms of film and media, such as theatrical films and broadcast television, are also distributed through streaming social media platforms. That means that a traditional broadcast production, like the Olympics and other global sports events, are also distributed through streaming, social media, and sometimes other forms such as podcasts. Guess who gets to steer this very large ship? The editing and post-production team.

If you are an experienced filmmaker reading this who already has a deep understanding of media forms, you may want to skip ahead. Or not! In fact, the people who might best understand media form might be undergraduate

DOI: 10.4324/9781003473152-4

and younger filmmakers who grew up with dozens of social media platforms, streaming through sites like Netflix, going to a movie theater, following YouTube channels, and watching a documentary on a laptop. They might have a stronger and more inherent sense of each of these forms tell stories differently, and relate to the rhythms of varied forms far more naturally than generations who did not grow up on so much digital content. Either way, the starting point for post-production is to know your form and then determine how it will influence your story structure.

## Types of Structure

### *Structure for Your Media Assets*

Most students and early filmmakers want to jump right to the fun part – editing the story. But the first thing you must do, in order to develop the kinds of habits that will allow you to have maximum creative expression, is to create a home for your media files. You need to structure where you store your files, how you name them, and how you back them up. This is loosely called workflow, but a more precise term is *media management*. Managing your *media assets* – a general term referring to everything from original footage to archival clips, music, voiceover, etc. – is the key to making sure your entire production flows well. Despite the fact that the post-production phase starts with "post," media management begins the moment the card is put into the camera and the archival footage is obtained. In other words, post-production begins in pre-production.

Media management is one of the hardest easy tasks that can be the underpinning of an excellent production or the downfall of a lot of collective effort. It is organization, consistency, and careful attention to detail. By "hardest easy task," I mean it is also the step many people want to skip, or simply just leapfrog on their way to cutting their footage. This is understandable but also not a habit that will serve you well. If you already started, you can go back and re-organize, but the bigger and more professional the production, the more you need to do this right from the beginning.

#### *Organizing, Naming, and Sorting to Drives*

Naming your files seems so simple. But, as an editing professor, this is likely in the top three questions I am frequently asked. Particularly for people making documentaries, which have so much footage, but for all media productions naming files and organizing them on drives is a crucial first step.

Start by creating a consistent *naming convention*, or a consistent, simple, and informative way to name files. Most cameras have a way to designate the file names of each clip; typically setting the camera to record with the date embedded in the file name is the most efficient way. For archival or stock footage, determine if you need to track the source or include the original name in your file's naming convention. Continue on with every photo, piece of music, sound effect, etc. When every file comes to you with a different name, like A0013483.mxf, A0013484.mxf, music.wav, newmusic.wav, 148897063847-dogbarking-soundpro.wav, tempsfx.mp3, and IMG_8054.heic, this does not help the editing team. If they are named in a consistent way, you can tell from the file where they belong in the film.

For example, a naming convention might include leading prefix numbers to show the type of material, along with scene number, type of shot, and (if necessary) original file name, as listed in Table 3.1.

Many editors use numerical designations to sort media into categories like original footage, archival footage, audio files, music, sound effects, photos, and so on. The exact type of naming system is going to vary considerably and is quite different for fiction films, which have a natural system of sorting by each scene of the script, versus documentary, reality television, wedding videography, broadcast news, and other types of shows.

In general, good file naming conventions typically include a mix of the following: 1) filming date, 2) a project name, 3) a subject, scene, or person's name, 4) the type of shot, 5) the camera, 6) original file name, 7) audio, and 8) clip number. You may not need all of these, or you may have additional categories. The point is to create consistency at the file name level, something everyone can understand, and it is easy to follow through all your types of media assets.

While media management might be a bit confusing at first, once you start following a system it makes enormous sense and is quite easy. More to the point, on independent or student films with tiny or one-person editing teams, there might be room for files to be named in idiosyncratic ways.

*Table 3.1* Sample Naming Conventions for Media Files

| | |
|---|---|
| 01_01_CU_A0013483.mxf | Scene 01, take 01, closeup, original file name |
| 01_02_WS_A0013484.mxf | Scene 01, take 02, wideshot, original file name |
| 002 sc01-kids-sing-happybirthday.wav | 002 to designate an audio file, Scene 01, the song name |
| 002 sc01-classical-score-chopin.wav | 002 to designate an audio file, Scene 01, the song name and composer |
| 003 dogbarking.wav | 003 to designate a sound effect file, the SFX name |
| 004 Sc01-group-photo-blowing-candles.heic | 004 to designate a still image, the photo name |

On large-scale professional productions with multiple people working on a film, there is no room for poor file management. See the Naming Conventions Chart in Appendix 5 for more details and examples.

**Box 3.1 Software to Help Rename Files**

An app called "A Better File Rename" is one excellent tool that allows for bulk renaming of huge bins of materials, and has many options from being able to keep the original file name, to adding prefixes, suffixes, and more. There are free and paid versions (see Figure 3.1). There are quite likely many other file-renaming apps findable through a quick internet search.

Why can't you just do the naming when you bring your footage into your editing system? There are several reasons. While filming, you will be offloading the footage on a daily basis and this should be done immediately. The role in the film industry is generally done by a *DIT* or *Digital Imaging Technician*, but might also be done by a production assistant or even someone who will be the assistant editor and come on set for this specific task. Another reason is that editing systems can sometimes tolerate renaming, but often if the file name is changed during the ingest or after it, the software will lose the *filepath*, or the series of folders that link back to where the file is stored. In other words, you can break the connection between your software and your media assets. In recent years, major professional software has become more capable of relinking to files with new names, but most work best when files are imported and not renamed or changed.

Some productions do the renaming process during *transcoding*, a step where footage filmed in one format is converted to another format for editing. Adobe created Media Encoder and Prelude for transcoding and renaming in one step. If using Avid, the file renaming is likely to come first, as transcoding can done during the ingest into Avid Media Composer, which provides an option to either link to original files, or to transcode all material into Avid's native *codec*, called DNxHD.

Once you ingest, or bring the footage into your editing system, you will create a *bin structure* and sort files there as well. Avid uses "bins" and Adobe and DaVinci use "folders" but they serve the same purpose. Once your footage is ingested, you will also create bins or folders similar to those on your hard drive: interviews, audio clips, archival, photos, special effects, and so on. Understanding which workflow to use and how to manage your media is the first discussion to have with your team, as the decision is affected by the editor, director, entire post-production team, and the standards of the industry.

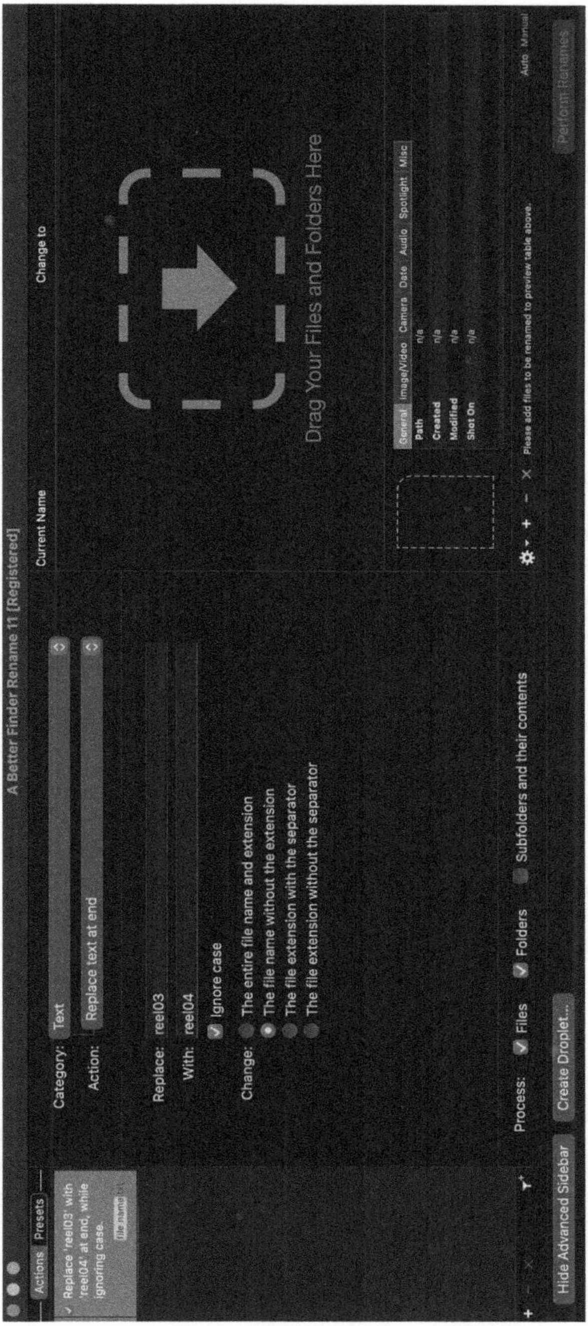


*Figure 3.1* A screenshot of "A Better File Rename." Image by author.

You might be working on a production where the dailies are brought to the editor immediately and the post-production process begins during filming. You might be doing an all-archival project, which is becoming very popular, and receive a giant amount of footage to sort. You may be working on your own film, and need to sort the footage you filmed. In all of these situations, setting your naming conventions is a first line of defense against a disorganized, frustrating mess, and the first step toward the fun part: creating the movie.

### *Offloading and Backing Up Your Media Files*

Your workflow also involves backing up your media assets. Once you have offloaded your footage to drives, named following a consistent naming convention, you will start backing up immediately. Most professional teams use a *RAID drive*, which stands for "redundant array of independent disks," which is an elaborate term for a series of connected hard drives. RAID drives were developed to create multiple versions of files as a backup system, because individual hard drives can fail. There is no good outcome with a hard drive fails. Your footage is lost and gone forever, and while some places claim they can recover materials from damaged hard drives it is the exception, not the norm. Backing up, like file organization, is another one of the hardest easy tasks. Resist the temptation to skip it, or to procrastinate and do it tomorrow. You are creating a home for your footage. Your backed-up files are insurance and mental peace. You are creating good habits that will support you and your more expressive, creative work.

On a high-budget production, if the footage is lost forever, it can mean enormous costs if a scene needs to be redone. On a low-budget production where a unique moment was captured in a documentary, it means that moment is gone forever. Backing up footage does not seem like it should be an important part of a chapter titled "Create," but if you lose footage you will have nothing to create with. So, the first thing to create is a secure system for storing all of your media assets, and a continual and secure way to back them up, such as a RAID drive or duplicated separate hard drives. If you are using two identical hard drives, make sure the file structure is exactly the same on drive 1 and drive 2 so that you can, if necessary, re-attach media files easily. Once you set up your file structure, look for software that duplicates "data" (the computer word for media assets) and will maintain your file structure. The one I use is called Beyond Compare, and it is widely available for any type of backing up, but there are various ones out there. The most important thing is that, once you set it up, it copies all of your new footage, graphics, audio, etc. and maintains the same file structure so you maintain identical duplicates.

The minimum level is to purchase two identical hard drives and copy the footage to both of them immediately. Once you are back in your office or production headquarters, you can do this in peace. If you are on a documentary field production, you would not be the first person to do a field offload in the back seat of the car or on a bus or train. If you are doing the offload in the field, make sure your computer and drive are on a stable surface: if the cable jiggles or falls out it can cause the offload to fail, at best. At worst, it can corrupt a file in mid-transfer. Finally, if you are doing a "field offload," it might be tempting to try to offload a huge pile of footage all at once, but it is wise to do it in smaller chunks that allow the files to transfer in a few minutes. If your file transfer says it will take an hour, and you are in a car or on a laptop with low battery, there is a predictable and quite unpleasant outcome.. If your whole system crashes during the offload process, you also risk losing footage. The sorting and renaming are best done in a quieter place, however, the offloading and backing up are often done as soon as the filming concludes.

### *Structure and Form*

Traditionally, the type of production, such as film or television, defined the job for the editor and post-production professionals, if not their entire career. Contemporary film professionals might work in multiple types of production, from television documentary to fiction, online series, and music videos. Where your film will screen is still the most important *external structure* you will work within, and this information on film duration and type of production will come from the director, producer, the broadcast team, or production company.

The two paths of television editor and film editor still exist, with another third large category of episodic editor. There is overlap, but the structural and technical differences in these media forms can be vast. Even with three main categories, there are dozens of forms, ranging from 30-second commercials, to five-second Instagram stories, to three-hour theatrical features or episodic shows with multiple seasons that must maintain consistent narratives and character arcs from season to season. While some editors still work exclusively on one form, such as fiction theatrical or episodic, that is swiftly becoming the exception, not the typical career path. So, the first question in making a film or media project is "*Where will this screen*?"

Also, pay attention to the difference between "content" and "form." *Form* is the means of distribution or production, like television broadcast, streaming episodic, social media channel, podcast, and so on. *Content* is the type of show: news, fiction, sit-com, drama, music video, documentary, advertising, live programs, and reality/unscripted television. Some types of content, like music videos and advertising, are unique in and of themselves.

Both might have versions for broadcast and social media, with social media versions having much more creative latitude, and broadcast still adhering to television broadcast standards. Advertising will also vary based on where it will go: a commercial or ad destined for Instagram will be constructed and edited quite differently than the same commercial for mainstream broadcast.

To understand the basics of form: it is where a piece will exist in the world of media. With the exception of experimental or installation filmmakers, filmmakers are not painters who can make any canvas in any size. We make programs to specific canvases, aka forms. The most common media forms are rapidly evolving, and streaming and YouTube channels are as important of media forms as traditional television and theatrical film. Most of these have many subcategories and branches into other forms. An editor working in broadcast television does not necessarily work on hour- or half-hour scripted programs, they might make news segments of three to four minutes. An editor working on streaming content might make a one-off feature of 90 minutes, or an eight-episode limited series of 22 minutes per episode. One of the biggest influences in the last decade is that runtimes changed when Netflix, Amazon, and Hulu, which began as streaming services that distributed films, started making their own content. Runtime had been determined by broadcast television slots that would start on the hour and half-hour such as the 6 pm news, the 11 pm news, and 3:30 pm children's programming. Broadcast television runtimes of 22 minutes for a half-hour and 44 or 52 minutes for an hour were created to fit in the commercials and still meet these times. These programs had to rigidly adhere to these runtimes.

Streaming programs and social media changed that. As on-demand content, it did not matter what time it was when someone watched a show. Subsequently, program runtimes evolved. A show could be any length that audiences will watch. As streaming services evolved over the last decade, runtimes also evolved and changed, including seeing many fiction films have three-hour-plus runtimes, such as the 2019 Netflix film "The Irishman," which clocked in at three-and-a-half hours. For YouTube channels, there is no specific duration or runtime, as content varies widely not only in duration but also in number of episodes and frequency. This evolution in specific runtimes has had an enormous impact on content creation, particularly on post-production.

### *External Structures*

As an editor or post-production professional, you are likely going to work within a specific form on each project, such as a feature documentary, a YouTube series, a short fiction, advertising, and so on. You might do marketing videos and social media stories. These forms are set externally by the type of production. Based on your destination form, your team will construct your *story structure* as well as your *technical structure*. Story structure is how you set up a beginning, middle, and end to your piece. Technical structure is how you set up your timeline, media assets, resolution, and delivery. While it is possible to change from some forms to other forms midstream, it is done primarily in advertising or types of media which are less form-specific. Changing forms is not common in major productions. And, when the form is changed, it is typically at the script stage not the post-production stage. Here is an example, in a 2015 interview with Forbes magazine, Sam Esmail, showrunner for "Mr. Robot," talks about how he envisioned the story as a feature film, but when he started writing the script, he realized that the story needed much more time as he was on page 90 and still in Act 1. So, he made it into a series. Changing forms during post-production, however, is not desirable, efficient, or easy.

When you start your editing process, you should know the form: where it will screen and the intended structure. If you are a student reading this, you will either be making a film based on your class assignments, or to the specifications of the kind of demo reel you would like to have: short fiction, web series, etc. The destination determines many important questions: how many people will be on the post-production team, how long the editing process will be, what kind of equipment is needed if you will need a dedicated person for visual effects, if you will translate your film, and dozens of other decisions. If your final form is episodic or for a network, you may be working with a team of other editors, and will have to decide among team members how to handle the storylines and continuity. At the end of this chapter is a list of common story forms, and a class exercise.

### *Your Editing Software*

The other structure that is often set for you by the type of production is the editing software. The tools you will use, like everything else, vary considerably based on where you work in the media industry. There are three common professional editing programs in wide use these days: Avid, Adobe Premiere, and DaVinci Resolve. Apple's Final Cut Pro is another common tool although it is not frequently used by professional houses, and mainly has its niche in prosumer and freelance work.

There are dozens of books, manuals, and online video courses for learning software. This book is intended as an overview of the principles and workflow that are universal to media and film, no matter which software you use, and if you need deeper training in specific software there are many places to find it. I will keep this section brief and touch on the relevant highlights of each software. Each of these are *NLEs*, or *non-linear editing systems*. What does that mean, in a digital generation? Editing used to be very linear, when editors would cut celluloid film and glue it together. If you had to move something from the middle of the film to the end, it was a major operation. NLEs came about in the 1990s as a way to edit film digitally. There is much more history and context, but for most readers of this book, it is a history as ancient as talking about typewriters. The more important question: *What software should an emerging filmmaker learn?* My answer: as many as you possibly can.

Software evolves and improves, or a new version comes out and professional editors flee. What you learn today might not be the best one to use in four years when you graduate and are looking for a job. While it is frustrating to think you have to know all the software, what you really have to know are the basics, and how to apply the same principles regardless of which software. If you are relatively computer-literate, the best thing to do is "learn to learn." In other words, learn how to keep your skills fresh and try to have a good level of ability with the major tools listed here. Alternatively, if you are determined to work in one particular area of media or film, find out what the standard is for that field and learn that software.

The interviews in this book, and in the suggested additional materials, can provide much more insight into field-specific software. The three major software and other tools for contemporary film and media are listed in Table 3.2.

### *Internal Structure – The Spine of the Film*

Finally, you have your film in the can, on a hard drive, and you have set up backup systems. Now, you can start the fun part: creating the film. Why is it necessary to have so much set-up and organization? Because once you start the story editing, you will focus on that world. As you create your *internal structure*, and find a sense of rhythm, the organizational system means you can seamlessly find the clips you need, and you can start the artistic part of post-production.

#### *Structuring Story in Post-Production*

Most important for the editor is understanding the overview of the story and how it fits into the chosen form. There is a saying in film, "*A film is born three times. First in the writing of the script, once again in the shooting, and finally in the editing*." Attributed to Robert Bresson, a French filmmaker, this saying reflects the technology and workflow of his time. Today, a film might be made in multiple versions, and because editing can extend indefinitely, it is David Fincher's quote that is probably more accurate for contemporary post-production: "*Movies aren't finished. They're abandoned.*" Meaning that, at some point, we have to stop editing and move on, and we have done as much as we can to make it the best story possible.

*Table 3.2* Editing Software

| | |
|---|---|
| **Avid Media Composer** | The OG of editing software, Avid Media Composer was the first NLE to come into wide commercial use. There are many versions of Avid from Avid First, a free version, to Avid Media Composer Ultimate. There is a NewsCutter option for broadcast news, and Avid Huddle for groups to edit together. Avid's tools and names have changed somewhat over the years, but it is essentially the great-grandmother of all editing software. It is used by most major broadcast and film production companies, and less frequently used by freelance, marketing, and independent films. |
| **Adobe Premiere Pro** | On the heels of Avid, Adobe developed Premiere in the 1990s, but it was not used widely as a professional editing system until the 2010s. But today, Premiere rivals Avid in the professional world and is probably the most common software for students to learn on. It is also part of the Adobe Suite, and interconnects film projects seamlessly with other Adobe software like Photoshop, After Effects, and Audition for a complete film + VFX + audio suite. |
| **Blackmagic DaVinci Resolve** | The newest NLE to hit consumer markets, DaVinci Resolve actually has been around for a very long time, since 2004, but was only used for color correction and grading, and available only to the most high-budget productions. Blackmagic added in editing, sound, and, eventually, special effects in Fusion, and released DaVinci Resolve to consumer markets. It is a fully integrated NLE system and the first to be resolution-independent, meaning it was designed to work with any type of video file. It also captured the hearts of emerging filmmakers by releasing a very robust free version, and a pro version that is only a few hundred dollars. |
| **Additional Common Tools** | If you love software and want to keep adding tools to your belt, you might also learn *Adobe After Effects*, a special effects software that has been used for decades and is one of the most powerful and ubiquitous tools for filmmakers. *ProTools* for sound editing has also occupied a near-exclusive niche for film and television sound, with *Adobe Audition* also being a powerful sound editor. |
| **"Prosumer" Or Professional/ Consumer Software** | Prosumer editing tools are designed for ease of use and low cost. They include *Final Cut Pro*, *Sony Vegas*, *iMovie*, and apps for smartphones and tablets (these are too numerous to list). These are effective editors but not necessarily considered professional tools. On the other hand, if you make a great film, few people will ask "Wow, what did you edit with?" because all the audience cares about is the story. So, if prosumer software is what you have access to, use it to make a great film and apply the principles throughout this book. |

Story structure relates back to the media form. Television sitcoms, fiction features, documentaries, and every other type of media mentioned in this book have their own inherent sense of structure. Television is formatted for shorter attention spans and includes frequent advertising breaks. Fiction films for mainstream audiences follow a traditional three-act structure, which was popularized by Hollywood and is now evolving as streaming services offer more creative freedom to directors. Documentaries traditionally found their own sense of structure, often using a three-act structure but sometimes finding a more unique and idiosyncratic way to convey a non-fiction story, such as described by Carla Gutiérrez for "FRIDA" and Aashish Kumar for "Body, Home, World" (see Part 2). Newer forms include the limited series, often done for novels being adapted by streaming channels typically into six- or eight-episode series. The limited series differs from other episodic shows in that there is no plan to continue the series into seasons 2, 3, or more. Online media such as YouTube channels have a completely unique way of setting up a structure, while interactive stories defy traditional acts and allow the viewer to explore the story in a non-linear way.

Structuring a story is a process unique to each film. In Part 2, highlights from four editors shed insight into how they structured their films. Their full interviews (on the website for this book) share even more. With that said, there are certain principles that are throughlines. Some of these come from the director and script while others come from the editor and post-production team. The constants of structuring stories are:

**Beginning, middle, and end**: For all media productions, structure means you start in one place with the character's story, and end in another place. Things improve for the character, or they get worse. The job of the post-production team and editor is to know how to ensure the dramatic key points along the way land appropriately with audiences. What is your strongest way to introduce the story? Does it have set-up moments that later payoff, as appropriate to the type of story? Does the story give enough time – or too much time – to developing the character's inner world? Does the viewer know the key facts they need for the story to make sense? When the film ends, will the viewer have been on the entire journey with the character or story?

**Rhythm, timing, and duration**: Is this a fast-paced show with a lot of song cues, like Edgar Wright's "Baby Driver"? Is this a dramatic study that invites us into the minds and lives of the characters, like Céline Sciamma's "Girlhood," which uses slower-paced editing to show fast-paced action and cameras that move through the character's inner circles? Is it meant to use film techniques to point out story elements, like Alejandro Iñárritu's "Birdman," which underlined the artifice of the characters' lives by creating an artificial and highly dramatic "all one take film." For each, and for other styles, much of the story edit is to determine the shot duration, scene duration, rhythm, and the entire film or series duration.

**Story beats**: Emotional key moments that advance the story, well-timed story beats are how editors create tension, drama, and a feeling of being on the edge of one's seat.

**The magic is in the space between cuts**: Cinematic filmmaking is *showing* not telling. Cinematic productions take viewers on a journey. Some films will deliberately create moments to provide breathing space for the viewer, as emphasis for emotional story beats and to invite the viewers to engage with their imaginations to understand what is happening on screen.

**Cut to the chase**: Alternatively, some productions require *telling* not showing. These are fast-paced, to the point, and use strong emotional hooks to engage the viewers right from frame one. This approach is more common in television and social media, as these forms do not wait for the viewer to imagine the emotional journey of the character and follow along through a five-minute scene developing their character. Rather, they tell you right up front, clear and specific, as a way to cut through the noise of their very crowded media fields.

**Class Activity 3**

**Which Form for Which Story? A Review of Common Media Forms**

As you get started, you need to become very familiar with media forms: television, feature films, social media, documentaries, etc. For this activity, refer to the Story Forms chart in Appendix 1 to review, compare, and contrast the differences in each type of media, how they tell different stories, in different durations, and for different audiences.

**Class Activity**

- Review the story forms listed in Appendix 1, Table A.1.
- Which forms tend to have a standard runtime?
- Which forms have wide ranges for runtimes? What is that range in minutes?
- Have the class guess at the approximate lengths for types of content that do not have "typical runtimes" listed.
- What media forms might you add to this list? Which categories have additional subcategories?

**Discussion Questions and Exercise**

***Simple discussion exercise***

As a class, what examples come to mind when reading the list of types of content? What does something like "sports program segment" mean to you? Describe what you think of when you hear "social media video" or "documentary." Are there typical stories that each form tends to gravitate toward? Have the class list some specific programming that tends to dominate each type of content. Also list forms that might challenge this standard of which type of content in which form: if you said narrative fiction tends to dominate feature films or episodic, is that always the case?

Can you think of stories that were told in many different forms? Two examples: (1) "The 1619 Project" is a *New York Times* magazine article, a podcast, a book, a Hulu series, and has an excellent interactive site for education. (2) "League of Denial" and "Concussion" are a documentary and a fiction film about football players who suffered concussions; this story was also told through many mainstream media outlets. How did the story change as it changed media forms?

***Advanced exercise***

Each student keeps a media log for one week. List what you watch with a focus on content and form, and where you saw it (broadcast, streaming, social media, theater, other). What was the runtime, pacing, intended audience, production style, and story? After one week of keeping a log, look at your trends. Compile the classes results. What types did most people consume? Discuss why those were your choices – was it convenience? Something a friend shared? An unconscious choice? Were there common throughlines between the types of stories in each type of content? What do these logs reveal about popular media forms and the types of stories that work best in each form?

# 4 Cut

## How to Get Started with Your Story

One way to look at editing is that it is like putting together a puzzle. You are looking for the pieces that will fit in a certain way, to create the final picture. Only your puzzle has way more pieces than you need, and you are the one cutting the pieces to the sizes to fit together seamlessly. And there are many possible results, all of which could work. So the first few steps of your process are to determine what type of story you want, or the director wants, and to find themes that elevate the story from the factual into the spellbinding.

To do this, you need to start somewhere. One of the most excellent pieces of advice on storytelling comes from author Stephen King:

> Write with the door closed, rewrite with the door open. Your stuff starts out being just for you, in other words, but then it goes out. Once you know what the story is and get it right – as right as you can, anyway – it belongs to anyone who wants to read it. Or criticize it.

Editing is a long process and it is both highly technical and deeply creative. If it is fiction or certain types of broadcast, you will have a script to start with. If it is a documentary or archival film, you may be working out the structure and story during post-production. For shorter media, like music videos, advertising, web series, and promotional pieces, you likely will have a sense of structure already. The song is the structure for the music video, and advertising and promotional pieces are persuasive stories with their own story hooks. Online series will have an internal structure native to that series; for example, there is a series intro, the host (if hosted) introduces a topic, there is a brief demo or interview, and the piece wraps with a series outro. Yet for all of these, there will be a phase where you write with the "door closed," meaning you put together the version you feel is best. That phase may only be one day long, or it might be three months, but you need to give yourself and your team time to create that "closed-door" version. It might end up being a starting point, but having that first sense of structure, of

DOI: 10.4324/9781003473152-5

seeing the characters come to life on screen, of feeling the rhythm and possible ending(s) will give you a framework for what to do next.

Each media form has a unique spine that you will create in your first few assemblies. From there, your process will be: continue organizing, choose selects or the best clips, arrange them into assembles, revise them into rough cuts, tighten the cuts, and decide what to get rid of and and what to add and where. You will fix errors, add sound effects, add or compose titles, color the film to maximize the story, and mix the sound.

## Organization Methods for Hours Upon Hours of Footage

The previous chapter extensively covered organization, and this chapter expands on that only minimally to address how you carry that into your editing software and active editing phase. The reason to emphasize habits is that you need to continue organizing footage using the editing software's tools. Many great teams spend needless hours looking for a certain clip. Do yourself and your team a favor and keep track of everything as you go along, so that you know where to find every clip.

As mentioned previously this is not a software manual. If you are unfamiliar with your editing software of choice, you may need to spend some time learning what the various windows are, how to import footage, and how to do the basics of editing. There are dozens of resources to do this. This book assumes that you have fundamental basic knowledge of the navigation of at least one major editing software program. The examples in this chapter for footage, characters, and story come from Appendix 2, Ocean University Sample "Introductory Briefing." Please refer to it for context. It is also the basis for several suggested editing exercises.

### Box 4.1 Which Editing Software Should You Use?

This depends largely on which industry you want to go into. My recommendation to all my students is to be as software-agnostic as possible. Learn as many types as your brain can handle so you don't rule yourself out of a job because you don't know a certain type of software. That is not always possible because of time, computer capacity, and cost, although both DaVinci Resolve and Avid have very robust free versions of their software available, and Adobe Premiere has a one-month trial and a good student rate. (See Part 2, the profiles of the four editors, to learn which software they use.)

Since this question comes up a lot, and there are certain industries that are more reliant on one type of software than others, here is a way to decide other than just using what you like personally. Take this list with a grain of salt! Media industries, newsrooms, and filmmaking change all the time but there are some longstanding areas where each software dominates.

The previous chapter describes each software in more detail. Here are the main industries and notable films that have used each:

- **Avid Media Composer** – You will need to know Avid to work in broadcast industries, especially sports, mainstream networks like CBS, NBC, and ABC in the US, the BBC in the UK, and probably most traditional broadcasters. Avid has many versions, including a high-end one, "Avid Media Composer | Ultimate" for team editing. The free version is "Avid Media Composer | First," a robust option with nearly all the features of the full version for those who wish to learn this industry-standard software. Films edited on Avid could fill another whole book as nearly all Hollywood-made films are edited on Avid. All of the ten films nominated for the 2023 Oscars for Best Picture, nine were edited on Avid. Of the five nominees that year for Best Editing, four were edited on Avid. Do you get the picture? Avid is still the industry gold standard.
- **Adobe Premiere** – Coming up on Avid's heels, Premiere has taken a large share of the non-studio, non-broadcast market. While that might sound like small potatoes, it is not. Think of: music videos, YouTube channels, advertising, independent films, radio programming, podcasts, and dozens of other parts of the media industry. Much content made for streaming uses Premiere as well. "Everything Everywhere All at Once" was cut on Premiere. Easier to learn than Avid, Premiere is a globally used powerhouse software. It is also most people's starting point for professional-grade software.
- **DaVinci Resolve** – the newest software of this group, DaVinci Resolve, made by Blackmagic Design, is fast becoming a popular choice for many editors. Its market is similar to that of Premiere in that it is used as an editing platform mostly by professionals outside of studio or broadcast systems. DaVinci Resolve's origins are as a color correction platform, and it is still the industry-standard software for color grading. Films edited using DaVinci Resolve include "Bohemian Rhapsody" and "Roma." Learn it if you want a robust and versatile option that is gaining wide international use.

## Importing, Sorting, and Organizing Footage

Every editing software has tools that include *bins and folders* (these terms are interchangeable for the purposes of this book, Avid uses bins and Premiere and Resolve use folders, but they have the same function); *markers*, or ways to tag and make notes on footage, like adding Post-it notes to clips; and ways to code footage using *metadata*.

*Logging and adding metadata* takes your organization to a more granular level. Most editing software also now has metadata functions to code clips by characters, scenes, types of shots, and other key data. For example, you can code all of the footage from a specific character in a fiction film in the metadata, and code it again with shot types like "over the shoulder," "wide shot," "reaction shot," and so on. Then when you're editing and need to find a clip you can type the character name or type of shot into the software's search function and find all of the footage coded that way.

To set up your timelines and bins, for fiction films, the most common and simple method is to follow the script's *scene structure* and name the bins as Scene 01, Scene 02, and so on. For documentary and unscripted, as mentioned in the previous chapter, your team will need to decide on a clear and consistent organizing method, as it largely depends on the type of documentary. Most people find that organizing by date or location, and by characters work best.

If you are working on a *verité documentary*, with a lot of footage of action and activities filmed over several months and locations, you might start with dates/locations. For example, if the film is about a swim team during training and competition, you might have: "07-2024 Swim Meet Paris" and "09-2024 Swim Practice Oregon." For *interview footage*, organize by character and possibly date if there was more than one interview, for example: "SAM, Interview 07-2024" as a folder or just "Sam" or "Coach Amy" and all materials go into that folder so that interviews and live action clips are stored in the same place.

Whichever you choose, remember that this system is to support you and your team in the editing process. Editing software is a giant database. It holds a variety of material, sorts it, and uses the timestamps you add to create your film. And like all data and organization, if you put garbage in, you get garbage out. So, your good, thoughtful, attention to organizing now will repay you ten times over when you and your team are in the final stages, exhausted, looking to refine your film, and need to find that one special clip.

## Choosing Selects

The *selects* are your first takes when you watch the footage of what you think are the best clips. There are two kinds of selects. First, there are *must-haves*. This is the footage that you must have for the story to make sense. These are often factual clips or story setups, establishing shots, character introductions, and dozens of other types of material that create the spine of the film. The other kind of selects are your *creative selects*. These are clips that elevate the film and enhance the theme. They take a film from a series of factual moments to an emotional story, and emphasize story beats, develop the character, and provide unique insight. Sometimes they work to counter genre and enrich a story by providing humorous moments in a serious film, serious moments in a humorous one, and so on. They are the notes that make your film unique and add that special something.

To choose your selects, start watching your sorted footage. The two primary ways to sort down large amounts of footage into smaller piles are:

**Timeline method** – Have a dedicated timeline for each scene or character, and name it consistent with your team's overall naming convention. When you see something that grabs you for a creative select or is a key moment for a must-have select, put in and out points around that clip, and throw it in the dedicated timeline. Take this a step further by adding markers to the timeline using your software's marker tool (they all have a version of markers) in between each select so you can navigate quickly through them.

**Subclip method** – Follow the same process above, but instead of putting them in a timeline create a new folder or bin, and make a *subclip*. The name is pretty self-explanatory, subclips are shorter clips pulled from longer footage. Every major editing software has a subclip option, and they allow you to rename the subclip when you put it in the new folder.

Go with your gut on selects. You have to whittle the footage down to a more manageable pile but you are not yet at the point of eliminating a lot of footage, and it is important that you identify the most choice material from your *first* viewing. Remember, you will see this footage hundreds of times. As you watch it over and over, you start to overthink it and over-analyze what is good. But your audience will be in the same frame of mind you are the first time you watch it, as it will be their first time seeing it, and they are seeing it in the context of a story. If a clip grabs you in a certain way, and something about it really sings, particularly if you remember it after you are done with your editing session that day, then that clip is ideal material for your selects reel.

### *Finding the Gems*

As you watch your footage and start assembling your selects reels and folders, certain clips will rise to the surface as absolute gems. Another way to identify your gems is to ask the director and filming team to make a list after each shooting day of key moments that need to be in the film; a certain take by an actor or a particular moment shared in a documentary interview. As editor, compare those with your selects. Where do they overlap? If all parties agree that something like "the moment where Coach Amy walks away from Sam during practice" was a gem, then it probably is.

Your select reels will shrink your pile of footage into a more manageable pile. Your gems are the absolute best of those.

The gems are a way to structure your story. Once you find your gems, you can create scenes around them. If you find one gem per scene, they function as a story spine. For scripted content, the gems will be in the actors takes, the pauses and slight show of emotion crossing someone's face, the epic action shot, and other key moments. For non-fiction, finding the gems is absolutely crucial, because they will encapsulate your story and bring your characters to the screen in the most empathetic way possible. For documentaries, often these gems form the structure of your film.

### *Audio Selects*

Audio is half the film! As you watch your footage you are also listening. Audio takes can be ambience, it can be sound effects recorded in the field, it can be interview clips, or any other type of audio content. In a documentary, perhaps somebody said something before the interview began or after it was over, while they were still miked, that was much more natural and compelling than what they said during the interview. If the camera wasn't on them or was composed oddly and you can't use the image, you can still use the audio. Your audio is part of logging selects. For fiction, if you will do a sound design, this is the point to start working with the sound editor. If you are doing your own sound design, this is the point to start noting what you have that is cleanly recorded, what will need to be replaced by stock sound effects, and what can be enhanced by *non-diegetic sound*, or sound that is not part of the image on screen.

On a practical note, audio logging is also where you select *room tone* for various shots, scenes, and interviews. Room tone is another self-explanatory term: it is the sound of the room you recorded the scene in. Your production crew should have recorded room tone at the head or tail of a clip. You need to start collecting those in a folder or selects reel, as the room tones vary considerably. If your production crew also recorded event footage, for example, a swim meet with cheering crowds, announcers, and calling winner's names, that is *original field audio* that will bring your film to life in a very authentic and powerful way. Original field audio is exactly what it says, sound that is original to a specific scene and place and that cannot be replaced, or at least not replaced well, by a sound library. Depending on the production you may need a folder dedicated to original field audio.

During logging your audio, you also want to identify dialog that needs to be replaced. Perhaps something from your selects reel where a crowd was cheering but you need to hear what the swimmer said, and the sound is too mixed to hear the character. Or the actor was *off-mike* but the emotional value of the scene works perfectly. This is audio that needs to be re-recorded during *ADR*, *dialog editing*, and *sound editing*. All of this audio should be flagged so that if it makes it into your final film it will be *re-recorded* as a later step. While you will be working on sound through the entire film, if you do need to re-record audio, it is left to a late-stage step because there is no point in redoing audio for something that might not make it to the final cut.

**Stringing Out Scenes**

You've edited down your footage into selects reels and identified some gems. You're ready to start stringing out scenes. For fiction, this can be quite straightforward on the first pass. Start with the script and follow it with the best takes, to create the scenes. If you found gems in the reaction shots as opposed to the actor speaking, your first pass might include giving the scene to the actor who had the most compelling performance in each scene. The director, particularly if they are the writer, will want to see their work visualized and they might want to scene to be given to a different actor. These discussions will be a very large part of your editing process, but as a beginning point, the most important thing is to create the scenes, so you can see how the film plays out. And then have alternate options to consider and discuss.

For documentary you need to create key scenes for your story structure, for example, "Introducing Assistant Coach Harold" and "Introducing Ali." If you've done the gem method and know the absolute best moments, now you start by combining your gems with your must-haves. For example, in the scene "Introducing Ali," as we know from the introductory brief, he is a very diligent and disciplined individual. The film wants to bring this quality to the audience's attention. A gem for this scene might be his daily routine of warming up for his swim practice, doing his stretches, and taking those first warm-up strokes in the water. Perhaps it's an early morning and the sun is still rising. Perhaps he is the first one there and there is a shot of him as the only person in the pool. If you cut these visual gems together, and pull his introduction in as voiceover, perhaps in a clip that says "This has been my daily morning routine, every morning, except for holidays, with no exceptions. For the past 10 years." Then we cut to a sit-down interview of Ali, out of the pool, dried off, dressed in street clothes, and he introduces himself "I am Ali, and I want to be a professional swimmer." The sit-down interview and introduction are the must-have, and the daily routine at the pool is the gem. Combined they speak louder than they do individually to give us a glimpse into Ali's persona.

Congratulations! You just strung together your first scene. Don't worry about every scene being absolutely complete on the first pass. What you're trying to do is take the selects, must-haves, and gems, and sort them into the right timeline or portion of the film, and start creating structure.

### Scenes and Structure

Structure is the core of storytelling. The crucial first five seconds need to intrigue audiences and invite them to watch further. Perhaps even grip them in the suspense of the story. The first five minutes must do the same, and, for features, so does the entire first act. Similarly, the last act, the last five minutes, and even the last five seconds must also leave the audience with a clear resolution. Even if the goal is to create an open-ended story, the plot and characters must all have a resolution by the end.

Creating this structure is the heart of the entire editing process. Many films and TV shows did their story edit using 3×5 index cards (in the old days) and Post-it notes (now), with each note having the core element of a scene written on it: "A&B medal ceremony"; "B meets A's teammate at brunch"; "A's coach talks to B's parents after the meet." Then these cards/notes are shuffled as needed to create the story. Prior to digital editing, this was one of the many ways of doing a "*paper edit*," which means exactly what it says: editing the film outside of the software, on paper. Paper edits, while less of a mandatory step, are still popular. Why use an analog paper method when we have perfectly good digital methods? Because it simplifies the process by reducing choices. It provides a high-level overview of the entire story and is easy to shuffle without having to untangle carefully crafted transitions between scenes, or worrying about audio and video separating in the mix, or any other technical snafu. It allows the team to focus on the story itself. This is especially useful in documentary and other types of non-fiction, which are often crafted in the edit. The paper edit in documentary actually accomplishes what the scripting and table read process accomplish for fiction. It is a simple and story-focused way to check the story flow, the character introductions, the beginning, the ending, and the various plot points from midpoint to ending twists. For any long project, this is a highly recommended step. And guess what? The paper edit can be done digitally while keeping the benefit of simplicity and still accommodating for remote teams or just people who prefer digital methods. There are many mind-mapping apps and digital tools available for project planning or plotting out websites; these apps work wonderfully for plotting out story. In my own work, I use Miro to work the story out with digital post-its. If you do an internet search for "mind-mapping software" you will find many, many options and nearly all have free versions.

Whichever technology you choose, or just good old reliable index cards on a wall if that works for you, the technology of it matters less than providing yourself and your team with this high-level, easy-to-shuffle view of your story. Then, build time into your edit process for scene shuffling. A brief synopsis on each card allows an editor or edit team to restructure and experiment. What scene do you imagine as the opening? What if you moved that to the middle? What happens if you open the film with the end, and then work back to that? Are each of your characters being introduced in the first act? Do you have scenes that show the characters' motivations, inner lives, development, or whatever else you need to create an arc? Does changing the scene order make your story more gripping? Do you need an additional opening scene? Do you need to build more into the middle? Have you identified the ending scenes? Do you have scenes that lead up to that ending to create a "set up/pay off" structure, in which you set up a story element in one scene, leave the audience hanging, and come back to it to finish in another scene? If so, what is in between these scenes, and how long?

This is all possible to do on an editing timeline, to be sure. But doing it in an editing timeline means you will shuffle your actual film, which will take far longer than this pre-visualization of the film's structure. Even one hour of using the paper edit method can pay off enormously in learning more about your story structure, and save hours of revisions. You will, eventually, do the edits in your timeline. But hopefully by the time you go through a structural paper edit, you will eliminate some options identify options that seem promising, and have a few other possibilities you can work on. This gives you a priority order for the many revisions that a film can go through in your timeline and can help the edit team save not just hours but days or weeks of time.

### Stringing Scenes into Reels

Separating your timelines into shorter scenes and reels has many benefits. On my first film, I did everything on one big, long timeline, because that was how I learned from other documentary editors. On later films, I started separating timelines into scenes, based on how fiction editors work. It was a breath of fresh air for my timeline, my computer's processor, and my own creativity. Instead of trying to fill a 30- or 60-minute timeline I was able to work in smaller chunks and edit two-to-six-minute scenes. With that long timeline, when I needed to move something at a late stage in the film, I could do so, but it was more challenging. Audio can come unsynced, a title might no longer be aligned. Using scenes and reels for a documentary reduced this to being a non-issue.

It is also better for your computer. The longer your timeline, the harder your computer has to work. Depending on your computer's strength, a shorter timeline makes for smoother editing because your computer's graphics processor does not have to work so hard.

On large-budget productions, such as television shows and feature films where you work in teams, editing by scene and reel is standard. Each editor or team might work on specific characters, scenes, or sections of the film.

You will recombine all of your scenes later in the process into that long timeline, but to start longer projects, create timelines for each scene. Even for short projects, there are benefits to working scene-by-scene. In addition to the benefits already mentioned, it gets you thinking in terms of scenes, duration, and structure. More on that below.

Another option is to work in reels. *Reels* are a collection of scenes. The term "reels" comes from the traditional celluloid film projection method in which a film was finished and would screen from several reels of celluloid. There is no precise length for a digital "reel," but it is often a few scenes long, probably ten minutes is a reasonable amount for a reel.

If we are working with a ten-minute reel, the number of scenes will vary from production to production. A fast-paced film with scenes of two minutes might have five scenes per reel. A slower-paced film, with scenes of approximately five minutes might, be only two scenes.

Breaking the film into these shorter timelines also helps you immediately and tangibly understand the duration of each scene. If you have scenes of ten minutes, you are not really cutting a "scene," and you are still at the selects stage. Short timelines let your team know when you going too long with one section and it either needs to be broken up into two or more scenes. Also when another section is too short, and somebody needs to go back into the selects and find more clips, add archival material, or otherwise ensure the scenes are equally developed.

## Stringing Reels Into an Assemble

Using scenes in reels helps you get very quickly to what is called an *assemble*. Selects are the first big milestone to shrink your pile of footage into a shorter smaller pile. The assemble is the next big milestone, and a version of your film that is quite rough – not even close enough to be called a rough cut – but you can see the structure and the characters, and start to see the narrative arc unfold. Most of all, you can see how long your first pass is. If you need to hit 52 minutes and you are at 110 minutes you have to cut out over half of your material. But if you need to hit 52 minutes and you are only at 45, you need to find more scenes and material.

To do this, you gather each scene's timeline into one big timeline. Some people will cut and paste the entire scene, and this is one way to do it. Another way is to use nests (Avid and Premiere) or compound clips (DaVinci Resolve) to place each scene in the desired order on a new, full timeline so you can start viewing in sequence. You can move the nested/compound clips around to create a different order to the scenes without risking something coming unsynced. For longer pieces, you will use this full nested timeline as a temporary viewer and will return back to the original short timelines to edit. For shorter pieces, once you created your scenes, and you are getting close to finishing, you might want to start putting everything on one assemble timeline.

### Shot Duration and Cut Duration

With your scenes now assembled into one timeline you can start to see your entire film. The assemble allows you to look at scene duration and even cut duration, and to start considering the pacing of your film now that you have the basic structure. Do the scenes fit the desired pacing? Are they equal to each other? If a scene is too long, what is the most important about it? (In this case, go back to your gems). What can be broken out, deleted, or put into another scene? Does one character have too little screen time, or too much? This is where your team steps back and looks at the whole film, and starts the process of trimming, reorganizing, and cutting. Many teams also start bringing in music and sound design at this stage, although for some music and sound come in later. If you are going to do extensive visual effects, this is the stage where you must have that started, to ensure sufficient time for the visual effects team to work.

At the assemble stage, an excellent and very simple tool for analyzing your scene duration is to simply color code the nested/compound clips. Find your software's tool to color code a clip or nest, and color code every other scene a different color to see the weight and density of your assemble. Maybe your story needs to have longer parts and shorter parts, maybe it needs to be consistent throughout. This gives you a visual bird's-eye view of the density of the story and how long the scenes are in relation to each other.

For more details and examples, please see the chapters in Part 2, which share highlights from several editors' approaches, as well as the full interviews available on the book's website.

### When Is the Film Done?

If we refer to the Stephen King quote at the beginning of this chapter, this is the phase where we are getting ready to open the door. But we are not quite there yet. If we refer to the Bresson quote in the previous chapter, we are clearly in the midst of rewriting the script into a visual story. If we refer to the Fincher quote, we are not even close to abandoning the film.

The editing stages for nearly any film regardless of form are:

1 Selects
2 Assemble (feedback screening and rounds of revision)
3 Rough Cut (feedback screening and rounds of revision)
4 Fine Cut (feedback screening and rounds of revision)
5 Picture Lock

You're at stage 2 – the assemble. When can you say you are, officially, at a rough cut? Generally, when you are at or within a very close distance to your designated time limit. Unless you are a major Hollywood director who can make a three-hour film, you are going to have a time limit. Even if you don't have a time limit designated for you by someone else, you need to start feeling the story's internal structure. There are some editing teams who believe that absolutely everybody wants to watch their three-and-a-half-hour "rough cut." People will watch a rough cut but it makes little sense to try to bring in outside eyes and ears until you are very close to your desired runtime. Your team has to decide what the film's themes are, what the strongest points are, and how to get closer to that goal runtime. (See the Post-Production Workflow Guide in Appendix 6 for a more detailed chart of the stages of editing).

If you are the main editor, you will have to start making recommendations to the director. Even though streaming content has so much variance in story duration, and major fiction films seem to be hitting two and a half hours regularly, there are far more types of content that are ten minutes, 22 minutes, 30 minutes, or one hour. Even if you are making an independent film or a student film, and no one tells you a specific duration, you need to look at your story's internal structure. Are you accurately bringing to life the story? Do parts of the story feel unnecessarily long or slow? Are certain sections detracting from dramatic emphasis? Are there weaker moments that are simply not working and not elevating the main story theme? Your job is to make the best film possible, not to tell the full exhaustive story.

## Learning by Examples – Resources for Finding Case Studies

The next chapters on collaboration, color, and score/sound all address how to get to the rough cut, fine cut, and picture lock stages. The interviews with different editors in Part 2 help to understand how they made their decisions. There are countless ways that editors design and cut films.

For deeper dives into how editors in a variety of productions cut down their films from the assemble to fine cut, there are several excellent resources listed throughout this book and in the appendixes, including books, podcasts, and YouTube channels featuring editors from varied media forms. If you are learning, this is the time to start learning based on the profession you want to be in: if you want to be a television editor, start listening to interviews with varied television editors so that you can understand how that field structures and cuts to specific durations. If your goal is to be a documentary or music-video editor, do the same but with documentary or music-video editors, who have a whole set of different specialized questions and challenges.

## How Many Feedback Screenings and Rounds of Revision Does One Do?

How do you wade through the feedback and notes? How long does it take to get to picture lock? These questions are best answered, as indicated above, by the type of form for which you are creating your film. Once you are at the assemble stage, you have completed the hardest phases and also will very likely have strong opinions on what the story should be. You no longer need such specific instructions creatively and can start making judgment calls. Also, you may, as editor, have versions to share with your director.

Feedback screenings and rounds of revision strengthen films. They also add a lot of time to the edit process. The phase from "pile of footage" to assemble can be quite short – you might get there within a few weeks or even days if it is a fiction film and you started organizing footage on set. If it is a documentary, it may take you a month or two to reach an assemble edit. It really depends on the amount of footage, the clarity of the story/script, how long your final piece will be, the number of people on your team, their experience level, and dozens of other variables.

The phases from assemble to rough cut, fine cut, and picture lock tend to take longer. Again, this varies and is best informed by listening to the experiences of editors in the field you wish to work in. A year to finish a feature film is not uncommon if the editor is working full-time. For documentaries or independent films where the editor may not be working full-time, two or more years is not uncommon. YouTube videos can be done in one day. If there are many rounds of revision, and a large team of producers who will watch different cuts, this will no doubt improve the story and film, however, will add quite a bit of time to the production. On the other hand, broadcast productions, which have much shorter timeframes and much larger teams, may only take six months.

To best answer this I have included a quote from Paul Rogers, one of the most creative editors on one of the most idiosyncratic and resonant films ever made, "Everything Everywhere All at Once." Speaking at The Berkeley Forum, the moderator asked Rogers about his unique workflow. Rogers described the process as reading the script before receiving the footage, then once he started editing, he did not look at the script again, to allow for spontaneity and creative editing. Rogers followed up:

> This is going to sound so pretentious … and I always roll my eyes, but its true … the footage kind of tells you what it wants to be … And if you can watch it objectively and say "here's the way this stuff is putting itself together," sometimes you make some really cool discoveries.

He goes on to describe how he tries to understand the intent of the script and scene and then cut the actual footage to bring out that intent, even though sometimes that means changes to the literal script. While sometimes this approach works, other times it does not, and they might go back to the scene as originally scripted. But, this type of experimentation can lead to insights that might be used in other scenes. According to Rogers: "Sometimes it doesn't apply to a scene, but sometimes it introduces a type of thinking that can be used in other scenes."

This type of intuitive editing can reveal powerful emotional hooks and glimpses of universal human moments. It also shows how approaching editing with too much adherence to a script or rigidly following a pre-planned scene might mean missing some true gems. On the other hand, this is a much longer and more labor-intensive process that involves tapping into the artistic aspects of editing and going far beyond mere technical skills.

This type of experimental, semi-poetic, flow-with-the-footage approach is going to really resonate with some people and work very well for some productions. For other types of productions, however, which must follow a formula or script, or that have a specific structure, this kind of approach might only work for specific scenes or not at all. Still, this approach merits mentioning.

Flowing with the footage is fantastic if the goal of a film is to transcend typical types of storytelling and be a profound and unique voice in a crowded creative field. However, most films, shows, and other types of content do follow the formulas of their genres, or follow scripts, and stick to a very specific style because that is what the channel or production company requires.

As the editor, you are the captain of this process and will decide and navigate the next phases of post-production.

In the words of Paul Rogers, "At the end of the day all we are trying to do is make something really good, transcendentally good."

Welcome to editing. It is a beautiful, fraught, inherently flawed and unfair and yet completely limitless and intoxicating process.

**Class Activity 4**

**Paper Edit: Find as Many Stories as You Can**

In Appendix 2 find the Ocean University Sample "Introductory Briefing," an overview of 30 facts, details, relationships, and other information about a totally fictional swim team at a made-up university. This list represents the types of complex and layered information you will find as you edit a story.

**Activity**

Break the class into groups or have students work individually. Each will do a "paper edit," which is a written cut of the story. There are limits on the number of facts that the student(s) can use, emulating the time-limited nature of media. They must choose their story. How many versions can you get to? In Appendix 2 there are additional options to make this more challenging.

1 Decide if you will work in groups or have each student do this individually.
2 Break into the groups or work on your own, and create your story. Who is your main character? Who is left on your cutting-room floor? Pick a storyline and choose the facts that follow it through to the end.
3 Because all types of media have to fit the story into a specific time frame, you are limited to using only a portion of the information listed. A good ratio is 30 percent of the provided information, meaning each student or group can choose a maximum of *nine facts* to create their story. Clarify with your class how much of the information they can use, typically 20 percent to no more than 50 percent (for an episodic).
4 Once the groups or students have created their own versions, have them share their story with the class.
5 Share your stories – Each group or student shares their version of the story.
6 Reflection – Use the class discussion or a written reflection assignment to address how each story followed a certain perspective, and how the class saw opinion and possibly even bias play out in the storytelling process.

A few guiding questions for the discussion:

- Were there characters no one wanted to follow? Why?
- Were there characters everyone liked? Why?
- Were there people listed who seemed completely irrelevant, and others who seemed to have only a tiny amount of information but seemed to play a larger role?
- Was there one version of this story that most people gravitated toward? Why?
- What *gaps* and *flaws* did the class encounter in this process? What information was not included but would have enriched the story?
- If you were going to film this tomorrow, what additional information would you seek?
- What influence did time pressure have (if there was a time limit)
- What tools would have helped sort out their story? Would a story chart have helped?

# 5 Collaborate

## Filmmaking is the Most Collaborative Art Form

Filmmaking and media production are dynamic and multifaceted art forms, mixing performance with writing, music, photography, and sound design, and it is among the most collaborative of all art forms, as it takes so many people to create a film. Some roles are highly specialized like color correction, cinematography, and sound mixing, while other roles require a broad sense of story or understanding of literature and culture, like writing and directing.

Even DIY (do it yourself) films with tiny budgets and student productions must develop collaborations. These can range in size from having a crew to film a production with many actors to a tiny documentary team of one or two people, in a collaboration with the people in front of the camera.

Collaborations can take many forms, based on the film. In planning a film, the director and screenwriter collaborate to create the story, plot, and characters. Many directors who write their own films often collaborate with other screenwriters to tighten and sharpen the story. For television, teams of writers create series and ensure consistency from season to season. Collaborations can take many forms, based on your film.

### *Remote Work*

Remote work options expand collaborations into an almost infinite pool of opportunities. While there are pros and cons to a remote team, the work-from-home protocols from the pandemic shifted the industry in a new direction, away from always working in a production office or studio. This comes with improvements in broadband access, and in software that allows for real-time remote teams to work individually in their home offices and share timelines and footage. This is very much still in development, and it is not without its drawbacks. But there is no doubt that remote work and remote teams are here to stay.

DOI: 10.4324/9781003473152-6

***Highlights from Featured Editors***

For more descriptions of collaborations, refer to the full interviews with each of the four editors on the website for this book. A few highlights:

- Carla Gutiérrez talks about collaborations on the documentary "FRIDA," including being able to work with team members from and in Mexico while she edited in New York; this including a team of animators in Mexico, and a Mexican composer who lives in Los Angeles. This was important to her because Frida Kahlo, the subject of the film, is a cultural treasure and holds a special place for Mexicans, and as someone from Peru, Carla also had a deep appreciation for Kahlo's work and yet also understood the value of having people on her post-production team from Mexico, to contribute their talents to making a film about this iconic's painter work and life.
- Aashish Kumar also collaborated with two musicians on "Body, Home, World," one of whose music was a specific type of folk music from a region in India. He speaks about how this collaboration elevated the project, which was designed for South Asian audiences around the world, including people who would recognize this type of music – and would also realize the lack of it or a less authentic version of it.
- Allie Sultan and Ryan Rehnborg talk about the enormous amount of collaboration in creating the superhero musical "Incognita's Infamous Adventures." As a musical with a large cast, many locations, performances, costumes, props, sets, and visual effects, the multi-year production was intensely collaborative from conception to filming, including creating the visual superhero effects.
- Zeb Achonu talks about another type of collaboration, specifically about building networks to bring in junior editors. This is another important aspect of collaboration – the behind-the-scenes efforts to create paths to sustainable, long-term careers for people who have traditionally had barriers to getting jobs in the film industry. She shares how she found her own path into the industry through such a program, and continues helping build these initiatives, through her own networking, creating mentoring organizations, and sharing her own story as a way to support other people finding their own path to a career in the film industry.

## Collaborations in Post-Production – Technical Roles

As you read this book and listen to the interviews with the editors, and research other post-production teams, you will start to gather specific examples of how teams have collaborated. While collaborations can be creative, we will start by looking at technical roles and who does what on a post-production team. Below are brief, general descriptions of typical roles of each of these film jobs, and how they work together (note that the list does not address roles in other phases of filmmaking, like producer, director, writer, set designer, cinematographer, even though the first two of these are often very involved in post-production, as are some other on-set roles).

**Box 5.1 FRIDA**

As an example of a collaboration that combines creative storytelling and technical roles, Carla Gutiérrez worked with animators in Mexico to create "FRIDA." Among their contributions, this team created gorgeous subtitles for "FRIDA." to create gorgeous subtitles for "FRIDA." With the film destined for an English-speaking audience but spoken in Spanish, the director and animation team wanted subtitles that looked like handwriting. These were animated to blend with the rest of the paintings, photography, and other art, and placed in customized spots to highlight the words on screen. It is an excellent example of how subtitles can allow for an additional artistic layer and enhance the film, rather than having basic black-and-white words pop up over a lyrical, artful image. (Find the film on Amazon Prime or watch the trailer to see these in action.)

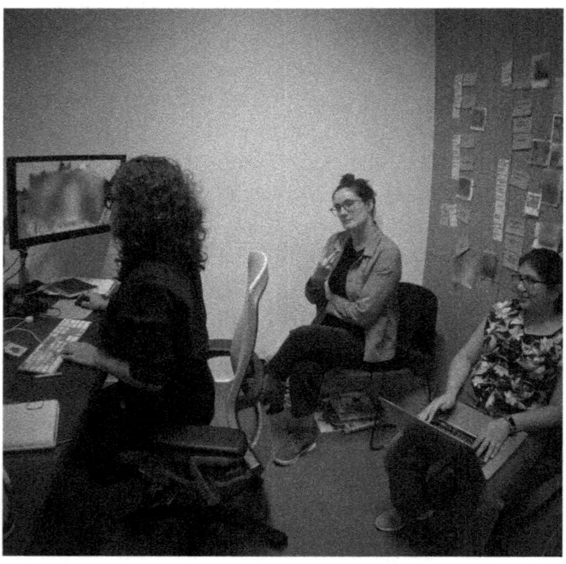

*Figure 5.1* Carla Gutiérrez editing with senior associate producer Laura Pilloni and producer Katia Maguire. Image credit: Paula Ospina.

***Primary Roles***

- **Editor** – The editor is the heart of the entire post-production team. They are the main person crafting the story, following the process from ingest to delivery, and ensuring that the story structure is creative and compelling. The editor is also the primary team manager unless there is a post-production supervisor, in which case they share the role.
- **Assistant editor** – The assistant editor can be anything from the entry point for emerging filmmakers to a career path for people who focus on broadcast or large-budget productions. They are the key to keeping the post process smoothly structured and efficient. Assistant editors organize and prep all footage, create logs, make transcripts (or have them made), sync audio, and organize bins and folders in the editing software. Imagine a reality television show, or a fiction film with large amounts of daily footage coming in – the assistant editors sort, name, organize, transcode, and otherwise make sure nothing is lost or corrupted. Without them, there would be a massive pile of disorganized footage. Assistants in some cases also work on graphics, trailers, select reels, finding coverage for scenes, music searches, supervising other roles like transcription and captioning, and other crucial roles.
- **Post supervisor** – The person in this role manages the post-production process, from schedules to delegating tasks and assigning roles, ensuring the whole process runs smoothly. It can be a somewhat technical role, such as making sure that the files in the finishing steps are correctly delivered to the colorist, sound mixer, and captioner, and they can also play a creative function in bringing together teams of animators, VFX crew, archival researchers and other specialists. The post-production supervisor role is sometimes done by the editor, or there might be two (or more) people working together to keep the edit process on track.

***Specialized Roles***

- **Story editor or story consultant** – This is a role within a team of editors, with a focus on tracking the story progress and character development. That means everything from scene order and the narrative arc – the set-ups and pay-offs within scenes, acts, and the entire film – to ensuring the film addresses the underlying themes desired by the director and producers. Story editors are often part of the post team for large reality shows. They often serve as consultants and a valuable outside perspective on documentaries where the story is created in editing and there are many choices to sort through to create a powerful, dramatic film.

- **Sound editor** – The sound editor creates clean dialog from interviews, for example, by editing out pauses, coughs, repeated words, and other unnecessary parts of the dialog/interviews. They also might be the person to record and replace lines with new ones in ADR, and to try to clean up sound files that have background noise.
- **Sound designer** – Similar to sound editor but slightly different, the sound designer creates an entire soundscape: music, ambience, effects, and non-diegetic sound. This is a creative role that adds to the film's story, and depending on the film, the sound design might start in the very first stages of post.
- **VFX team** – the visual effect team, who do everything from animation to compositing effects in post-production. While the completion of this role might take place in the finishing stage, a team that includes VFX specialists involve them early to ensure the creative development of the visual effects along with the other aspects of the story. (Note: *visual* effects are done in post-production; *special* effects are done on set or in camera.)
- **Music supervisor** – The person responsible for managing all music and licensing. (See Chapter 6, "Sound" for more detail.)
- **Composer** – The musician who creates an original score for the film, or allows their pre-recorded music to be used. (See Chapter 6, "Sound" for more detail.)

### *Finishing Roles*

- **Online editor** – This is a technical role during which the film goes through all its finalization and polishing steps. While today, an "online" editor sounds like a remote, virtual position, the name comes from days when most editing computers were expensive and editing was done in two phases: the very long "offline" phase, which resulted in a low-res version of the film, which then went through a much shorter, expensive "online" phase, which using the high-res original footage to recreate the film in a post-production house. While the online/offline phases somewhat apply today, the line is much fuzzier. Editors still work with proxy files, or lower resolution versions of their footage, and recreate the final film in an online process, when they work with an editor to recreate the film using high-res footage. Or, this role can also mean the person tasked with finishing the film – supervising the color, sound, and final music, matching everything back together, and creating all of the exhibition copies.
- **Colorist** – The person who creates the color palette for a film, adjusts all color corrections, and fixes other issues with the image. This is another role that has evolved significantly, color grading and correction used to be only available to high-budget productions but now is a normal step on most productions.

- **Sound mixer** – This is a technical finishing role, and the mixer is the person who finalizes all audio files, optimizes voices, and ensures the levels are all perfectly balanced for the destined screening environment (theatrical, streaming, broadcast).
- **Captioner** – the person or team who creates the captions. As captions become more and more common, filmmakers are starting to embrace the words on screen as another aesthetic of the film, including word choices and the look of captions.
- **Subtitler** – the person managing the translations and adding subtitles. Typically, these are the last step, but in some cases can be a vivid part of the film. See Box 5.1 on the subtitles in "FRIDA."

Clearly, roles change from production to production: in broadcast and mainstream production teams, roles might be very fixed and specific. There are hierarchies of skill, experience, and seniority that are necessary to work with speed and clarity, and people develop entire careers around doing one aspect of post. For independent films and documentaries, roles shift all the time and one person might do several roles on a team. Even for YouTube channels and online production, which often have only a one-person edit team, it can help to look at the division of labour to understand how portions of the filmmaking process can be delegated, and when it is best to do so.

## How to Collaborate on Long Projects?

You might think, "Sure, working with a composer or animator is a type of collaboration. That's wonderful. But editing is a time-consuming process, just like writing. How can a collaboration help shorten it or make it more efficient? Or do what we really care about and make it the best possible film and something truly memorable?"

### *A Few Ways That Post Teams Can Work Together*

#### *Traditional Workflow*

The sections below describe many varied collaborative workflows. Some are quite new, like virtual productions. Others are tried-and-true, like teams of editors working on a story. Before you start learning new ways to collaborate, first understand how filmmaking has worked in traditional collaborations.

Post-production has traditionally always had sequenced productions, meaning one phase had to be complete to move on to the next one. Daily footage was sorted, then cut, then sound and music was added and so on. While the timeframe is often not sequential anymore, many productions still follow those roles to collaborate. (For a detailed visual layout of the many steps in a post-production process, see Appendix 6: Post-Production Workflow Guide.)

The traditional post-production workflow is something along the lines of the following:

- Editors lead the post team. They work collaboratively with the director, producer, and commissioning editor to understand the themes, story subtext, plot, goals, and other creative aspects of the production.
- The editor and/or post-production supervisor develops primary creative collaborations with animators, composers, and graphic designers. They also build a team of assistant editors and production assistants who support the overall production and learn on the job. If there is more than one editor, they determine who is the lead, and what sections each other team member will take on. The next section has a few examples of collaborative story editing.
- Depending on the type of story, this team brings in additional creative collaborations like VFX specialists.
- As the rough cut moves forward, frequent collaborative relationships are with musicians and composers to create original music. This highly specialized skill greatly enhances the production. For productions using prerecorded tracks, the music supervisor fills this role.
- Once the picture is locked, the editor or post-production supervisor turns the film over to a colorist and sound mixer.
- The colorist might be brought in very early if strong color grading is needed, or it might be a shorter step, for a less extensive job (see Chapter 8, "Color"). The sound mixer does the last pass on the sound and masters the audio files (see Chapter 6, "Sound").
- Increasingly, captions are becoming more than a technical finishing step, and being made a creative part of the film by including vocabulary that re-creates the unique story world through the captions (see Chapter 9, "Transcripts, Captions, Subtitles"). This offers a new area for collaboration: editors can work with a captioning team to develop specific words to use on-screen to most effectively recreate the sound and music in words.
- At each step, the editor or post supervisor conveys the goals of the film, the feeling that is required in the music, sound design, artwork, titling, graphics, and effects, and otherwise guiding and centering the team. They are the hub of a massive network of people.

### *Story Editing Collaborations*

**Edit by Character**: Some teams of editors divide stories or films up by characters. So one editor will create all of the scenes for one character, another editor will work on another character's story, and so on. For a large-budget fiction film with an ensemble cast, this is one way to split up the work.

**Edit by Versions**: For a fiction film, the director and writer already created the script. For documentaries, the producer or director might do a paper cut, or a commissioning editor might determine the story. In television, the showrunner, writing team, and executive producers also have written the script. In all of these cases, the story is created by whoever serves as the showrunner (we'll use that term for all of these leaders, even though "showrunner" is specific to television and streaming). However, often when editing the first cut together based on the script, an editor will find other ways to put the scenes together or might spot some additional scenes or approaches that could elevate the story. This often happens. In this case, the editor might put together the director's cut and some optional cuts for each scene or act. The editor, director, producers, and other team members then review these versions. Sometimes they bring in a story consultant or other editors. Often they find that elements of the director's cut and elements of the editor's versions work best, and they decide to use those approaches.

**Edit by Episodes**: Television series often have teams of editors, and often have a much faster turnaround time. One common approach on a series is for the editing team to divide up the series by episode. Each editor takes on their particular episodes, sharing footage, notes, and story arcs, to turn around an entire series in a much faster time frame than a single editor could.

One example of collaborative editing is the television series "Beef" (Netflix, Lee Sung Jin, 2023), which is edited by Harry Yoon (ACE), Laura Zempel, Jordan Kim, and Nat Fuller. As shared in the *Art of The Cut* podcast in an interview with Steve Hellish (ACE), "Beef" was filmed and edited all at once, not sequentially. Meaning, rather than the pilot episode being filmed and edited first, then episode 1, then episode 2, and so on – the footage was all coming in at the same time, and the cutting was all going on at the same time. The "Beef" team had two editors work in turn on the pilot, partly to accommodate schedules, and each editor also took on different episodes. They worked at times as a remote team and at times together in an office, allowing the showrunner Lee Sung Jin to see and weigh in on cuts at various points. This complex drama used the emotional entanglements between characters as the driver of the story, and the editing team had to track the entanglements and references throughout the series, weave them in and out of the narrative so the story threads extend throughout the series and were referenced in the right order. For example, there is an epic car chase as a climactic scene and a pivotal story beat, which was filmed toward the end of production. Hints of this scene were foreshadowed in episodes early in the series, creating a set-up/payoff structure that elevated the tension of this award-winning series. This kind of complex story and editing process is only possible with excellent communication between the editing team and the showrunner(s), and a clear sense of how each editor needs to constantly be ready to adjust based on how the storylines develop across episodes.

"Beef" is just one example of the way teams of editors collaborate. For more on how collaborations in fiction filmmaking work, see the highlights of the interview with Allie Sultan and Ryan Rhenborg in Part 2, where they describe how they made an effects-heavy superhero musical with a collaborative team during the pandemic.

At the end of this chapter there is a suggested class activity to research other specific ways that editing teams have "divided and conquered" their stories, using the best resource of all: the direct experience of editors working in the field you would like to focus on. The full interviews included with this book all provide insights into different approaches and collaborations. Two other excellent resources for learning about specific productions are the *Art of The Cut*, podcast mentioned above, which is also a book and a YouTube channel, and the *Manhattan Edit Workshop* podcast and YouTube channel. Both profile hundreds of contemporary editors in fiction, television, and documentary, and include deep-dive interviews with editing teams who describe how they divide up the editing workflow (among many other things). If you are interested in a specific film, find out who the editor(s) are and start searching, as there are many interviews with editors available online. Another resource, The Berkeley Forum (an undergraduate-run forum hosted by the University of California) did a deep-dive interview with Paul Rogers, editor of "Everything Everywhere All At Once," in which he shares how they edited that exceptional film as a remote team during the pandemic's lockdown. Search for what you are interested in – you just might find it.

**Box 5.2 Remote Collaboration Expands Teams**

Carla Gutiérrez found opportunity in collaboration and also a way to mitigate the limits of remote work There is a natural storytelling flow that a production team has when they are all in the same rooms together that is impossible to recreate in a fully virtual environment. In editing "FRIDA," as mentioned above, part of her team was in Mexico. Others were in California, and the main team was in the New York City area. She shared how they softened the distance and made the team feel connected:

> I knew that I needed to work in collaboration with somebody else, especially if I was going to both direct and edit at the same time. So he [story editor David Teague] became instrumental in finding the voice of the film. My producer also was really involved in the

creative aspects, the story, but then our composer was remote (Los Angeles), our animation team was remote (Mexico), and we had very intense conversations over Zoom, but we also … got together with the animation team. And I think that was really important. We traveled to Mexico and we met them. And just having that personal interaction, it just … opens up the communication, and then your virtual meetings become a little bit different and more vulnerable and more direct in the way that you're expressing your opinions. It's not as careful as when you really don't know each other … we made jokes together and really get to know people's personalities.

## Remote and Virtual Production

The global lockdown that started in 2020 pushed the film and television industry in a direction it was headed already – toward remote workflows. Managing post-production in remote environments is full of new opportunities and challenges, and the acceleration to work-from-home set-ups showed that remote work on films and television shows is more than viable. However, as mentioned in Box 5.2, it can feel limiting as well. Zoom calls do not replace office conversations and while scenes and cuts can be easily shared through links, it is still not the same as pulling someone into your office to watch a scene revision.

At the time of writing this, there are many ways to work in remote and virtual environments:

### *Remote Teams*

Each team is distinct and has its own portion of the process, such as on "FRIDA" where the animators had a specific role in the production. The footage is shared and team timelines are updated through each person's workstation. All major editing software has options for remote video editing and shared timelines. Essentially, teams of editors share timelines and different ways of sharing footage. As they edit, the timelines update for everyone on the team.

There are several versions for remote teams, depending on their budget and team size. The entry point for a small team is shared media files stored on duplicated media drives, with identical file structures. Often the drives are shipped to the team members, or the footage can be shared through an upload/download. Teams work on shared timelines or team projects that update remotely on other team member's computers. Remote projects offer features like locking timelines to ensure that editors do not write over each other's work. These names of the options have changed quite a bit in the past couple of years, but currently Avid calls it Edit on Demand, Premiere calls it Team Projects, and Davinci Resolve calls it Collaboration.

The next level is cloud-based collaborative tools like *Frame.io* and *LucidLink* which create instant access to shared files stored online, eliminating the need for shipping drives. These tools use newer methods of reading footage in the cloud without the need for long upload/download times, local storage, or syncing drives.

This technology and techniques are constantly improving, becoming more integrated with local desktop systems, and developing more secure and efficient ways to ensure this is productive and not a technical nightmare. Most of these, by the time you read this book, will probably even have new features!

The challenge that many teams face now is isolation. Creatives already spend long hours staring at screens, and while work-from-home has many benefits, the synergy of a team environment suffers. It is very hard to get to know your team, develop rapport, share insights into the project, and really develop good creative energy when you are on video calls. As mentioned previously for "FRIDA" Carla Gutiérrez took her US-based team to Mexico to spend time with the animators and forge creative bonds. When she returned to New York to continue editing, the rapport and energy between team members had significantly deepened. Hybrid options like this can bridge some of the worst aspects of remote productions. And, by the time you read this book, perhaps there will be new platforms for creative collaboration that mimic the feeling of being in a room together.

### *Virtual Production*

Virtual production is real-time television and film production in which advanced cameras and computer graphic systems recreate an on-set production experience into an entirely virtual environment. Think of a stage play, with LED backgrounds, and each actor possibly on a different set but combined in a virtual environment. The backgrounds include CGI that is rendered in real time and that can be changed instantly. Think about the kind of rear projection that Hollywood has used for decades to create special effect backgrounds, such as Alfred Hitchcock's famous crop-duster attack scene in "North By Northwest." In that film, Cary Grant was filmed in a studio with the image of the plane projected on a screen behind him, and the sound effects and action made the scene into one of the most famous in film history.

Virtual production is this, exponentially advanced. Using technology like *volumetric stages* – three-dimensional performance stages that use multiple cameras to capture the performance from many angles – and *LED walls* that range in size from 10 feet tall (3 meters) to 30 feet tall (just under 10 meters) – productions filmed on virtual sets are a unique combination of incredibly real digital environment and incredible fantasy realms made in just an afternoon. "The Mandalorian" (Disney+, 2019) has become the standard-setter for virtual production; it used virtual sets to create digital backgrounds that were instantly changeable from a mountain to a desert to anything else, with digital foregrounds that also are instantly changeable and can move realistically with the background. Actors in virtual sets can interact with each other for natural performances. Performance shows also use virtual production, as do music videos. Virtual productions take the months of post-production that typically goes into an effects-driven fantasy or CGI production and puts it all into the camera: the action, imagery, actors, and CGI is captured in real time and immediately viewable.

These technologies are costly and not for everyday productions. They also require advanced computers, similar to virtual reality and gaming computers, and specialized software that combines virtual and physical productions together. While the cameras and environments are expensive, some of the most common virtual production tools/software, like the real-time three-dimensional platforms like Unreal Engine and Unity, which have free entry-level versions for students and beginning users to start learning. See Box 5.3 for how Allie Sultan used virtual production at Middle Tennessee State University.

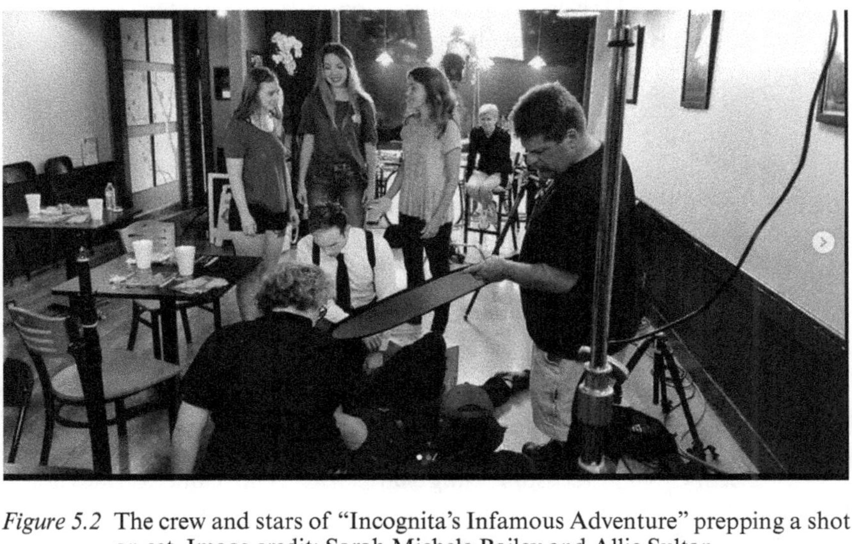

*Figure 5.2* The crew and stars of "Incognita's Infamous Adventure" prepping a shot on set. Image credit: Sarah Michele Bailey and Allie Sultan.

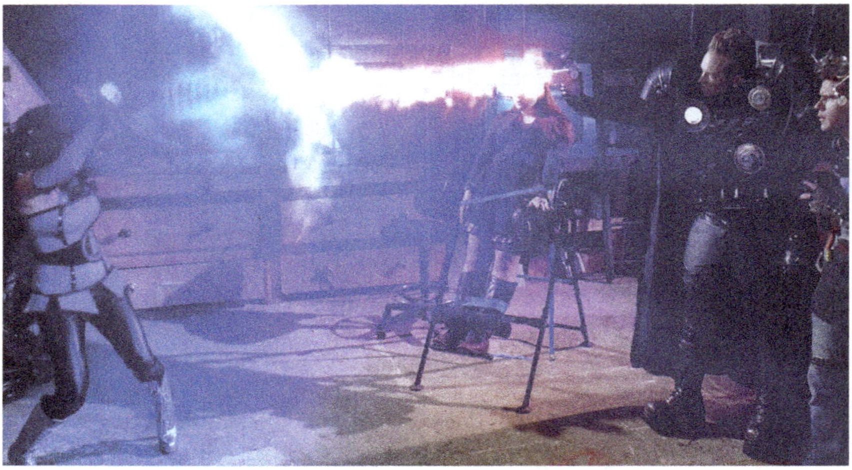

*Figure 5.3* Sarah Michele Bailey and Christopher Bailey face off as Incognita and Baddio. VFX shots like this take enormous amounts of pre-planning and collaboration. Image credit: Chris Hollo and Ryan Rehnborg.

**Box 5.3 Getting Started with Virtual Production – and its Pitfalls**

Allie Sultan, director, VFX supervisor, and Professor at Middle Tennessee State University, had a rare opportunity to start a virtual production program for her university. She shares some of the excitement and also a few pitfalls:

> We actually, during COVID, we got some federal funds for our university … a previous department chair used a million dollars of it to buy a virtual production stage. So we're like … the first in the state of Tennessee to have this virtual production stage. And many of the faculty members were terrified of teaching this because no one knows how this works. And it's server-based, mapping to the wall, but there's also motion tracking. And then Unreal … we've been offering a class in Unreal Engine for filmmakers, which is really great. I created a class called Virtual Filmmaking and Production Design. So we've been collaborating with this Unreal Engine class to make films on this million-dollar wall.
>
> Second semester something happened. The camera tracking wasn't working. The wall's not functional. Everything grinds to a halt. And we are a public university with no tech support really, other than a senior staff engineer and the assistant engineer who are running around putting out fires everywhere.

> So in many cases I've been like … just get me a green screen … I could do the same thing on a green screen and we'd be done. There's so much post that comes now in pre-production with virtual production. I don't know if it's a time saver in Nashville. Those stages are $50,000 a day. So they're not for independent filmmakers, they're for the record labels. But our students are going to get jobs in it because it's new. The older folks are not going to want to learn … LED systems. But our students are younger and more interested in that technology.

### Collaborations for Joint Projects

Other types of collaborations include joint projects in which a filmmaker and a mission-driven organization or social group team up to create a film that elevates values, supports a cause, or shares an important and overlooked story. This sometimes functions as a "work-for-hire," in which the organization hires the filmmaker to make a film they have written, however, a true collaboration is more like a commissioned project. The difference is that in a commissioned project, the group shares their goals for the film: the story, the character, the values, and so on, and develops a partnership with a filmmaker who then translates these ideas to the screen.

In his interview in Part 2, Aashish Kumar describes how his first paid job was developing this type of partnership with an organization working to elevate the visibility of South Asian communities to address hate crimes. He started as a consultant on the project, and then quickly realized that he wanted to do more than consult on the project. The film they developed together became a powerful and widely screened story highlighting a virulent stream of hate crimes in New York against anyone who appeared South Asian or Arab, beginning after the 9/11 bombing of the World Trade Center. For him, this signature project was personally meaningful and a way to collaborate and share skills with a group working toward goals that he shared, while also creating a way to establish himself as a filmmaker with a particular voice and topic area. (See the highlighted interview in Part 2 for details.)

### Collaborations for Networking

Collaboration means more than just working with a team, it also means that the industry is working with film schools and universities to create programs for emerging filmmakers. These are important points of entree and help create friendships and professional networks. The film industry traditionally used apprenticeships and learning on the job, and these two traditions stand to suffer and maybe even disappear as work environments shift to remote, or become heavily remote. Collaborations come from networks, and networks are built by being on the same team together, sharing resources, and finding a community of like-minded people who want to work in the same types of film you do, and who share your work ethic and style.

Apprenticeship and mentoring programs have always been critically important points of entry for people in film production. Zeb Achonu, (BAFTA Award Winner, "White Nanny, Black Child"), mentioned her entree to her career came through a BBC post-production trainee program. She recalls:

> "It was a full-time job, but it was learning on the job. And so that was great. And then I guess when it got serious, when I started editing seriously was still within the BBC because I stayed with them for nine years. It was making children's programs. So I would make a lot of the preschool programs and cut the sort of bedtime stories that are short stories read by celebrities … And so that was my beginning, and it would be sort of sound and music and rostrum images, putting those together and then moving from there into slightly older children's programs like 'Blue Peter' and … children's programs about science and things like that where you'd be putting little packages together of journeys that the presenters had taken or experiments that people had done."

What used to happen naturally in jobs is less likely now, and students entering the editing workforce need to be prepared for how to approach these working environments. Carla Gutiérrez sums up this challenge:

> "I'm learning continuously by looking at other people's films. I love, love, love going to to screenings because I'm able to see behind the scenes whether coming against what are the issues that they have, how are they working with the themes and the narratives of the film? And that's just kind of like a lesson when you see other people's process and you also see how hard it is for everybody. So that's what we're losing with some of the remote stuff that is happening. We're losing that personal contact of the assistant editor to be able to be in the room where the story is being discussed. If you give an assistant editor something to cut, how do they know how that scene is going to fit into the larger picture, the larger story? I feel like that's one of the downfalls of remote because apprenticeship is not as normal anymore and [junior editors] are getting stuck with just the technical aspects of it … on 'FRIDA,' we did a lot of remote work, but mostly the core team was in New York, and it was important for me to get together."

Working in London, Zeb Achonu echoed this sentiment:

> "So many of us work remotely, which means we lose the opportunity to train people on site. I can't have someone shadowing me as often, which is a huge loss because it's so important not just to see what buttons I press, but to see how I communicate with my clients, that kind of … customer service, all of that comes into it. And so we've lost that. So now I think it's so important to find a community or a network that will tell you about opportunities … who know what it is that you want to do. I think it is good to learn obviously how to edit the basics, but I think a lot of it, again – I used to really struggle to teach myself how to do things because it wasn't real. Nobody cared if it didn't look great, it was just me, I cared. But as time went on, knowing the basics, but having the opportunity to put them into practice with someone else going, 'Oh, I don't quite feel how that works, or maybe we could try this.' It's that experience that you have to get."

As remote work is not likely to disappear any time soon, there are other options for developing collaborations and networks. One solution is simply to remember that many people cope with this sense of isolation, and find professional groups, social media sites, and meetups to help form a network. Zeb Achonu shares how she, as do many people, at first hated this kind of awkward, stilted social situations that come from professional networking, but then found a way to make it more natural and even normal:

> "I think that our industry is without a doubt, whether we like it or not, it's run on who you can get to know. And so the networking side of things is huge and it's always been huge. And I used to say, 'Oh, I hate networking, I hate it.' Which everybody says, until again, on one of those mentoring schemes, someone pointed out that you are just getting to meet new friends. And if you go in with that mindset, it is a lot easier depending on where it is. It can still be awful walking into a huge room of people you don't know. But when you're just making new friends, the ones that you like, you'll chat and then you get to work with your friends rather than forcing yourself on someone that you just cannot vibe with. That you're going to have to spend three months in a room with or nine months in a room with. So that's always been quite good. So I find networking has been really, really useful and making sure the industry's so different to when I started.
>
> "But for me, I think the networking and finding out who's doing what and who you might want to get to know, I guess talking – as you can tell, I love talking … During lockdown, with the British Film Editors Guild

I was involved in some Zooms as well. People would come together and have conversations. And so you sort of learn that the editors that you looked up to were human and you could actually send them a message on Twitter or Instagram or whatever, and they would more often than not respond. So the community became closer. And it does also mean that if I see something I'm really interested in and I check the credits and I think, 'Oh, that's such and such an editor, I'll drop 'em a line.' And if they're in my area, I might try and meet them for coffee or just tell them what I thought, because who doesn't love praise, but just trying to make those connections or just learn who they are and see what other work they've done so I can get some inspiration from the way that they work. And so I think it's all those things. I think it's networking, it's reaching out to your peers and it's really studying the art of the people that you admire."

All is not lost! The industry that needs networking will create ways to network. Both Carla and Zeb have been instrumental in creating organizations to foster this type of mentorship. (For more details see their highlighted interviews in Part 2, and the full interviews available at the associated website.)

**Class Activity 5**

**BTS: Listening for Collaborations**

Find an interview with an editor describing the process of making their film. It can be from a variety of sources – the editors interviewed for this book, other books, podcasts, or YouTube channels interviewing editors. These are all sources that are current and detailed, and share the editing process and more context of the production like the budget, timeframe, intended audience, and other important details.

**Activity**

1 Find an interview with a team of editors. Listen to the interview and make notes on how they address collaboration.
2 How is the collaboration structured? Is there one lead person, who directs and supervises the other do some of these collaborations work? It can be with the director, the sound designer, and other crew members. The goal is to find more examples from contemporary stories.
3 Take notes to share with your class.

**Resources**

The full interviews with the four editors included in this book (see the publisher's website for the audio versions of these interviews: www.routledge.com/9781032640037)

- *Manhattan Edit Workshop* – podcast or YouTube channel
- *Art of the Cut* – podcast
- *The Rough Cut* – podcast

**Discussion:** Share some unique collaborations in class. How did they work together? Did they share how they connected? Did they provide insight into the nature of the collaboration?

# 6 Sound

## Soundscape

Even silent films have a "soundscape": the silence that echoes slightly, allowing our imaginations to fill the space. The filmmaker who neglects their sound makes a flat film and misses half of their creative opportunities. In many ways, sound is more powerful than picture, and can be evocative, haunting, challenging, and set the rhythm of the entire film. On the practical side, it is also easier and less costly than ever to have a fantastic soundscape and score.

Audiences desire deep ambient sound immersion, and particularly in theaters with excellent speaker systems, the quality and layers of a sound design will transform a film. In fact, studies have shown audiences will put up with murky images but not murky sound. Try it: play a film with your screen brightness turned down. You might find watching it a bit challenging, maybe even less pleasant, but you might still watch, as long as you can follow the audio. Now, play the same clip but crank the audio so it is obnoxiously loud. Or replace it with a scratchy buzz. Perhaps even envisioning this makes you cringe. Not only will audiences not watch films with poor sound, but they might flee the room or demand that someone "shut off that noise."

## Signal versus Noise

So what is good sound? In film, good sound equates to "signal versus noise." The broadest description is that *signal* is whatever you want, even if it is a scratchy buzz (which generally is not what you want). *Noise* is everything else. In creating your soundscape, you decide what the signal in your film and use it to elevate your story, invite the audience deeper into the world you create, and enhance the suspension of disbelief. The opposite – poor sound design – involves unexpected or undesired audio elements, lack of ambience, sound levels that draw attention to themselves, choppy audio cuts, and production sound that has a lot of interference from traffic, people talking, and

DOI: 10.4324/9781003473152-7

other elements including poor recording levels. No matter how carefully constructed the dramatic arcs are, the film will fall flat if the audio does not correlate. As the editor, you are looking for the best signal – the good lines, the best dialog takes, the most insightful interview soundbites, and the sounds of the world you are trying to create.

**Box 6.1 Close Your Eyes and Listen**

There are many exemplary films for sound design. As you read this chapter, pause a moment and look up scenes from some of the following films, and listen to their incredible soundscapes:

"A Quiet Place" (2018) – part of sound is silence, and this horror film uses minimal sound and anticipation-filled silences to increase tension and drama.

"Apocalypse Now" (1977) – this epic used a moody, off-genre soundscape to add poignancy to a film about the futility of war.

"Baby Driver" (2017) – tempo, diegetic music, and audio rhythms sync with visual rhythm in this heist movie, creating an extraordinary soundscape.

"The Matrix" (1999) – the sound of a slo-mo bullet and other hyperreal elements immerse audiences in this futuristic blockbuster.

"Whiplash" (2014) – a dark musical with the sound design coming from the on-screen performances in this taught, percussive drama.

## Diegetic and Non-Diegetic Sound

Film and media divide all sound into two large categories: *diegetic*, something you can see on screen within the story; and *non-diegetic*, meaning something you cannot see on screen but are choosing to make a part of your story. An example of non-diegetic sound is if you had a scene of an artist or performer in the space that they will perform in, and you want to indicate that they are imagining their success and fame, using the sound of a cheering crowd while they look into an entirely empty auditorium will indicate that through non-diegetic sound. If using diegetic sound in the same scene, a way to indicate they are imagining their future would be through dialog, possibly with another character like a teacher. The artist tells the teacher "I think I am going to have a fantastic career," or something literal and visible. The choice of using diegetic versus non-diegetic sound is entirely up to the design and theme of the film, and while non-diegetic sound is a technique that is much more common in fiction, there's no reason a nonfiction film cannot use non-diagenetic sound.

## Roles in Sound – Who Does What?

Sound design involves several roles, like sound editing, sound mixing, and sound design. Music composition and music supervision are also aspects of sound. Not every production will use every aspect of sound design, particularly online videos such as YouTube channels that tend to have one person as the editor. Even in feature films, sometimes the editor performs many aspects of sound, but this depends on the editing team, the amount of time for the process, the budget, and plans for sound design. Typically these roles are shared with many people, particularly sound mixing which is the most highly specialized.

The roles in the tech sound design process are:

- **Sound designer** – The creative aspect of sound is done in sound design. This role, often done by the creative editor, involves the overall sound approach ranging from the sound effects, ambience, musical approach, and other creative aspects that contribute to the story. This phase is done in tandem with the rough cut/fine-cut story edit as the sound and image must weave together to create the full story. Just as there is a rough cut for picture there may also be a rough cut for sound design, in which a temp sound design created by the editor is replaced and polished in the final sound mix by the sound re-recorder.
- **Sound editor** – The sound editor is the person who cleans up poor-quality audio and replaces it with better audio. For example, if there were wild lines recorded on set in a quiet atmosphere it is the sound editor who will match them back and sync them to the image. In the news show or podcast, this clean-up involves removing "ums" and "uhs" from interviews, and sometimes trimming desired interview segments that are too long down so that you say the same thing and get the essence of a quote in fewer words and assure a specific timeframe.
- **Sound mixer or re-recording supervisor** – The sound mix is when the fine-cut sound tracks are exported and sent to the sound mixer, also called the audio re-recorder or re-recording engineer. They clean up any last issues with voice and dialog, enriches the audio, and balances the levels. Sometimes the sound re-recorder adds in additional sound effects. During the sound mix individual audio tracks are mastered to make them sound the best possible. Then those tracks are mixed down together into a stereo mix for television, streaming, or online video, or stereo or 5.1 surround mix for theatrical.

- **Composer** – The composer creates an original score for the production. On large-scale productions, like a Hollywood film, a composer may work with an entire orchestra. On smaller budget productions a composer may actually perform all of the music that they compose.
- **Music supervisor** – A different type of music approach includes using songs to create a soundtrack, as opposed to creating an original score. A song is created by a musician for distribution on its own, and several songs constitute the soundtrack of a film, while a score is a type of music created specifically for use in a film or media production. As with every other aspect of filmmaking, there are distinct creative advantages for using songs and a soundtrack, and for commissioning an original score, and it is a question of design. Some productions mix a soundtrack with a score, for example, having an original opening or closing score and a soundtrack of songs throughout the film. The music supervisor also manages all aspects of licensing songs for a soundtrack by contacting musicians, clearing rights, and licensing the music for the film.

**Name That Sound – Various Types of Recordings**

Your timeline often has more audio tracks than video ones. Skillful editors layer sounds including ambience and room tone to sound effects, music tracks, and dialog. There are actually many types of audio recorded in film and media production, each with slight variations of its origins, goals, and role in the production. Familiarizing yourself with the various types of audio elements allows you to plan how to approach your sound design.

The most common types of audio recording are listed in Table 6.1. Many of the names for audio files are used interchangeably but there are important distinctions between various types of sound used in production and in the audio assets used in post-production.

As the editor, you will receive many if not all of these kinds of audio. Your track breakdown may be somewhat different but the principle still applies to keeping similar audio files together on the same tracks in your timeline. Color coding helps with this organization, and can also indicate temp audio files. In fact, "temp" might be a designation for one of your tracks, so that you can easily find audio elements to be replaced,

Editors are the managers of the post-production process, and on large productions there might be a senior or supervising editor and several junior editors. On smaller productions it tends to be one primary editor. Regardless of the team size, the editor(s) will be sorting through all of these audio elements to construct the soundscape. Editors are also in charge of the process of re-recording sound in ADR and managing the talent in an ADR recording session. The actual recording session might be an additional team

*Table 6.1* Types of Audio

| | |
|---|---|
| **Production sound** | The sound you recorded during your filming: the talking, walking, fighting, joking, laughing, breathing, and any other actor vocalization. The term is the broadest of all audio categories and refers to any type of sound you recorded on your set or location, including wild sound, sync sound, and even room tone. |
| **Sync sound** | Production sound that is synced to the person speaking, either an actor or person being interviewed. The key distinction is that sync sound refers to lip-syncing the audio to the video, and it does not necessarily mean a synced sound of an object, machine, room, or other inanimate objects. It might be used in something like an action scene however when you need a specific type of sync sound because of the action. |
| **Scratch track** | Audio recorded on set or location with the intention of re-recording it in a studio. It differs from sync sound in that quality might vary considerably and not be very good. Scratch tracks are usually recorded because the environment is noisy and you are unlikely to ever get a clean sound. They also speed up the process of filming considerably by reducing retakes due to environmental noise and interference. |
| **Wild tracks and wild lines** | Audio that is recorded on set or location that is not synced to the image, and often recorded only as audio. *Wild lines* are "pick up lines," meaning an actor is off camera and performs their lines in an audio-only recording. They are also another way to back up sync sound. For example, to ensure good production in a noisy environment, like on a city street or crowded office, an actor and sound recorder might go to a quiet, closed location like a car or conference room with a door that closes, and record wild lines that might be matched back in editing. *Wild tracks*, on the other hand, are ambience and environmental noise that is recorded to provide options in editing. Its purpose is to provide natural sound for the environment depicted in a scene, serve a type of room tone, and create consistency from scene to scene. The audio recorder walks around the location to get clean audio of specific environmental elements. For example, at a sporting event, perhaps the cheering crowds have a unique tone or chant, and that might be recorded as wild tracks. It might also be the sound of a playground, park, specific natural or built environment, or something else with a unique sound. |
| **ADR sound** | This stands for "automated dialogue replacement" or re-recorded lines that replace scratch tracks or sound that was corrupted or damaged. ADR is recorded in a sound studio with the actors mimicking exactly and precisely the words they said: the timing, the emotional quality, breathing, and all other aspects so that it syncs back perfectly to their lips. They are usually watching themselves on a video replay in order to do this with precision. Despite the name, it is not a terribly automated process and can be very time-consuming and expensive. The difference between ADR and wild lines is that ADR is much more precise and controlled, and done in a studio setting, while wild lines are on set, and much more challenging to do with perfect lip-sync precision. ADR is also quite costly while wild lines only take time and planning but don't add much to costs. |

(*Continued*)

*Table 6.1* (Continued)

| | |
|---|---|
| **Room tone** | Exactly as the name says, room tone is the sound of a room, recorded cleanly for a minimum of 30 to 60 seconds, if not more. Unique room tone provides an enormous amount of information to the story: the type of space from the size to the other occupants; the neighborhood and what is nearby, from a city street with layers of noise coming into quiet breezes in a country setting. Room tone balances audio levels by providing a standard base for each interview or dialog clip. Every room and space has a unique audio signature, from the low hum of air conditioners in offices, to the sound of a meadow with songbirds or a distant train, to a warehouse with concrete floors, machinery humming, and dozens of people working. Room tone can be recorded in outdoor areas as well; and the more unique the space, the more special attention should be paid to capturing adequate room tone. If you are filming at a rodeo, for example, you may need to gather a lot of different wild tracks and room tone to ensure the unique mix of audio is authentically portrayed on screen. |
| **MOS** | A slang term for video recorded with no sound, with its origins in the German-influenced "mit out sound." You will often see visual-only clips labeled MOS and will have to add sound to these clips. |
| **Music** | There are many types of music as well, which are part of their overall sound design. As music is not typically recorded during production, the various types are detailed below. |
| **Stems (audio mix)** | Stems refer to separated out tracks. In film production it is common to keep each audio element on its own audio track. For example, the dialogue will be on tracks 1 and 2, and possibly up to tracks 3 and 4 (or more, depending on the number of characters). Sound effects will be on their own dedicated tracks, as are voiceover, ambience, foley, and music. The reason for this is if something needs to change to a specific element it is easy to find that element. When you send your sound out for your sound mix you generate out each of your audio tracks as its own stem so that the audio mixer has the flexibility to change every element individually. Stems are also important for films that are going to be dubbed or re-recorded in other languages, for example, if the dialogue or voiceover/narration needs to be translated and redubbed, then a version of the film will be made without those tracks in the audio, and stems in the new language will be added. |

member or might be done by an in-house sound team. Either way, the editor(s) must prepare the script and specific files for re-recording, and manage the process of matching the sound back.

Similarly, editors are tasked with identifying other audio elements that need to be replaced because the original audio recording was not of good quality. For example, if there is background noise in an ambient track or a sound effect is not clear or evocative enough.

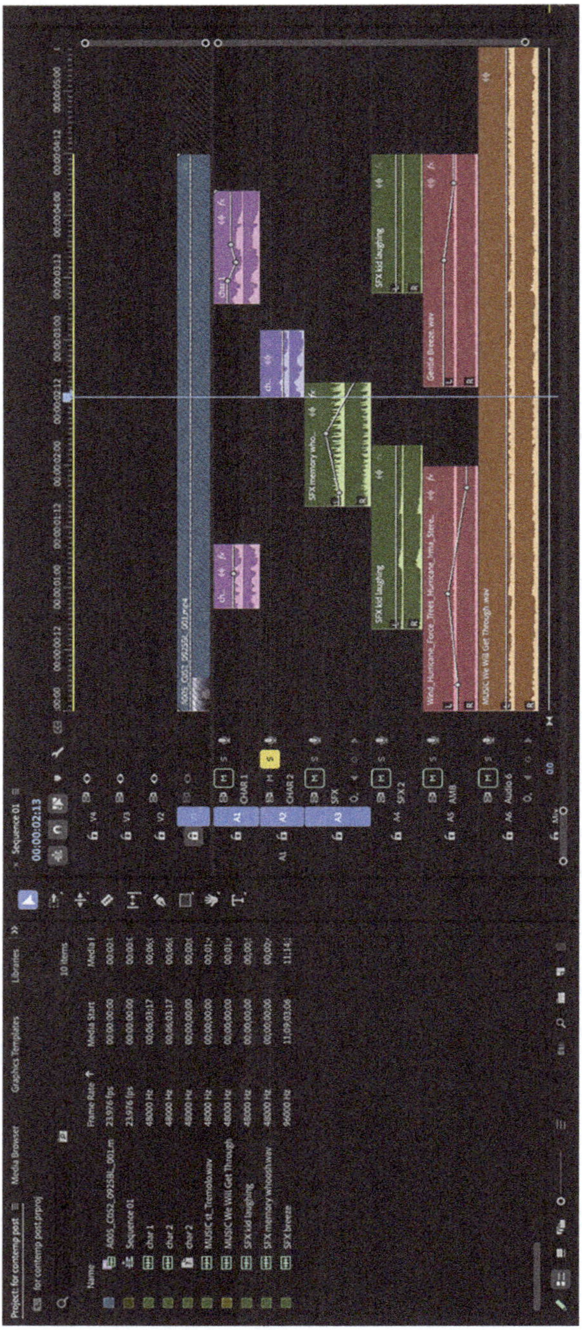

*Figure 6.1* An Adobe Premiere timeline with six tracks sorted by dialog, SFX, ambience, and music. Image by author.

**Layers of Sound – Where to Begin?**

Once you have your production sound, wild tracks, room tone, music, and all audio elements, you are ready to begin your sound design. Since many editors do much of their own sound design, and add ambience, music, and room tone to the rough cuts, the soundscape edit ideally starts at the same time as the picture edit.

Many people assume the natural starting point is your production sound. And for some films that is the starting place for building the sound to the image, particularly in dialog-heavy films and documentaries (more on this below).

But first, consider another approach: start with the ambience of each scene, or with the music. The ambience is incredibly powerful in determining how audiences interpret the tone of the scene. Faint background noise can indicate the type of neighborhood somebody is in, and their environmental and social influences, for example, if there is constant heavy machinery or the sounds of a crowded and lively street as a backdrop. Probably everybody has seen a film that includes a scene with a mournful foghorn, indicating loneliness and isolation. Ambient sound also serves as a type of reflection of the character's inner world. For example, if a story is about a family divided over an issue where they disagree, and you have a highly emotional scene in which a teenager in the family is revealing something difficult to their parents, rather than using a straightforward basic room tone you have the choice to add ambience like traffic, rainfall, or more dramatic weather elements, or even something slightly surreal like the creaking of a house. If done in a smooth and non-intrusive way, this adds another layer to the story. Depending on your specific story, you might take a non-diegetic sound approach, for example by using playground noises, a child's song, or remembered conversations from decades prior to add subtext to the scene, and indicate that it is about the teenager's memories, coming of age, and current emotional state.

Similarly, music will also create a powerful mood. Starting with the music and then cutting the images to the already-established rhythm and timing can shape the visuals in a very natural way. This clearly will work best with music-forward films such as soundtrack-heavy features, music documentaries, music videos, and some advertising. Some editors start with a "temp track" of scores, loops, and other sounds, and build the film around desired music, then take that temp track to a composer at a near-final stage. Others work with composers or music tracks right from the beginning, as they prefer to use the music to pace the scene, and do not want to have to replace the music at the fine-cut stage. Still other editors prefer to use music as a sound effect and bring it in and out like ambience or a sound effect. This entire sound design process is integral to the content of the film.

The suggestion to start with ambience or music is rooted in creating atmosphere and audio structure in the scene and then layering on the specific sounds that need to be present. In the examples above, for the performer in the empty theater, footsteps might provide a sense of the space, and specific sounds to indicate things like the time of day (is there distant traffic noise or late-night silence) and how many other people are around, if any (for example, noises of people working in another part of the theater). For the teenager telling the parents something difficult, their breathing might be an atmospheric addition along with the noises of the house. Are there other people there? What are they doing? Is someone cooking dinner? Is the TV or radio on? If so, what is playing? Is it loud and distracting, soothing, or almost like white noise?

Once you have your music and ambience laid into your tracks, then start laying in the specific sounds. These come from your actual production sound, for example, footsteps or other production sounds. This is the point where the editor and director can see if they have everything they need in the production sound, and what might need to be replaced from a sound library to make it more dramatic, clean, and specific. As you start creating the specific and actual sounds and mixing them with your ambience, and then with any offscreen or non-diagenetic sound, you can continue building your sound design with additional effects if that is relevant for your production. Changing pitch, adding a little reverb to create a sense of space, or even slowing down a sound can alter the feel of the film, as does adding in subtle non-diegetic sound effects.

While the methods of creating a sound design are as numerous as the methods of creating all stories, the lesson here is that you need to put as much thought into your approach to your sound design as you do to your visual story. The ambience, production sound, non-diegetic sound, effects, and types of music are critical to the production, and can be one of the most creative parts of your filmmaking process. And in creating that sound design, the order of how you design it is also important to create structure and work as efficiently as possible.

## Dialog-Heavy Films and Documentaries: The Radio Edit

Starting with ambience and music can work well for many types of filmmaking including documentaries and nonfiction. But the reality is that most broadcast-bound pieces, documentaries, news clips, and sports programming rely on interviews and dialog. For these pieces the most common starting point is the *radio edit*. And this is when you start the structure of the film based on your audio selects, and begin by pulling soundbites or dialog, and then structure each scene based on the voice as opposed to the picture.

The radio edit does not mean you forget about image. Rather it is a more efficient way to start structuring a film when your primary content are interviews or a dialog-heavy fiction film. It means you start the edit with the audio — what people say — and create scenes by just laying the clips down with the interview image. For the moment, disregard jump cuts because you will cover the image with other footage once you have created the audio structure. It also does not mean you forget about scenes, arcs, or narrative structure for your film. Those still apply and can be done in the audio version. Essentially, the radio edit is a starting point for creating all of these.

When you start your radio edit, you still need to create reels and scenes. For example, based on the Ocean University example used in other parts of this book, perhaps you create a scene about Sam and her mom Molly through their interviews, about how their family has always been swimmers and was a major part of their life. The radio edit of that scene is on a timeline by itself. Then you create another scene using your interviews, for example about how the swim team members cheered each other on at the national competitions and how their moral support for each other helped them do their best in their races. Each of these are on an individual timeline. If you keep going this way, organizing content into scenes based on theme or story elements, with each scene structured on individual timelines, it becomes much easier to structure the whole film because you can shift the timelines around and change the order of your scenes.

Once you have created your scenes, established the order, and are comfortable with that part of the storytelling, then you can put them all together in one timeline. There are a couple ways to do this. The most obvious is that you can carefully cut and paste the footage into one big timeline. Before doing that, you might want to try grouping the scenes. All three major professional editing software programs allow you to group clips together, meaning the software locks the clips and you can move them around like one single clip. If you group each scene and then put the grouped clips on one timeline, it is easier to shuffle them without losing something important or accidentally knocking something out of order.

So essentially, if your Ocean University radio edit has eight short scenes, you can group the clips and pull them onto one timeline. Then on your "full-film" timeline you can shuffle the order of the eight scenes until you are content with how the story flows. If you set up your project by just cutting everything together in one long timeline, then shifting the order of the scenes can be messy and challenging. If you want to move scene 2 after scene 8, and then bump scene 7 up to where scene 2 was, and all your footage is in one timeline, you will have to redo a lot of editing. You might lose some of your visual transitions and need to put them back in the new order. You might also lose audio sync or titles. When you have your final story structure, then you start layering on your visual footage, create transitions, add additional *vérité* scenes that might link some of these interview scenes together, and so on.

It is not going to be a surprise that the radio edit is a common technique in broadcasting. It is expedient, draws on your primary resource (the interview), and is much faster to edit. It is an excellent approach in situations when time is of the essence. Even in post-production schedules that are not under the pressure of broadcast, a radio edit can be an elegant way to create the structure for your film. It is a sort of blueprint that allows you to see exactly what type of visual coverage, music, sound effects, animation, graphics, and other footage you will need.

**Class Activity 6**

**Create a Soundscape Using a Sound Library**

Watching and listening will only take you so far in learning sound. For this activity, you will create your own soundscape. Using a free sound library and a movie clip, your own short film, or a Creative Commons film, design a soundscape.

Suggested resource:
Freesound is a free, global, collaborative sound library (https://freesound.org)

**Activity**

1 Find a short clip in a movie – your own film, a mainstream release, or a Creative Commons video. It should have no talking in it so you can focus on the sound environment and not dialog. A clip of one to two minutes is plenty for this exercise; it can take a long time to match up every sound so make sure it is short and has a variety of options. Animations are a great choice, as the sound does not have to be as realistic as live action.
2 Pull it into your editing software and strip the audio off of it.
3 Go through your clip and identify the needed sfx: ambience, footsteps, "room tone" for space, motors, animals, and so on. Also identify any non-diegetic and expressive sounds you might need: beating hearts, train whistles, that mournful foghorn. Start creating a list of your sounds.
4 Head over to your sound library. Use any sound library you have access to — if you have a professional one available, that certainly would work, but you can also use Freesound, which is very extensive, or even the YouTube sound library although that is somewhat limited. Start searching out the sounds you need.

5 Start cutting your soundscape and practice separating out your audio tracks. If you have people in your clip, dedicate a track to each character, another track for SFX that are not clearly shown, another for ambience, etc.
6 Use your software's audio mixer to monitor the volume of each separate track. You don't have to create a full mix but you should balance your levels so the sounds are at appropriate volumes. (Note that the *audio mixer* is not the same as the audio meter that shows you the overall volume; the mixer shows you the audio level of each track.)

In class, watch each student's sound design, and discuss the results (see questions below). There are many skills learned in this, from the creation of the sound design itself to the sound effects (SFX) search, to the many types of audio files and how they work together. Make sure you watch on a real projector so you can hear it outside of an editing computer. It is valuable to hear how your audio design sounds through a projector, because it will be different than your computer headphones. Hearing this firsthand is the best way to understand how a mix sounds in different speakers.

**Discussion**

Was the audio design believable? If so, why? If not, why not? What sounds worked best? Were they literal sounds like we see a dog and then hear a dog bark, or more evocative like we see a dog and then hear a reverb whistle of someone calling a dog? Each student might even share what they had to type into a search bar to find the correct sound, because the vocabulary might not be obvious. Was there anything surprising you had to look up to find a sound that fit?

# 7 Score

## Score

### *Music – Scores, Soundtracks, Songs, and Loops*

Your music is one of the most important post-production decisions that you will make for your film. It shares equal ranking with all other elements that go into filmmaking, because a music track is a story in and of itself. A music track will have a theme and an arc, with progressions, tempo, builds and falls, and an end to the arc.

The reach of the film score can be greater than the reach of some films – consider the main theme track from the score for "The Good, The Bad and the Ugly." Audiences worldwide will recognize Ennio Morricone's evocative composition, even if they've never seen the film. For that film in particular this recognition extends to nearly every track in the score.

Even if you are making a much simpler more straightforward media piece, such as a YouTube channel, and using downloaded songs or loops, your music choices are crucial. Before starting, consider the different varieties of music for film, as they are not all the same (listed in Table 7.1). Understanding the difference between songs, scores, loops, and ambience, can help you communicate with a composer, or do a more effective search in a sound library.

You can practice your skills at scoring with Class Activity 7 at the end of this chapter.

## Dear Composer: This Is What I Am Looking for

We know that music is one of the most evocative parts of the film. Yet, it can be quite challenging to convey what type of music is desired by the composer. Take any of the examples throughout this chapter; for example, the 2023 musical "Barbie," which won multiple awards for its soundtrack, included songs talking about soul-searching and understanding one's purpose in life. It all makes sense once on screen, but how does one convey that to a composer? For the 1966 epic spaghetti western "The Good, The Bad,

DOI: 10.4324/9781003473152-8

*Table 7.1* Types of Music

| | |
|---|---|
| **Scores** | Original music composed specifically for a film. Scores are created to fit the story shape and cut to the timing of scenes. While film scores can and frequently are released on their own, their origin is part of the film production. |
| **Soundtracks** | A variety of songs are cut to a film, which have independent musical lives outside of the film. For example, "Barbie" has an original soundtrack with songs like "What Was I Made For" by Billie Eilish, plus many more songs which were specifically created for the film. The songs were released as *Barbie the Album*, a soundtrack album released on the same day as the film. Soundtracks are not necessarily all original music to the film and can mix songs created specifically for the film with songs that have had long lives before the film. A different example is a film like "Pulp Fiction" which mixed eclectic pop songs like Kool & The Gang's "Jungle Boogie," Dusty Springfield's "Son of a Preacher Man," and a wide assortment of other rock, blues, and soul songs to create its unique and highly memorable soundtrack. None of this music was created specifically for the film, although the mix of this varied collection became synonymous with the film, and many of the songs gained a second life from being included in *Music from the Motion Picture Pulp Fiction*, the 1994 soundtrack album that enjoyed its own commercial success. |
| **Songs** | Individual tracks of music within the soundtrack. As mentioned above they can be from popular sources outside of the film, or written as part of the script (as in the "Barbie" example). Using songs to convey dialog is the hallmark of musical films, when the dialog is delivered through a song performed by a character, making it part of the script. Additional instrumental music might be added as part of the film score. Another example of a music film which used songs to convey dialog was "LaLa Land," which featured musical performances in nearly every key scene. |
| **Loops** | Short instrumental musical segments that are played as transitions or as part of a scene to add atmosphere. Loops typically refer to music or ambience tracks that can be played endlessly, as opposed to scores or songs with strong builds and musical climaxes. |
| **Stock music** | Pre-recorded songs that are widely available for purchase from sound libraries. |
| **Scratch tracks or temp music** | Songs an editor uses in creating the rough cut, with the intention that these will not be used in the final film and will be replaced by an original score. |
| **Composer** | A musician who works with the film team to create a score unique to this film. Composers might work only on the opening and credit roll score, or they might create tracks for every scene in the film. It is quite common for composers to perform and record the music as well, although on high-budget films a composer might work with additional musicians to perform and record the score. |

(*Continued*)

*Table 7.1* (Continued)

| | |
|---|---|
| **Leitmotif** | A melody or sound effect in the music that is repeated throughout the film, typically in association with a specific character. Think of a film like "The Hobbit," with varied leitmotifs in the music for each specific characters: Bilbo's theme includes warm harmonies in the shire and more rhythmic ones as his adventure develops, while Thorin's character features strong horn calls, and a dark low rumble is used for Thorin's nemesis, the Orc. These leitmotifs help to add personality to characters, help audiences distinguish between characters, and signal emotional turning points in each character's arc. |
| **Stems (music)** | Stems in music refer to having each instrument or track separated, for a multi-instrument composition. For example, if you have a rock track and you want to isolate the guitar, drum, bass, so each has its own separate stem so the editor can further weave the music into the film. Composers can generate many different types of stems – for example, isolating out vocals from the rest of the music, or creating stems for each instrument. Stock music tracks are often licensed either in a mixed-down version, with everything combined, or with separated stems for each instrument. A custom score might use a leitmotif for various different elements of the story, separated out into stems, and then bring those stems together into the full composition at key moments in the piece. |

and the Ugly," what might Sergio Leone have said to Ennio Morricone to convey the theme and mood of the score that ended up being one of the most famous compositions of all filmmaking history? Starting with questions like that might provide both the director and the composer with some guidance, although these types of thematic questions are challenging to respond to with clear and succinct answers.

There are easier starting points to talk to your composer, including specifics and practical aspects that will determine your sound. One of the best ways to start to build the sound of the film is to create a playlist of *temp tracks* or "*sound-alike*" tracks. This is a term for music that sounds like what you're seeking. You can use nearly any kind of music for your sound-alike playlist, including pop songs and tracks from one of the dozens of online music libraries, as long as you know those are temp tracks that can only be used during the editing and must be replaced for the final film. Even for films that cannot afford to license copyrighted music, sound-alike tracks create a way to experiment with cutting a certain theme or tone of a song to your picture. It also allows you to start to refine creative aspects like *rhythm*, *instrumentation*, *tempo*, *builds*, if the tracks have *lyrics* or are *instrumental*, and the *duration* of the track in question. Creating a playlist of temp tracks provides a way to start detailing the specifics of your desired music.

If you know some of these aspects already you can start working with a composer. Examples of what you might tell the composer are "fast-paced guitar music with a country and western vibe," or "a deep soul rhythm and bass driven ambient track," or "ethereal ambient pulses that build to a deep swell." It is also important to know these are starting points, but only starting points. Your music likely will evolve once you start working with a composer. You may cut a fast-paced country western guitar track into your scene and realize it doesn't work (which is one reason that many post-production teams start with temp tracks). On the other hand, if your composer understands the theme of your film and how you want the music to weave into the story, their role is to be a *creative* contributor. Proving a mix of story guidelines, temp tracks, and creative freedom can result in music that surprises you and also fits the scene perfectly.

To understand how this works in practice, see the "Examples of Sound Design" section below, which illustrates how four editors approached their sound design. A few guidelines you will need to provide a composer are in Table 7.2.

*Table 7.2* Guidelines for Composers

| | | |
|---|---|---|
| **Instrumentation** | Types of preferred instrument and how many instruments are in the sound design. | A single piano, a four-piece rock band, a full orchestra, a specific type of drum, guitar, or other instrument. |
| **Duration** | The length of the particular track or opening or closing theme. | This can include if you need the track to fit a specific scene's twists, for example: "Start slow and at exactly 13 seconds the rhythm slowly speeds up to double time by 19 seconds." For these types of very specific composed music the composer needs the final scenes so that they can be watching the visuals while they work. |
| **Rhythm** | Fast-paced, building to a specific tempo, slow-paced, looping and ambient, etc. | How much noticeable rhythm do you want in the music? Or, do you want it to be atmospheric without an aggressive rhythm? Some very intense rhythms will dominate the visuals, and some intensely rhythmic visuals will lack energy without similarly timed music. |
| **Culture and history** | Do you want the music in your film to reflect a specific culture or type of music? An instrument that is common in a particular culture but not elsewhere in the world? | Is there a way to find a musician from the specific place portrayed on screen? This will produce the most authentic version of this type of music, and also provide an opportunity to work with a musician beloved in a specific culture or community. |

## Examples of Sound Design

### *How the Featured Editors Used Sound in Their Films*

Your approach to music or sound is as profoundly unique as your approach to casting, story development, finding settings, and every other aspect of your film. Each of the editors interviewed for this book shared a bit about their approaches to using sound. This section shares highlights on how they did their sound. (Please see the complete interviews for even more detailed accounts).

### *Aashish Kumar On Creating the Music for "Body, Home, World"*

***Author:*** **For your interactive, intergenerational story-telling platform, "Body, Home, World" how did you find music and how did you work on the score for that?**

*Aashish Kumar:* There were two types of music that I was looking for in the project. One that would be part of the documentary shorts, which is more traditional, but I also needed to make sure that the site in which the stories live, they have … they're not just divorced from the music that is in the stories and the non-diegetic music that I'm using within the stories. So I found a composer [Ravi Krishnaswami] whose main work had been for video games. Somebody who understood the value of how you create a composition that has stems, and those stems occur in different pieces and different parts, and then they also come together. So that approach was very valuable in creating pieces that used the entire composition.

But on the website, we were using a stem or a sound that you may have heard in the piece if you paid attention. Of course, the idea is never to identify something very, very clearly, but overall it coheres. So that approach really paid well. He [Ravi] had done the music for each of the short pieces, and they were all unique. They had their moments, and he was able to take my cues and make transformations in the existing pieces so that the foregrounding and the backgrounding of instrumentation, of poignancy … those were taken care of.

But, when it came to the website, the interactions themselves had to be in some ways punctuated. It's tricky on a website, if you click on something and you don't get some type of a feedback, whether it's a click or whether it's a sound or something changes on the screen, and if it's too silent, then it kind of eerie because all of a sudden the video playback begins and that's full of sounds, but the website is silent.

So he [Ravi] was instrumental in working through that process. For instance, the website has a mandala, which is comprised of WebGL three-dimensional particles, and you can actually take your mouse, or if you're working on a touch device, you can turn the mandala in the other direction. That turning has a sound that comes from reversing one of the music beds that was used in the film. So you went about it kind of thoughtfully, not borrowing or cobbling together pieces, but working on a piece whose stems served in various directions.

For the piece that I was working with in Assam, I was very clear that I wanted sounds from the region and that people would identify. That there wouldn't be just generic music… I was really lucky to find a composer [Ron Cha] who was from Guwahati … who had studied jazz at the Berklee College of Music and was able to take folk compositions, but also do improvisational work that made it more contemporary. In the documentary world, you have to work with the blessings of the entire world because the money is not going to make it all happen.

I wrote to [Ron], and all I told him was a brief of the film, and his immediate response was, you're welcome to use the work because you're doing it for awareness and educational reasons, and I'm happy to be part of it. He didn't even ask to see a cut of the film to approve how I had used this film.

I was really blessed because I just sent him the finished cut of the film, and in a very respectable way, I sort of said, I'm giving this back to you with trepidation because I have changed the context of your music. I have used it in a different way, and he wrote me a beautiful email saying that he was so happy to see how thoughtfully his songs had been used and how they had been given a new life in the context of this film that he hadn't even thought of.

I do think that looking for things that you believe belong within the film and not being satisfied until you find them, and, of course, luck is a big part of it. Finding this composer was, for me, a big stroke of fortune, and it really impacts the film. I mean, don't let anyone tell you that music is an afterthought. It is the sound of the film, right?

***Zeb Achonu on Editing Music for Broadcast Documentaries and TV Shows***

*Author:* **When you work with music, do you start with music? Early on, I was taught to slap in a track at the end. But when I did my own films, if I structured the scene to the music, it just worked a lot better. What is your method?**

*Zeb Achonu:* I come from a music background, so I will cut a tune down to fit what I need, which can be frustrating. I've worked with directors who've been like, just cut it and fade it. And I'm like, "No, because the flow doesn't work" … if you know the song, you know what the lyrics are, you know what the rhythm is, and I can't do that … When I started, I remember being told, just choose a track, lay it down, they'll sort it out in the dub. Someone else will sort it out, which was what we did.

I love it if I can start with music, but I also really enjoy working with composers who send me their temp tracks, but are going to basically recompose everything at the end or refi everything because they own that. And I love that, but I know what the mood is that we're working with … I know that if I put down a lot of temporary tracks, I never know if I'm insulting someone, they're like, "I'd never write that," or "Why didn't you use the stuff I sent" or whatever.

I will just begin. And … what gets really frustrating is … maybe once a year I'll be on something where I'm coming in to finish something and it's all very quick and they need different music and there's no time and dah, dah. And then … so what's been really helpful took me, again, years to realize that this was an option … is to have contacts at the music libraries who I can just email and say, "I've got a scene, and we're in a market in Nigeria, but I don't want traditional old school. What do you expect it to sound like? I need this feeling. It's this time of day and I want this, and there's these people walking. Can you help?" And it is someone's job there to make me a playlist of things they think might work from what I've explained. Or I might send them a clip or they might come in and look … and will send me some ideas and whether I use them or not, it's just someone else has done that initial brainstorm for me because I haven't had the time. And I really enjoy working like that, even though it sounds like a cop-out that someone else is doing the work. But it gives me a new starting point. And sometimes it's brilliant. Sometimes I'll go, "These are great, but actually if you could get me something like this, but I dunno, less drums or more guitar," whatever. And that can be really fun, a really fun quick way because it is, it's not having my music assistant in the room, but they're … part of the process and it just gives me a different perspective. I find that quite useful when I'm working at speed.

It's so rare to have enough time to do the music on anything. It's lovely when I'm in a feature doc and they've got a composer on board from the start, and I can chat to them, and they'll give me some temp or I'll say, "I've cut this, I've put nothing on it … What does it spark in you?" And I just can build up that creative relationship. And I really, really, really enjoy that. I really enjoy that.

It's a real mix. I've had music supervisors … it is great when you've got 'em on board. It's so rare that I seem to have them on the projects that I'm on, but then you'll have something like continuing drama will be quite fun. Something like EastEnders because they will already have in the system for you … the latest pop hits or others that have been sent to them. And then it's my job now to know the program and know the feeling of, like, "In this scene, we are in the cafe and it's this time of day. And I feel like the radio would be playing these tunes." Whereas in this person's bedroom or their house, they're in this mood. That's sort of setting a mood to the person … to where they are and building that, as opposed to laying the sound bed or the soundtrack to a documentary where you are just trying to move the emotion on a little bit or keep the film moving. They're very different ways of working and it's all fun.

***Carla Gutiérrez – Working with a Composer for "FRIDA"***

***Author:*** **How do you find music? Do you tend to work with a composer or do you ever find yourself just buying stock tracks? Or do you start with stock tracks and then take that to a composer?**

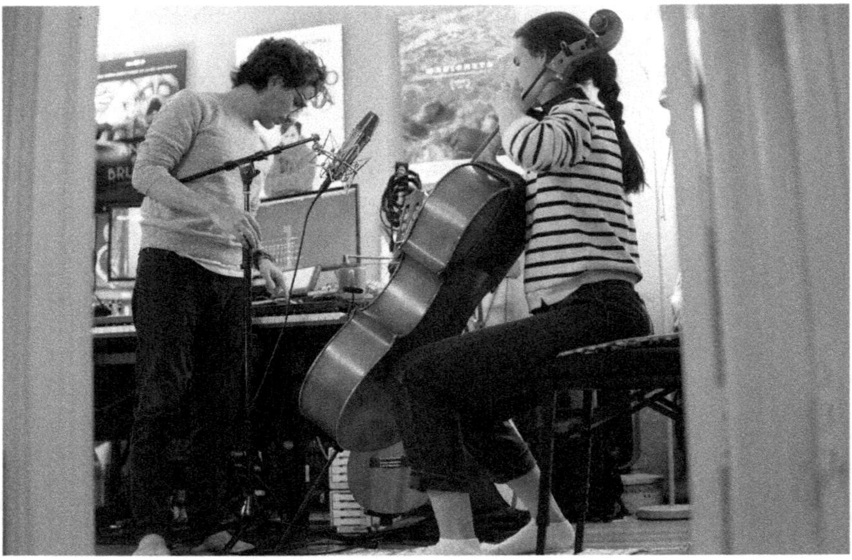

*Figure 7.1* Víctor Hernández Stumpfhauser, composer for "FRIDA," and cellist Alexa Ramírez recording the score. Image credit: Víctor Hernández Stumpfhauser.

*Carla Gutiérrez:* Our composer was in LA. And I mean, that's the beauty of remote. It has its limitations ... some of the collaboration is beautiful to do in person, but it also allows you to be able to work with talent that is not near you. And that was really important to me to be able to pull in talent from Mexico. Or Mexican talent that was anywhere in the country. Our composer (Víctor Hernández Stumpfhauser) is from Michoacán (Mexico). He lives in LA. And that's the beauty of remote ... not only be able to talk in virtual calls, but also just share work so quickly. It's just so fluid now. And I was able to work from home and also jump into the office.

Sound to me is really important in the edit, and it ... sound very much changes the way that we experience time, how time moves when we're seeing something. So either sound effects, for example, I always cut archival with sound effects. I can never just only have the video and say, "Oh, the sound team will add stuff." Because I know that once you add layers of sound, and depending on what decisions if you want to go abstract, poetic, or very literal to what you're seeing, sound just kind of changes the experience that we have in terms of the rhythm of how things move and how time moves.

So I start cutting with music right away if that's something that I want to try for a scene or not. Sometimes I have to be careful not to use music as a crutch … with temp music, it's difficult. With "FRIDA," it took us a while to find something that kind of got toward the path of what we wanted to try out with the composer. And then the composition was very different from our temp music, but it just kind of gave us some ideas … this is what we want to explore. So with temp music, you never get everything that you will get with composed music. It's very different, but you can at least get a little bit of rhythm and a little bit of emotional mood and maybe a little bit of the texture that you're going for. For "FRIDA," we used a lot of temp music that didn't work at all, and we found some temp music that was working a little bit better. And then we started working with the composer kind of early on, with a couple of cues, just to be able to get the voice. And then he worked really fast for the rest of the film, but we already knew that we got it with those two cues, and we worked those two cues for a long time. For us, the music in that film was another voice of "FRIDA," and it just kind of took us a while to really capture her voice with the music as well.

***Allie Sultan – Working on the Musical "Incognita's Infamous Adventures"***

***Author:*** **How do you work with music? Do you work with composers? Did you have a composer or score?**

*Allie Sultan:* I'm really lucky to work with students at Middle Tennessee State University because we have a commercial songwriting program, we have an audio production program, we've got music scoring classes, and in Nashville, there's a ton of music supervisors whose job is to get music placed in film and television, mostly for the country music industry. But these are folks who are skilled and who are friends you can look toward to get advice. But in almost every film I've made, I've initially used unlicensed music and it has hurt me. In my most recent film, I am collaborating with a student who's writing stuff for it. But yeah, music's so hard. I think having a composer is so critical.

***Author:*** **Since "Incognita" is a musical, how did you approach the music differently?**

*Allie Sultan:* ["Incognita" was filmed] going around Nashville … there's music in every clip. I'm like, "How can I use this?" Really looking at fair use now I'm going to have to run everything through a lawyer to make sure I am not violating copyright or even privacy laws with the people in the film … But, luckily … we had original music because Sarah (Sarah Michele Bailey), who stars in this film, also wrote all the music. And then we worked with David Weinstein, who's a composer who had done a lot of work with Nashville Children's Theater, and he also teaches at Belmont University … I think has since left to start a camp theater camp in Maine … He did some orchestrations with strings.

Because we're in Nashville, Sarah's got a music studio in her backyard. We all have these sheds in our backyard where we record really amazing music. So I will say Tennessee has passed an incentive for scoring. If you use musicians here in Tennessee, you can get a tax rebate for composing for film, TV and games … there are lots of composers in Middle Tennessee.

**Class Activity 7**

**Re-Score a Scene with Several Music Choices**

Using a Creative Commons music library like the three listed below, experiment with how different music changes the mood of the scene. Do a "music search" – which is exactly what it sounds like – and is an excellent skill to practice as plunking a poorly chosen track under your footage will degrade your entire project. A music search can take anywhere from 15 minutes to a month, depending on what you want and where you are looking. By practicing with easily available online tracks, you can learn how to understand and refine your approach to music, and be prepared to talk to a composer when you are ready for that.
Suggested Creative Commons music libraries:

- Free Music Archive (https://freemusicarchive.org)
- Incompetech (https://incompetech.com)
- Ende.app (https://filmmusic.io)

**Activity**

1 Find a non-dialog scene in a film or TV show, or pull a stock clip, archival clip, or Creative Commons short film from internet sources. (In my classes, we often used the film "Wall-E" because it has so little dialog. Or, find a Creative Commons animation online.) It is important to not have dialog so you can put in music without lips flapping with no audio, which will ruin the effect. You could do this with a short film you created, but it is easier to practice and change the sounds on clips that you are not as passionate about, so you can really explore this without feeling like you are actually choosing the final music for your film.
2 Determine some basic music parameters: Orchestral? A cinematic military track with many horns and huge builds? A mellow jazz track or a discordant one? An ethereal chorus of angels singing? A lone piano? As you look through the music libraries you will start to see some of the terms they use to describe different types of music. Some let you search by instrument, most have beats per minute, and nearly all have music genres like reggae, jazz, funk, soundtrack, etc.
3 Do your music search and find at least three to five relevant tracks to re-score the scene. As you go through the music libraries you will start to understand how you can search out the best options and maybe even find some new ones.
4 Pull your scene into a timeline, delete the audio, and bring in your music tracks. Start cutting and layering to make your "score."
5 As you lay the tracks to the clip, using the "solo" and "mute" buttons to turn the new score on and off and see the results. Keep going and cut the new tracks to different parts of the scene. Perhaps have one at the beginning, another in the middle, and a third to create a climactic ending.
6 Have the class share their re-scored scenes and discuss how the results changed the story.

In this, you are looking for ways that the music and image interact, not to dominate the image or try to push emotion that is not already in the scene. An intense soundtrack will not necessarily make an everyday scene (for example, an early morning swim practice) more cinematic if the image and music do not relate to each other. On the other hand, you can experiment with off-genre music, like a slow or ambient track to a fast swim race.

# 8 Color

A hint of aqua in the shadows. Enhancing the golden and pink glows of magic hour – or even creating it artificially. Creating deep black shadows and brilliant highlights, or a subdued palette of russets and ombres for a period piece. The color, saturation, and color density of your story are elements of the story that were previously available only on the highest-budget films. But now, productions of even modest means build in a color-correction phase or even a full color grade.

## Color Correction versus Color Grading

These two terms are often used to mean the same thing, or to generally mean "doing something with the color." They are, in fact, quite different. They come into the post-production process at different phases, have different roles in the story, and also have practical differences in terms of time and cost. Color is one of filmmaking's best tools after story and music.

### *Color Grading*

During your post-production phase, your team has painstakingly considered the themes, subtext, and genre of your story. Likely you debate the character's emotional life and how to put it on screen with the images, audio, and music. Now, you can also emphasize those with color. What emotional elements would you like to reference with your color? Color can create comfort and discomfort. It can excite the audience and signal adventure. It can indicate that the scene is about intimacy and romance, nostalgia, or cold, hard, reality. Or maybe it will show a world that is a bit richer and better than regular reality. All of the shades and hues referenced above – aqua, ombre, russet, pink, gold – come from doing a color grade to enhance footage filmed in ways that prepare it for a color grade. That last part is important – while most footage can be color-corrected to some extent, to do a proper, fully designed color grade, the footage needs to be filmed in the appropriate way to ensure

DOI: 10.4324/9781003473152-9

the best results. Color grading can accomplish many, many types of changes in post, although it cannot do everything, particularly if the footage was not filmed in the correct way. Like every other aspect of filmmaking, color grading and correction require a careful, well-conceived approach. For films where color is meant to be a very important part of the storytelling, the most successful teams pre-visualize key scenes, and do tests with various camera settings and lighting to see how a location and the actors look with certain color treatments, and what camera and lighting adjustments might be needed to ensure the final footage turns out as planned.

### *Color Correction*

You were lighting an interview with sunlight and then it got cloudy. Or the camera's white balance was off, or you are matching footage from five cameras, have an important shot that is underexposed, or have an issue with a spot of dust on the footage. These are issues for color *correction*, which is different than color grading. Correction is simply fixing problems, errors, and issues, doing basic balancing between shots, especially from different cameras. A color correction ensures that the overall aesthetic matches. This is not a small job, however, in most cases it is not as extensive as a color grade.

Some key differences:

*Table 8.1* Differences between Color Grading and Color Correction

| | *Color Grading* | *Color Correction* |
|---|---|---|
| Amount of time | Nearly the entire production, depending on the extent of the color design and film. Ideally, a color grade concept starts in pre-production, the director does tests to ensure the lighting, costumes, and production design are also optimized for the grade, and the colorist can work with dailies to correct any production-related issues. The film footage must be shot in raw, flat footage, which is a professional standard, and the colorist might start working on concepts at the storyboard stage and continue through the final days of post. | A few days to a couple of weeks, at the end of the post process, depending on the issues and duration of the film. Minor common issues like white balance, saturation, and brightening shots are quite fast. Complex issues like removing dust or flaws from shots are far more extensive. |
| Skill level required | This is a highly skilled, advanced job. | For most corrections, this is an intermediate-level skill. |

(*Continued*)

*Table 8.1* (Continued)

| | | |
|---|---|---|
| Expense | Due to the skill level and creative input desired, this is a very expensive process. | Basic color is quickly becoming something that many editors can do, and while color correction still can be an additional cost, this is a shorter process than a full-color grade and therefore less expensive. |
| Preparation | Footage must be filmed as raw, flat color space. Typically, full-color grades involve the production designer, cinematographer, director, and edit team in the pre-pro stage, so that they can collaborate on set aspects of the color process, lighting, and create the overall palette. | Basic color correction is an expected step in post, and prep means simply ensuring the footage is at the fullest resolution and all proxies or low-res clips are transcoded.<br>Correcting complex problems means identifying clips during the editing phase that need work and getting them to the color correction person with time to see if a fix is possible. It is best to do this before getting to a fine cut, so if the clip is not fixable the team can replace it. |
| Software | DaVinci Resolve is the gold standard for color grading. Avid and Premiere have wonderful tools for adjusting color, however, DaVinci was the first, has been the standard for decades, and remains unparalleled in this capacity. | All professional editing software – Avid, Premiere, and DaVinci Resolve – can do basic color correction. |
| Specialization | This is highly specialized. | This is somewhat specialized. |
| LUTs | LUTs or "look-up tables" are instant color grades that are applied to flat footage to get it to a standard broadcast color space, or to grade it quickly. They are something like a professional version of an photo filter in that the goal is a "one-click" type of approach as opposed to a fine-tuned scene-by-scene manual color grade. Or, some colorists use LUTs as a starting point for more extensive customized grades.<br>Many colorists develop and sell their own LUTs. | Not as widely used in color correction as LUTs are intended for creating "looks." But a basic color correction on a specific type of footage, shot in a certain light on a certain camera, can create a LUT for that film that can be applied in a "one-click" way on most of the scenes and then individually adjusted, significantly speeding up the color process. |
| Footage and media | Should be ProRes 444 10-bit. | Ideally, should be at least ProRes 422 10-bit or higher resolution. Corrections can be done on lower-resolution footage although the quality will not be the same. |

## Creative Color

### *What Is "Right"? Using Your Eyes and Using the Scopes*

This is a frequent question when getting started with color. The option to make many changes in color does not mean you necessarily have to create a complete color grade for every film. Full-color grades with a detailed palette are most common in music videos and feature films, and, while documentaries and streaming episodics use color correction, full-color palettes are infrequent. So, when you are doing that color correction, how do you know you have it "correct?"

**Box 8.1 Feast Your Eyes – Exemplary and Gorgeous Uses of Color in Film**

A selection of films that stand out because of how they used color as an additional character in the film. As you consider how to use color in your story, watch a few of the following for inspiration:

"Call Me by Your Name" (2017) – The soft pastels of the Italian countryside in summer are both desaturated and full of intense heat, yet still feel natural in this heated coming of age by Luca Guadagnino.

"In the Mood for Love" (2000) – Wong Kar-wei's poignant romantic tragedy is like a living painting and masterclass in using color to convey story, with deep saturated reds and golds punctuating through a dark aesthetic to signal passion, mystery, and romance, and blues and greens spilling out to signal other emotional shifts. Watch for how the director used color to signal the emotional beats of the film and make one of filmmaking's most notoriously romantic films with barely a kiss in it.

"Moonlight" (2016) – The color scheme asserts itself as a character with its own dynamic arc in Barry Jenkins' coming-of-age romance drama. Deep pinks and yellows play out in scenes of family alienation, while blues, purples, and an aqua-tinged conversation on the beach show how the character's emotions drench every frame of this powerful story.

Every film by Wes Anderson – The singular design of a Wes Anderson film, from the saturated pastels of "Grand Budapest Hotel" (2014) to the autumn hues of "Moonrise Kingdom" (2012), makes his body of work uniquely notable for their production design and exemplary color schemes.

### *Correct for Faces First*

Typically, a color correction centers on making the imagery look like it should in real life. The north star for the colorist is *skin tone*. How do the people in the shot look? Design your correction around exposing properly for faces. If a shot is lit with strong sunlight, and one side of someone's face is overexposed but the area behind them is too dark, how do you balance the shot? The first correction is to bring the face as close to good exposure as possible, even if it means that the underexposed area becomes a bit darker. There are tools to work on just the face and to separate it out from the background, which are a bit more time-consuming, however in a situation where the colorist makes a decision as to what to correct, the first priority is the faces.

### *Using Scopes*

Using your eye to see how an image looks is like using your headphones to balance the audio – in other words, they can be a reference but are not the best final measurement. Premiere, Avid, and DaVinci Resolve all have scopes to measure exposure and saturation. The *waveform monitor* shows the level of exposure by measuring the levels of black and white in the image. When "flat" footage is brought into a timeline, the waveform monitor will show why the footage has this name – all of the luminance and color is compressed and the waveform appears flattened out in the monitor, without the peaks and valleys of correctly exposed footage. "Correct" based on the waveform monitor means the peaks hit above 90 percent exposure and might just barely touch the top of the waveform monitor, as these measure the brightest areas of the image (assuming the image has a wide dynamic range). The valleys measure the dark areas, and also should be just barely touching the bottom of the waveform monitor for the most shadowy areas of the image. Again, this is for a standard image like an interview, which is lit to have bright and dark areas. If the image does not have a wide dynamic range, for example, a moody shot at dusk, with a misty sky, then the waveform monitor will not have peaks and valleys, but it is still needs to be within acceptable exposure ranges in the waveform monitor. The waveform is also useful to balance the color, as the lines in the scope show the amount of red, green, and blue in the shadows, midtones, and highlights. If you feel a shot looks muddy and murky, and notice that the waveform shows a lot of red in the shadows, for example, you might try adjusting the green (the color opposite red on the color wheel) in the shadows and see if it improves the look. If you notice that an actor's skin tones seem off and the waveform shows a lot of green in the highlights, which is common if filming was done under fluorescent light, and you can adjust the amount of the opposite color — purple or pink — until the skin tone looks balanced. In this way, the waveform is a tool to speed up adjustments as it can help identify what makes a scene look "off."

The *vectorscope* measures the saturation of clips – similarly, flat raw footage will show up as unsaturated clips with little depth, and the vectorscope will have a tightly clustered set of measurements. Adjusting the saturation and vibrance until the image looks correct, will show up in the vectorscope as a good overall range and distribution of colors.

*Then Correct for Feel and Overall Issues*

Color correction has many, many possibilities. With all these options, what does it mean to do a "basic correction?" And how can a post team most efficiently approach this step if they did not budget nor plan time for an extensive color phase?

There is a priority order to the type of adjustments to make sure the image is correct. They are:

1 Correct the exposure – adjust the white/black levels, shadows/highlights, and curves until the waveform shows good overall exposure. This simple adjustment can correct many issues with somewhat flat or dull-looking footage.
2 Correct the white balance – make sure the shots match and any incorrect white balance issues are adjusted.
3 Correct the saturation and vibrance –The difference between these two is that saturation raises the overall color levels of everything in the scene, but colors that are already deeply saturated will be raised along with less-saturated ones. Vibrance, on the other hand, balances the amount of saturation by raising the less-saturated colors to be more balanced with already-saturated ones. For footage to "pop" (if that is the desired look), raising the saturation by 10–15 percent can do wonders without looking garish or oversaturated. For footage to look atmospheric and moody, try reducing the saturation or vibrance by small amounts. Experiment with both of these – you might find that vibrance is the "pop" you want, while saturation works best for very strong overall color palettes.

These three steps are going to bring most footage into a level of exposure and color that looks "correct." A handful of additional steps that are often done in basic correction include: adding vignettes around images, masking off areas of the image and adding shadows, stabilizing handheld or moving footage, resizing images, blurring faces or words, and creating dynamic masks that track to people's faces to brighten them. While describing how to do each of those is beyond the scope of this book, there are dozens of online tutorials to learn these relatively simple intermediate-level skills.

#### *Dear Colorist, This is What I'm Looking For*

Similar to the composer, starting with story goals and themes is important to let the colorist share in the creative aspects of the film. Also similar to the composer, there are many practical ways to talk about your footage, goals, and vision that are easier starting points. There is no specific or standard color treatment for a romcom or a horror movie, and you will need to let the colorist know what you would like. Some starting points: *color temperature* and the *warmth* or *coolness* of the overall look, a cooler look has blue tints, while a warmer look has golden or orange tints. *Level of contrast* and the *density of the shadows* and *highlights*, for example, deep shadows with strong contrast, or lower contrast and softer highlights for a muted look. *Saturation* and *vibrance*, do you want a natural look, deeply saturated tones, bright candy colors, watercolor-style pastels, a dated, muted, under-saturated vibe, or other color treatment?

These starting points are also vastly improved with visual references. As you might do for "sound-alike" tracks, find some "look-alike" scenes that you would like to emulate. Bring these to go over with the colorist. Also make a clear, time-coded list of "problems": shots you want to be stabilized, blurred, masked, and other corrections. Deliver all other director's notes as a clear list, do not expect the colorist to figure out what you hope to do with the footage.

You may not be able to fix every issue or create every look you want, but having the visual references and some ideas of what you want to achieve will provide the raw materials to make this a productive conversation. You will learn what you can accomplish in a simple color correction, which might be everything you need, and also learn the "next level" options that are only possible in a more elaborate color grade.

### Technical Color

Are you inspired? Do you have a vision of your palette? Have you found some comps for your desired look? Good – now hold onto those images. In order for this all to work, you must prepare your files technically to get the best results.

#### *Software Comparison of Tools: Davinci Resolve and Nodal Editing Versus Avid's Effects and Premiere's Layers*

First choose your software. For most films, using the embedded color correction tools is an excellent place to start. A detailed description of how to use each software's tools is beyond the scope of this book, and this section focuses more on preparing files and meeting the technical requirements for your color correction or grade. But to offer just a short overview of each software:

- *DaVinci Resolve* is the original color grading software that has been used by the film industry for decades. With that kind of deep experience, it is no surprise that DaVinci is the gold standard and leading software for adjusting color. It differs from Premiere and Avid in two important ways: one, it has all the different work areas set up in tabs across the bottom of the screen, with "Color" as its own tab. Two, it uses a *nodal structure*, allowing the colorist to build an extensive color design with many layers and options, which can easily be adjusted by turning the node on or off, or by bypassing them, duplicating them, and sharing them.
- *Premiere* and *Avid* also have color panels, and Premiere's Lumetri Color is in a dedicated panel with quick options for doing basic adjustments like vignettes, saturation, white/black levels, and using color wheels. Avid's color workspace also has a dedicated color panel with two tabs: one with color wheels for shadows, mid-tones, and highlights, and the other with many other options. For both Premiere and Avid, it is best to adjust color on an additional layer inserted into the track. These "*adjustment layers*" serve the same purpose as DaVinci's nodes – to turn them on and off to test looks, easily adjust various color effects, and be able to apply a successful look to many clips by copying/pasting.

### *Resolution and Technical Preparation*

#### *Color Information and Color Subsampling*

To do an excellent color grade, you ideally need to have ProRes 10-bit 4:4:4 footage, but ProRes 10-bit 4:2:2 will work. Color grading will not work well on 8-bit footage or H.264 footage, which is 4:2:0 or 4:1:1. If you do not know what any of this means, keep reading to learn more about the color information embedded in a video clip that makes it possible for a color grade to work well.

**Bit depth**: Your video file has what is called "color information" or "color depth" which is the number of pixels that show color. This is expressed in the type of footage in two ways: *bit depth* and *subsampling*. Bit depth refers to the number of bits, or computer information, recorded in the video file; 10-bit footage has an exponentially higher amount of color information than 8-bit footage, which means to properly grade your footage it is crucial to have shot the film at 10-bit. While you can up-res 8-bit footage and export out a 10-bit version, it does not add anything that was not there when the film was captured.

What is "color information?" Consider how many shades of blue there are in the sky. Every time a cloud crosses the sky, where the cloud and the sky meet are hundreds of shades of blue. Your eye can see and process the entire gradient of white-to-blue. Your camera cannot. A sky filmed in

*8-bit footage* often has what is called "banding" or long clear bands of color that make a sky look slightly color-blocked. This is because the image quality of 8-bit cannot capture this range. Film the same sky with a *10-bit* camera and you will see a smooth, natural gradient with no banding, a much wider dynamic range, and a richness of color that is unmatched with 8-bit footage. Your file will also be much, much larger as 10-bit raw footage files are huge. The pixels stored in a 10-bit image mean the image has access to thousands of shades in its RGB channels (red, green, and blue) – 1,024, to be exact – which allows it to show over 1 billion shades, making that range of white-to-blue as clear as if you were looking at the sky itself. The more common 8-bit footage has a range of 256 colors in its RGB channels, resulting in a total of 16 million possible shades. If you ever wondered how many shades it takes to represent a sky, apparently it requires more than 16 million shades to do so without creating banding. If 10-bit is not enough for you, and you have the budget, you can upgrade to 12-bit, which has 4,096 colors per RGB channel, and about 60 times more shades than 10-bit footage. Your media files will be similarly huge, and you may not even be able to play them on a regular computer, but you could see every single speck of dust and gradient found in nature.

This same dynamic range (or lack of it) can show up in dark areas, which have their own type of banding when black areas of the screen look crushed, with little range of grays in the black. Adequate color depth is one of the most important aspects of filming for an excellent color grade: if you have this depth in your original footage, your color grade will offer you the most possible options.

**Color subsampling**: Similarly, the subsampling of a media file is an important part of it being optimized for color grading or correction. Subsampling refers to luminance, or light, as opposed to bit depth, which relates to color. Subsampling, expressed by the numbers 4:4:4, 4:2:2, 4:2:0, or 4:1:1, is about how a level of compression is applied to footage to make the file sizes smaller and more manageable without losing image quality. (See Table 8.2). More compressed files – 4:2:0 and 4:1:1 – look fine to our eyes. In fact, most streaming video uses this level of resolution. But because the subsampling removes some of the color data from the video clip, footage with lower subsample levels is not ideal for adjusting the color. They have a more limited dynamic range, and, while you still can correct or grade the footage, it will more quickly start to pixelate, create banding, crush the shadows or blow out the highlights.

Footage that is subsampled at 4:4:4 has all of its color information, making it the best for color grading, while 4:2:2 footage also has half of its color data. Many people find that 4:2:2 10-bit footage is an optimal

*Table 8.2* Color Subsampling

| *Subsample type* | *This number refers to the luminance levels or the amount of light in the image* | *These numbers refer to the color information subsampled in the clip* | *Quality of resolution and use* |
|---|---|---|---|
| *4:4:4* | 4: | 4:4 | Full, very high-end, large files |
| *4:2:2* | 4: | 2:2 | Most common professional-grade footage |
| *4:2:0 or 4:1:1* | 4: | 2:0 and 1:1 | Pro-sumer camera, streaming content, and proxy level footage – looks good but not ideal for color grading |

choice, as clips that are 10-bit 4:4:4 are so huge that they can be unwieldy. For a high-end project, most likely the capture on camera is at 4:4:4, and there is an offline edit at a proxy level, maybe even an 8-bit 4:2:0 version to make the files faster to cut, then a relinking to the original full resolution for color grade. For moderate budgets, in-camera capture is likely at 4:2:2 and 10-bit, while prosumer cameras are often 8-bit 4:2:0. But, this has changed significantly in the past few years and cameras with higher resolutions and bit rates are always becoming easier to find and cheaper to purchase or rent.

### *Translation to Codecs and Types of Video*

These standards of color resolution and subsampling extend throughout various codecs, with the most common formats – Apple's ProRes and Avid's DNxHD – each having its own versions. For example, ProRes 10-bit 4:4:4 is called ProRes HQ (high quality), while ProRes proxy and LT are 8-bit. Just plain "ProRes" is 4:2:2 but has other data parameters as well. Avid's DNxHD and DNxHR also have their own flavors and variations, with additional variations like data rates, frame size, and frames per second. There are dozens of types of camera-specific footage, each with their own technical specs. To find the precise type of footage from your camera, refer to its specs, the manual, or an internet search. If you bring a clip into your editing program, you can also find this information in the metadata.

Your editing team will need to establish the codec you use for editing. If you are tasked with preparing or delivering the fine cut to the colorist for correction, you will need to confer with your team to ensure you either relink back to original high-resolution files or transcode everything in the timeline to the same high-resolution format. Or if you are doing a basic correction in-house, you need to transcode all the footage to the same, highest possible resolution for even the basic color correction. It works better, prevents computer crashes, and provides vastly more creative options for your film.

### *Prepping for the Colorist to Correct or Grade*

When you are at picture lock and ready to start the color process, there are several ways to prepare your files for transfer to a colorist.

**Add a 2-pop**: At this point, make sure your timeline includes a "2-pop" which is a countdown that goes to the number 2, then there is a "pop" sound, and then it goes black. This "2-pop" is the sync point for your fine cut when you separate the image from the audio. Your image will go to the colorist and the audio to the sound person. The 2-pop allows for easy re-syncing. Many people also do a "tail slate" which is another sync point at the end of the piece, for added insurance.

**Get transfer details from your colorist**: There are two primary ways to transfer the film to a colorist. Confirm with your colorist which they prefer:

1. **Export film as individual clips and XML file**: You create a timeline with each clip exported as its own discrete, high-resolution clip, and send the timeline as an XML file transfer to the colorist to recreate in their machine. This means they receive only the footage that is used in the timeline, not the additional raw footage, and will have just the final clips.
2. **Export the full film for scene cut detection**: Export a *textless version* of your film out as one complete file, at the highest resolution possible. Make sure to turn off any graphics, lower thirds, titles, dissolves, and all text layers that go on top of the image so they are not burned into the image itself. Since you will be adjusting the color, you need to remove the words so they do not also change colors. Send this full textless film, with the 2-pops added, the director's note, and the reference video, to your colorist. How can they work on each scene? Most editing software has a tool that does "*scene cut detection*," in which, during the footage ingest the software looks for changes in color and light to know when there are scene cuts. The software then generates a list of scene cuts, and the colorist goes through them one by one to accept or delete the auto-generated cuts. This means they can cut up your film into scenes for color correction. It is an extra step for the colorist although avoids any chances of footage going out of sync or a missing shot in a more complex XML file transfer.

**Prepare the notes**: Send the director's color notes and specific requests for each scene

**Prepare a reference video**: A reference video is a lower-resolution version of the film with time code burned in, which serves as a reference for the director's notes, the sync, and all other aspects as the colorist works on the film. They are used to address questions that come up during the color correct.

*Additional Options for Image Correction at This Stage*

While most of this chapter focuses on entry-level color correction and grading, it would not be complete without noting that there are other forms of correction other than just color. These are more advanced skills and also cannot be addressed fully given the scope of this book, but if you need any of the following you can start researching or discussing these with your color team. While there are literally thousands of additional corrections that can be done during the color phase, some commonly used options are:

**Noise reduction**: reducing grain and digital noise in underexposed scenes
**Relighting**: adding new "lights" to a scene using effects and tools. These can be fantastic options for a run and gun production that did not have adequate lighting on set.
**Face masks**: DaVinci Resolve has tools designed specifically to adjust faces, which are pre-configured tools that map precisely to the face, meaning there can be subtle individual adjustments to eyes, forehead, under-eye areas, and more. Under-eye lighting can be a powerful subtle correction and significantly brighten an image with a tiny boost to the light
**Blurring faces, words, license plates, etc.**: If it is necessary to blur and pixelate faces or other information for privacy, all professional editing programs have a blurring tool that puts a mask on whatever needs to be blurred.

**Class Activity 8**

**Color a Film Two Ways**

This is ideally done using flat footage ready for color correction,* although you could still see the effects of using other types of footage. You can film the footage yourself or find it online to purchase as stock footage. Alternatively, you could do this exercise with archival footage from the public domain or NASA, although the effect will not be the same as using footage filmed specifically for color grading. However, if you are just getting started learning color grading and correction, the tools will still work on any type of footage. Just play around with it to start to see how the different looks affect the story.

**Activity resources (choose what footage to use)**

- Editstock.com color pack
- Original footage, preferably show it flat or raw mode
- Archival footage from the public domain

**Activity**

1 Cut together a short scene or two using your footage.
2 Try to create 2–3 different color treatments for the footage: perhaps a BW version, a "normal" color look, and a "dramatic" color look.
3 Compare the "color palettes" with the class – what worked well? How did they create their looks?

**Conclusion and discussion questions:**

What process did each student use? How did they come up with their looks? Did they choose one item in the shot to enhance? How did they revise the color process as they went along?

* An excellent source for acquiring footage for color correction is Editstock, which sells packages of raw footage for class projects. They have several packages for color correction.

# 9 Transcripts, Captions, and Subtitles

## What and Why

Industry-shifting entities like Netflix, Amazon, major film studios, and major broadcasters in the US now all require captions, leading a shift for the entire industry. With captions as a required post-production step for any film or media piece intended for broad distribution and streaming, and subtitles in one or more languages being increasingly common, the post-production team has to add this to their workflow.

## Captions versus Subtitles

To begin, the starting point is to know the difference between *captions* and *subtitles*. Captions are *text descriptions of the audio aspects of the film*. They make media and movies accessible for people who are hearing-impaired. Subtitles are *translations* of the dialog and on-screen words but do not describe the audio aspects of the film.

As filmmakers, we know that sound carries half the story, and many films that are not dialog-heavy rely on sound design and music to advance their story. Captions go far beyond subtitles to provide a way for those with hearing impairments to experience the full creative story. The legal requirements are the push to create these. Like many tasks that are pushed and required, a post-production team that does not see the bigger picture for captioning or resents the additional step, which is a considerable amount of work, might create captions that are done with little thought or effort. Consider instead the "pull" – the advantages and benefits for creatives: captions and subtitles expand the reach of your work. Your film can now reach people who could only experience half of it before. It can reach people from other cultures and countries. You can show it to international audiences through online viewing platforms. This is a wonderful expansion of the reach, inclusiveness, and audience development. The ability to do this is unprecedented in film and media industries.

DOI: 10.4324/9781003473152-10

First, let's clarify terms. Often these two words are used interchangeably but there are important differences for those tasked with making and editing in the subtitles and captions. For example, with subtitles (translations), the person creating them has to include signs, inter-title graphics, news articles, and any other text that appears on the screen. If a character is wearing a T-shirt or hat with words on it, and those words are important to the story because they reveal something to the audience, the T-shirt needs to be translated and included in the subtitles. Captions, however, are intended to make the media piece accessible to people with hearing impairments and are for creating visible means to "hear" the film. Since words on a hat or T-shirt are legible they would not need to be in the captions. But captions include text describing the audio, music, and sound effects, along with all of the dialog. This means that while the same original *transcription file* (a transcription is a text version of the dialog in the film) can be a starting point for both, caption files will have information that is not in subtitle files, and subtitles will have information that is not in caption files. While many people use these terms to mean both things, these are the definitions this book uses: "captions" are a written version of the film, in the viewer's own language and describing the audio; "subtitles" are translations, including translations of words on the screen.

## Captions Are for Everyone, Everywhere

Captions are not just used by people with hearing impairments. Many people with perfectly good hearing turn on captions. In fact, it is becoming the norm. A small media cycle in 2022–2023 included articles in several publications with variations on the headline "Why Does Everyone Use Subtitles Now?" These publications ranged from mainstream outlets like *The Guardian*, *The Atlantic*, and *Vox*, to film-specific ones like *IndieWire* and *NAB Amplify*. Many of the articles cited a study by Preply, a language tutor and training company. The study interviewed over 1,200 Americans about using subtitles, with compelling findings that will convince anyone making contemporary films and TV shows that subtitles and captions are a crucial new creative aspect to your film. Preply found that 50 percent of Americans turn on subtitles most of the time, and 62 percent use subtitles more often with streaming services than regular TV. A startling finding revealed that 74 percent of Gen Z viewers watch shows in public and turn on subtitles because of the background noise of a public environment. Take a moment to consider that: this is the highly desired "youth demographic," and three-fourths of them will watch your film with the captions on! That is enormous. If you need convincing that your captions should be more than an afterthought, consider how many people are using them.

The Preply study and articles in the media cycle detail several reasons, ranging from watching films in noisy places like public transit to the need to use captions to follow the plot because of mumbling or dialog that is not easily understood. The *Indiewire* article discusses that audio mixes for many films are for theatrical spaces with excellent speakers, and when these films are streamed the sound mix is less clear so it is harder to hear the dialog. (The articles and Preply study are listed in the citations of this book and available online for anyone curious to know more about why this is happening.)

It is also not just Americans. In 2024, RTE, Ireland's National Public Media, ran an article saying exactly the same thing: everyone is watching TV with subtitles on. They cite data showing similar trends: a UK-based study found that 85 percent of Netflix customers in the UK use subtitles. Netflix's own internal metrics show that 80 percent of customers use subtitles monthly, and 40 percent use them all the time. These statistics should reinforce that this step is no small matter. In fact, Netflix created a dedicated staff role, "Director of Product Accessibility," to guide this process, and in an article with Yahoo Entertainment, the first person to staff this role shared how growing up with deaf parents showed her the importance of not just having captions, but *good* captions.

With creating captions becoming a routine part of film delivery, the field is now evolving to understand what "good" captions are. We can look at what the industry giants are doing; for example, Netflix leaned in so heavily to create good captions that they created a style guide to ensure consistency among the many people who perform this task. One show noted for its excellent captions is the series "Stranger Things," a series that blends drama with sci-fi and horror, and explores supernatural forces. Enormous time and effort go into realizing this world visually and sonically, and when it came to doing the same through the captions the "Stranger Things" team put in the same level of effort. The show is noted for its visceral descriptions like [Tentacles undulating moistly] and [wet footsteps squelch], which elevate a simple caption to a creative description. In a 2022 article with *Vulture.com*, the subtitle team for "Stranger Things" shares their commitment to this task and their creativity with language, including how they created a "*word bank*" based on sci-fi and the game "Dungeons and Dragons." This allowed them to use consistent and creative wording to convey the world-building in the captions, and translate the creativity of "Stranger Things" for deaf and hearing-impaired people. (For those interested in a deeper dive into the commitment of this team, the article is listed in this book's citations.)

**Transcripts versus Captions**: A transcription is a literal, word-for-word written version of the film. A final transcript is used for many purposes, from captions and subtitles to cut-downs of the film.

While a transcript file is similar to a caption file, notice there is only one time code and the breaks for each line of written text follow what the person says. Captions break spoken sentences into specific character counts to ensure legibility. They also space the words over scenes to create correct timing and duration for the caption. See Figures 9.1 and 9.2 to see what transcripts and captions look like.

```
[00:00:00] MARY: We want to be a part of the solution. I love that
line. If you sit on the lid of progress, be prepared to be blown to
bits.

[00:00:27] COSTA (2): We need to move away from fossil fuel electric
generation.

[00:00:31] MARY: I think most people's dream is to actually have some
type of solar equipment on their rooftop. The problem is being able to
afford it.

[00:00:39] CHRIS: Clean energies become politicized. It's beyond me
because it's an American story.

[00:00:49] COSTA (2): More than we currently have, right?
```

*Figure 9.1* An excerpt of a transcript. Image by the author.

```
1
00:58:16,618 --> 00:58:19,829
[Quiet wind]

2
00:58:24,918 --> 00:58:28,129
[Wind intensifies]

3
00:58:28,963 --> 00:58:30,715
- We wanna be a part of the

4
00:58:30,715 --> 00:58:32,217
- solution.

5
00:58:33,468 --> 00:58:36,304
- I love that line. If you
sit on the lid of progress,

6
00:58:36,304 --> 00:58:37,889
be prepared to be blown to bits.

7
00:58:38,139 --> 00:58:39,224
[Boom and big bang noise]
```

*Figure 9.2* An excerpt of a caption file. Image by the author.

With all of this said, at the time of writing this, a typical caption standard is 32 characters per line, and no more than two lines, with a minimum of one second on screen.

**Subtitles**: Unlike captions, subtitles are not necessarily a delivery requirement, however, they can be very desirable to include. Subtitles are dialog translations, also synced to the film and the speakers. As with captions, AI subtitles have made this step much easier to do. However, as with captions, AI can only do so much and the final subtitles need to be reviewed by a human for accuracy.

**Open and Closed Captions**: Captioning expands on transcriptions to create a time-coded written description of the film, including music, sound design, and important non-dialog audio. *Closed-captions* are embedded into the final export of the film, but are invisible until turned on and off by the viewer. Think of the "cc" button on a YouTube video – those are closed-captions. *Open captions* are burned into the image, and exported out as part of the final film. They can be useful in theatrical settings where a caption is required but audiences cannot just click a button. Open captions are sometimes done on the image itself, and thus need to be placed in a way that does not interfere with other titles and lower thirds, and also formatted in a way to ensure legibility. Alternatively, an additional space can be added under the image, such as a black bar, and the open captions placed in that box. This essentially makes a 16×9 image into a 4×3 image with a dedicated area for the captions, with the benefit of making them very legible and not interfering with other parts of the image.

**Box 9.1 Captions Versus Subtitles**

Captions describe sounds, music, and things that someone cannot hear. Subtitles are translations, and must include every important written word on screen, such as signs and inter-titles. Captions re-create layers of sound, including sound effects and music. When making captions, because there is only so much space to put the words on the screen, sometimes the editor/captioner must make a judgment call and decide which sound is the most relevant to put into the captions. Typically, captions show the dialog, however, sound effects and music are also important parts of the film. If there is dialog, and a dog barks in the background, perhaps the caption for that shot only shows the dialog. But, if there is talking, and a dog barks and it is an important part of the story, the sound effect might take precedence over the talking. For example, if the story is about a missing person, and the team is walking through a field, and their dialog is incidental (such as "here?" and "you go that way"), but there is a dog as part of the search team, and the dog's bark shows they found someone, then the caption might indicate [Dog barking] and prioritize that over the incidental dialog.

What is relevant? That decision is made based on the specific story. While AI can help this process along, the final significant story elements require a human to decide. For example, when a person is walking through a yard or park, and the audio design has a light breeze, birds chirping, and gentle ambient music the captions might say [Birds chirping] or [Gentle ambient music] as one of these two things is likely the most relevant. As the story advances and the audio changes, the captioner uses the story cues to decide what is most relevant. For example, the birds are interrupted by jackhammers, the caption changes to [Jackhammers interrupt birds]. If the music darkens and becomes more ominous the caption might read [Music grows ominous].

**How to Create with Help from AI**

Now that AI has grown into regular use in editing and post-production, these are easier than ever to do. An editor can simply export a low-resolution version of their film, or even just an audio version, and upload it to an AI transcription service. It "listens" and spits out a semi-decent transcript.

At the time of writing this, AI can still only produce translations and captions that are, at best, perhaps 80–85 percent correct. Accuracy of AI depends on the nature of the film and its content. AI is at its worst with dialog-heavy content with many place names, specific vocabulary, people speaking colloquially, and slightly off-mike audio that was not recorded with the same clarity. It also does not do as well when people speak fast and mash words together, nor is it as accurate in languages other than English (although that is changing swiftly). No doubt it will continue to improve in all these ways, and improve fast. However, all things related to story rely on human understanding to fully interpret the meaning and put the story into the correct context. Many people, including professional translators, start with AI translations and captions and revise them, which speeds up the process enormously but has not yet replaced human translation or captioning. Humans still need to decide what is relevant, proofread and fix errors, and ensure the spirit of the scene is not lost in translation.

Practically speaking, captions are prepared differently than transcripts, as captions are time-coded to exactly where the dialog, sound, or music occurs. They are delivered in many formats – *.srt* is the most common, as are *.scc* and *.vtt* files. These sync to the original film and are designed to meet *legibility requirements* by broadcasters, streamers, museums, and other institutions. Legibility requirements are exactly what they sound like – standards to ensure the captions are easy to read on-screen with images moving behind them. If you have ever seen a graphic title used in a film that extended to four or five lines, in complete sentences, and felt the need to hit "pause" just so you could read it, then you know how hard it can be to put story elements into text. Typical caption standards include 1) how many characters per line, 2) how many lines, and 3) how long each caption must remain on screen. The most important aspects are: that the captions sync with the sound, the dialog is in tiny bite-sized chunks and syncs with what the person actually says at the time they say it, and the captions are accurate to the actual speech. For example, captions should include incorrect grammar, slang, and verbal shortcuts, and not correct them in the writing. This is critically important to convey the actual audio of the film, and to ensure that a person captioning a film is not editing by removing or changing key elements, nor are they editorializing by interpreting key elements through a lens of what the captioner believes to be correct. If someone says on-screen "ain't" or "wassup" or "g'day," that is what the captions should say. Accuracy and lack of editorializing also extend to sound and music, and captions should describe music by adjectives, feel, and instrumentation, not through a perceived culture; for example, a percussion-heavy soundtrack caption might say [Fast-paced snare drums] or [Slow steel drum melody], which are more accurate and culturally neutral, rather than [Patriotic drums] or [Caribbean music], which are perceptions that come through one's culture, are too generic, and create a sense of adding meaning to the music that did not come from the filmmaker but from the captioner.

Additional requirements for captions might include: speaker names; word case, for example, you cannot use all capitals; and maximum duration of the caption.

A final technical consideration is the font size and screen placement. Unsurprisingly, these also vary. Font sizes should be measured by their ratio of the screen size and not an absolute "point" value as one does in writing. A theatrical screen is much larger than a television screen or a streaming service, and the font needs to be legible on the intended screen size. The font color, whether there is a stroke of black or gray behind the words, and other formatting can typically be included for streaming but not for broadcast. Broadcast distribution may require captions with no formatting at all, as formatted caption files will come through with the format codes embedded into the caption, and end up displaying on the screen in a very messy way. For most broadcast outlets, captions will display only in the font of the broadcaster, not the font you use. Formatting for streaming, however, may include placement on the screen, as some standards indicate that captions should not cover faces, important story elements, or other text. A common final step in captioning for streamers is either moving around the captions so they are placed correctly, or creating a version of the film with a caption space under the image and putting all of the captions there.

These are a lot of requirements! And you might be frustrated reading how many times this section says "It depends" and "It varies by distribution" and "may be required, or may not." That, unfortunately, is the case at the time of writing this. While there are some industry standards, the final specific requirements depend on the distribution venue. For films going to multiple venues, there might need to be different captions. For example, Netflix, as one of the largest distributors, has their own standards and specifications for legibility for both captions and subtitles, while a broadcaster might have other specifications for captions, and a film festival may not have any requirements at all. And standards like these change often. It is crucial that, if tasked with creating captions, you check with your distribution, festival, broadcaster, or streaming service for their specific requirements.

**Workflow for Captions and Subtitles: Which Goes First?**

A method to save time on your captions and subtitle workflow is to create the dialog captions, and do all the necessary trimming, correction, and timing. Generate from your editing timeline an unformatted .srt file.

Give your translator a .txt file of the captions that include the time code, and ask them to be diligent about maintaining the sentences, line breaks, and nuggets of dialog, and to ensure they do not delete any of the time code. They can return the file to you once it is translated, and you can then import the subtitles and place them with the original dialog. This is not a fool-proof method, as some languages have longer or shorter words, and do not as easily fit into character counts. Or sometimes idiomatic sayings do not translate in the same number of words, or a sentence that starts on one shot and continues on the next shot does not translate as neatly to the subtitle. If you are with a production that can afford a translator to check the words against the image, and make a final round of corrections, that is incredibly valuable to ensure the film is presented as best possible in the second language. And if you are with a production where the primary intended audience speaks a language other than what is spoken on screen, this is more than valuable: it is necessary to convey the story.

Subtitling may be bi-directional if more than one language is represented on screen, and also needs to include any signs on screen, written graphics, inter-titles, and any relevant written elements. If a stop sign is shown, and the word "stop" is important to the story, that sign needs to be translated, as do all other relevant screen graphics.

Knowing your audience is important, and subtitling will translate from the main language spoken on the screen to the main language of the intended audience. If you filmed in a country different than the one you will show the film in, or the film will screen in multiple countries at the same time, or you have more than one language on screen, you may need to do translations in different directions. For example, if you filmed in France and will show the film only in England, then you will translate all the French in the film into English, including any signs and on-screen graphics. If you filmed in both England and France, and people speak both languages on screen, and you will show it in both England and France, then you will need to do two translations: one into French, and one into English, including all the signs and graphics. If you filmed in both countries and will have a worldwide release on a streaming service, you may need to translate into many languages, also including all graphics and on-screen signs.

Subtitling is a consideration that traditionally comes at the very end. In contemporary films, however, it is moving up the priority ladder and should be budgeted adequately to ensure the story is presented authentically to all audiences. At the moment, AI translations are not as accurate as cash-strapped, budget-conscious producers would like them to be. While this might improve over the years, ensuring human review at this part of post-production is the only way for the director to know that the story is being portrayed in the way they intended.

**Class Activity 10**

Use GenAI to make captions for a short film. Develop the vocabulary for your film.

What you need:

- a short film or video clip and
- an account with an app that does AI transcription and captions, like Rev or even YouTube (look for ones that do free trials)

**Activity**

1 Using your GenAI app of choice, upload your short film to the transcription/captioning site
2 Set it to do a GenAI transcription for captions. Note that transcription and captions are different and this may be two steps (first transcription, then captions).

3. Once the AI transcription is completed, compare it against the film's audio by listening in the transcription app (most allow you to listen while you read through the transcription). Correct the incorrect terms, noting where the AI made mistakes.
4. *Optional*: create a word bank for your film's audio, which is a collection of descriptive words that portray the qualities of the audio environment in ways as unique as your soundscape.
5. Using your word bank (if you made one) add the rest of the captions – the sound, music, and any other descriptive audio.
6. Generate/export your .srt file
7. Move to your editing software and import the film and the .srt file
8. Create a subtitle track (follow your specific software's instructions for creating subtitle tracks, as it varies slightly).
9. Bring the .srt file into the subtitle track, syncing the captions back to the video.
10. Watch through the newly subtitled track. Move and position the captions on the entire track to a good spot overall in the frame, usually the center lower third. You may need to individually adjust certain captions so they do not appear over other words on the screen.
11. Watch your film with your new captions added. What do you have to adjust? How creative were your captions?

**Discussion Questions**

How many things did GenAI get wrong? How useful was it, and what did it get correct? What would you do differently for a different film?

# 10 Exhibit and Deliver

## Exhibition and Deliverables

Congratulations! Your film is complete! You have gone through many, many months of cuts from rough to medium to fine. You got to picture lock, finished your color and sound master, and created your captions and maybe even a subtitle file. Your film is ready to go! Now, you can just hit "export" on your timeline and your beautiful movie will be out in the world. Right? Well … not quite.

When you are starting to exhibit your film, which simply means to screen it, although your "exhibition" phase usually means public, competitive screenings like a film festival, you need to do the final step, known as "delivery of exhibition versions."

First, make sure you understand the differences between "*exhibition version*" and "*deliverables*." They are similar and related but mean slightly different things. To put it into a bit of historical context: back in the early days of filmmaking, when people filmed and cut actual celluloid film, the editing process included a phase where the film was clipped and glued together. This made for a very delicate version of the film, the "work print," which would be transferred from one projector to another to a new roll of celluloid film. Reel by reel this transfer would be completed, and this "answer print" would be used to make the "*exhibition print*," or the screening version of the full final film. Depending on how much money you had you might make one of these, or you might make 50. These exhibition prints would be shipped from theater to theater, and a film could screen in as many theaters as there were exhibition prints. So, a studio film might make dozens of exhibition prints to open in a national release, while a small independent or art film might have one exhibition print. The term "exhibition version" still is used today and is a fancy term referring to the actual film that is screened in the theater

DOI: 10.4324/9781003473152-11

or film festival. Note that this term is not commonly used by broadcast or streaming services, and those industries might use "master file" to refer to your final film.

This mini-history lesson is provided to give contemporary filmmakers a sense of context for today's exhibition prints. Does shipping prints around the country sound expensive? It was. Time-consuming? Yes, indeed. Potential for things to go missing, be damaged, and potentially even stolen? Those all happened and were all flaws of that system. Today the exhibition copy has been largely replaced by the DCP, or Digital Cinema Package. The DCP was created when digital projection started to become widespread, and involves more protections for filmmakers. See below for more detail.

Now, a filmmaker or broadcast professional will have to provide several other *media assets* (another fancy term that just means different video files, along with posters and promotional items. Collectively these are called *deliverables*, or sometimes a *package* or *delivery package*. You get the point. Instead of shipping one film to a theater, a filmmaker now has a list of *deliverables* or their *package*. Precisely what is in this package depends on where you are sending it, but there are standard types of deliverable packages that are relatively common. They all still include delivering an exhibition cut of the final film or television show. But the most complicated deliverable is the DCP, or Digital Cinema Package.

## Digital Cinema Package

A DCP is an encrypted "Digital Cinema Package." This special format was designed for screening movies on digital cinema projectors, it was developed when movie theaters started to use digital projectors as opposed to celluloid projectors. The industry hit a hurdle when they realized that sending digital copies could save a lot of time and money in making exhibition prints, but that digital copies are also incredibly easy to steal. The DCP was created to provide security and a way to protect the intellectual property of filmmakers. A digital version of a film made it easier than ever for "pirating," which means stealing a film with the intent to sell or screen it on your own. Even delivering through password-protected streaming portals allowed a window through which hackers to access the video file and potentially download it. Studios that invested millions into making the latest blockbuster needed to ensure that their films would not be pirated before they could even have their premiere. This led to the development of other technologies in addition to DCPs like digital rights protection and watermarked copies of films, to prevent pirating.

DCPs are an extremely high-resolution version of your film. They are meant to emulate the quality of a 35-mm exhibition screener in a digital file. While the DCP original file can be exported from most editing systems, the creation of a DCP includes encryption, and sometimes an additional KDM (key delivery message, or a passphrase) for screening windows. For example, if a festival has a screening window from June 1 to June 30, the KDM will allow the DCP to be opened from June 1 to June 30 and then it will expire. This level of encryption is not readily done from the typical editing system, nor are some other options in a DCP like captioning and subtitles in various languages. A DCP export typically takes several hours, depending on the duration of your film.

Many DCP creation companies have emerged that use the latest software to make DCPs with all the added options, and most filmmakers send the highest possible resolution version of their film to one of these companies. The company then generates out the encrypted DCP with all the required features. DCPs are used for theatrical events, like film festivals, because their projectors require DCPs. Broadcast channels and streamers have other technology and deliver their films behind firewalls that protect them. Social media and YouTube channels do not require anything like a DCP.

### *DCP Delivery and Naming*

DCPs are a bit costly to create, depending on the requirements and timeframe. They are very large files, upwards of 100GB. Due to their size, they are delivered either through a digital download or on a formatted, encrypted drive. Creating a DCP can take as little as one day and as long as a week, and the upload/download times can be significant. If you need to deliver a DCP plan a very substantial amount of time so you can quality check, confirm that the recipient has been able to download the file, and that it was tested and works.

DCPs also have unique naming conventions that will look very confusing to the untrained eye, but to a professional it is code that includes several key pieces of information. The most important of information in the DCP's name include: the movie title (abbreviated); if it is a short, feature, trailer, or other type of content; the aspect ratio; the primarly language; if there are captions and which type; the studio that made the film; and date of creation. See Box 10.1 for an example of a DCP name, and Figure 10.1 for a chart that breaks down this code. Standardization of this naming convention is very helpful for theaters and festivals that receive dozens if not hundreds of DCPs and must be able to organize them based on the name.

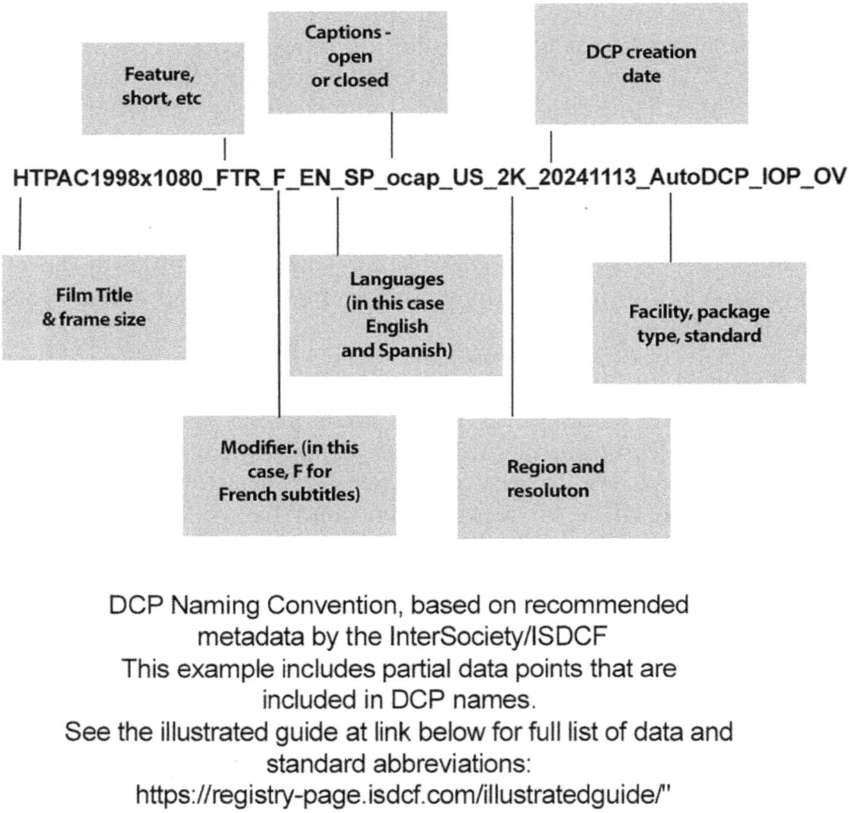


*Figure 10.1* A standardized chart showing a common naming convention for DCPs.

**Box 10.1 An Example of a DCP Name**

A film I recently delivered, a feature documentary, has a DCP name of:
HTPAC1998x1080_FTR_F_EN_SP_ocap_US_20_2K_20241113_AutoDCP_IOP_OV

This is not something I came up with on my own. Rather, I followed the standardized naming convention shown above meant to put all technical details into the file name. The chart in Figure 10.1 shows the naming method suggested by the InterSociety, and breaks down suggested naming conventions for DCPs. (Note: this chart can be found in a fuller resolution at www.registry-page.isdcf.com which has other very good guidance on issues of international standards in digital cinema.)

**Typical Deliverables Package**

This is not an exhaustive list, nor it is meant to be a prescription for what all films have to deliver. Rather, it is intended as a guide to understanding how to finalize a project and hand it over for the next phase.

A typical package of deliverables includes:

- DCP of film (theatrical) or high-resolution export of film, meeting broadcast/streaming/social media standards (in ProRes, DNxHD, and/or sometimes H.264).
- Trailer(s).
- Promotional clips.
- Promotional stills in various sizes.
- Social media-sized versions of promotional stills.
- Social media-timed exports of key scenes, such as five- and ten-second excerpts.
- Caption files in the original language.
- Subtitles in second language (optional).
- Caption files in second language (optional).
- Additional captions and subtitles in other languages (optional).

For delivery to distributors or within independent markets, the final delivery may also include marketing materials. While these are not necessarily something the editor creates or manages, as items that are often part of the delivery process, the editor or post supervisor may also need to keep these items on their radar for completion of the final delivery.

- Poster (vertical, high res).
- Poster (horizontal, high res).
- Poster (vertical, low res).
- Poster (horizontal, low res).
- Images for use on social media, in various sizes and aspect ratios (optional).
- Postcard (optional).
- Official logline, usually one sentences.
- Official summary, usually under 100 words.

To see a more detailed chart of distribution by media form, see Appendix 7: Post-Production Guide by Form.

# Part 2

# Creative Aesthetics

# 11 Interview: Aashish Kumar – "Body, Home, World"

## Bio

***Aashish Kumar: Professor and Filmmaker***

Aashish Kumar is an award-winning documentary filmmaker and social action scholar whose work turns a spotlight on issues such as emerging democracies, social stigmas, globalization, migration, civic engagement, and grassroots advocacy. His films have been shown at film festivals in the US and internationally, used in grassroots community advocacy, and distributed to academic institutions. He has won several Fulbright grants to study in South Africa and India, including the Fulbright-Nehru Academic and Professional Excellence Award and the Fulbright Specialist Award. Kumar created an interactive documentary entitled "Body, Home, World: South Asian LGBTQI Journeys" that explores the dynamic of South Asian immigrant families in the United States navigating issues of gender and sexual diversity. In this interactive documentary, viewers are able to watch situations from the perspective of both an LGBTQI youth as well as their relative and how they have come to a place of acceptance as a family. [See this project at www.bodyhomeworld.com.]

## Summary — "Body, Home, World"

"Body, Home, World" first began to take shape following the 2010 suicide of a gay college student who took his own life after being secretly recorded in his dorm room by his roommate, a South Asian first-year student.

DOI: 10.4324/9781003473152-13

> This story was given wide press in both the mainstream and South Asian media and it made me think hard about how [the roommate] grew up and what kind of conversations were or were not happening in his family for him to be in that place. It opened the door in my mind for what I wanted my own son to know as my point of view as a straight, brown man. Instead of looking at others for them to lead the way, I decided I should be setting my own example by making a project about these issues.

From: "Professor Receives Second Fulbright Scholar Award," *Hofstra University News*, May 18, 2022.

## Interview Selects

Listen to the full interview and view the complete transcript on the associate website for this book. *Author's note: This interview was lightly edited for clarity.*

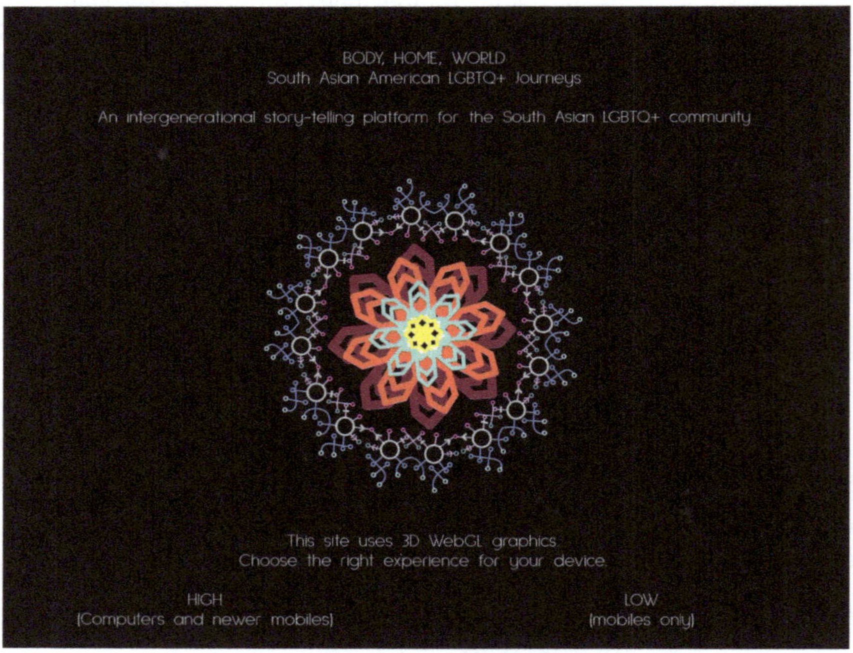


*Figure 11.1* "Body, Home, World" home page. Image credit: Aashish Kumar.

*Author:* **Could you introduce yourself and share your primary role in the film industry?**

*Aashish Kumar:* My name is Aashish Kumar and I am a higher education professional. I have been teaching in higher education for almost 30 years now. Currently, I'm a professor of television studies and production and immersive media at Hofstra University Lawrence Herbert School of Communication. I'm also an independent documentary maker. I have done several commissioned as well as independent documentaries on a range of issues going from bias crimes to mental illness to LGBTQI intergenerational stories.

*Author:* **Thank you. And then which of your credits or roles, whether it's editing or something else, make you the most excited and proud?**

*Aashish Kumar:* I think in documentaries, producing a documentary and conceiving the idea, but also then seeing it taking shape in the editing room. So those two roles, I would say the producing and the editing part I am most excited about because as you're gathering the material in the field, you're already thinking about how it might get shaped into the final narrative. It is daunting because when you're doing a documentary edit, there's like the material that's facing you is immense – but to be able to select and shape a narrative that is compelling and evocative of the story, to me that is really creatively very satisfying.

*Author:* **And your favorite aspect of post-production?**

*Aashish Kumar:* Once you get past the first assembly, when you actually start to listen and think about images and connections and relationships between what people are saying and if it's an ensemble cast that you are editing, or if it's even a story about a single individual or a few individuals around them, I tell my students also that the real excitement of edit begins once you have something in the timeline. Because till then, what are you doing is a lot of housekeeping, a lot of arranging, managing. So you have easily accessible material that you know where it lives, but it really sparks … really start to come alive and you start to really get buried in the story as you start to watch the timeline. And I have a colleague who sometimes refers to the process of making a story as a picture puzzle, and maybe he does that to make his students understand it.

I think that part always excites me as to how stories take a turn and how an image and word in the timeline speak differently. They may have lived in a different place, but once you put them together, I mean that's the true power of editing is when you place things next to each other and when they start to speak in a different way.

***Author:*** **Awesome. I love the picture puzzle analogy. I use it myself. And I always say you're not always just putting the puzzle together, but sometimes you're going out and getting the puzzle pieces. The other side of that – editing can be long and frustrating. What is your least favorite part of it?**

*Aashish Kumar:* I would say it used to be the transcription process. Back in the day there was no speech recognition software and it all had to be done by hand. And if you were working on tight budgets, you ended up doing some of that yourself. The advantage to that was that you are intimately familiar with the material and you knew exactly what people had said and it was kind of burned in your head as you went through the process, but it took time and it kept you from … because inside you wanted to just get to cutting the story and you couldn't do it because you didn't know word for word what was said. Thankfully, that's been taken care of with a lot of very smart transcription software at this point. My least favorite is logging and getting everything organized and labeled properly. I still err sometimes I still leave a bunch of things just broadly labeled in the bin, and I leave the contents kind of unlabeled.

I think those are the time-consuming things that as an editor, they will come back to haunt you because you'll be scrolling through a bin trying to find that clip that you know lives there, but you haven't labeled it … I think some of those parts are frustrating. I think toward the tail end of the post-process, once you have the film finished, again, depending on the budgets … I'm a complete end-to-end editor, so I will color-correct, I'll mix sound, but lately I've had some help. Sometimes the color correction process can be very time-consuming. You're going frame by frame and sometimes you have multiple shots from multiple sources. So I would say those two are not the most favorite parts.

*Author:* **How did you get your start in film and video, and did you do something before storytelling?**

*Aashish Kumar:* In terms of my start, I had a somewhat non-traditional [beginning] … I'm sure a lot of people have gotten into film from various disciplines and they might not have started out as a film student. I, for one, did not start out studying film. So I grew up in India, and at the time that I was in college, which was in the mid to late 1980s, there was only one film school in the entire country. You had to get into it right after getting out of high school. So it was a five-year … it was like a traditional old-style film school. I was doing sociology in college and I did my undergraduate and graduate work in sociology. And at the time that I was doing my grad school, I took a class in semiotics with an amazing intellectual and professor who is now teaching at Johns Hopkins.

She introduced me to my first cinema studies text and to the idea that cinema was something worth studying as opposed to … in India cinema meant the Mumbai film industry, which is known by its somewhat derisive term, Bollywood. And the idea that filmmaking was an enterprise in that you could not just learn the craft but also study it as a social text or as a text, as a cultural text. That excited me a lot. So my transition took place after grad school when I was looking for film programs and I came to the US to study – for the first time in my life – to do a grad program in communication. It took two degrees, I have an MS and an MFA in television production, after which I started looking at how I could find a place in this world of making creative work. And academia presented a nice option.

They both happened simultaneously. I had founded, with another South Asian friend of mine, a society for a South Asian Film and Video Association because we saw that there was a lack of community among many people in the diaspora. And we had a website, we got a lot of people to write in, and we were developing that as a resource for the community. And somebody saw that website, somebody who was in the activism, progressive activism kind of community, and called me asking if I would want to be a consultant on a documentary project that she was developing at the time about bias crime, about hate crimes against South Asians. And so we had a very long conversation, about half an hour, 40-minute-long conversation. And when I hung up, it occurred to me that I wasn't going to be a consultant on this. I wanted to do this.

So I threw my hat in, I wrote the proposal, I sent it in, and I got picked. At the time, my ex-wife and I, we used to work together on projects. And so we would always pitch as a duo. And that project really was a baptism by fire in the world of field production, it was a national spread. We traveled to four cities: DC, Chicago, LA, and, of course, within New York City.

That project was about hate crimes. The transformative part of the project was not that it was about hate crimes but that it took place around the same time as another transformative event happened – the 9/11 attacks and the hate crimes that spiked after that.* We were doing a history of bias crimes and hate crimes against South Asians. And we had a rough cut ready in October of 2000, August of 2001, and a month later, September 11th happened and there was a rash of attacks against people of South Asian descent, whether it was a Sikh, whether it was somebody brown, with a beard like me, whether it was actually … it didn't matter whether you were a Muslim or you just had to look like somebody who was one of the 19 hijackers whose photos were being printed.

And that really made me, in terms of filmmaking, when you have to transform the film midstream and its agenda shifts by real-world events that are happening. To me that was really powerful. And I'll never forget how that shaped me as a filmmaker, both in terms of how I responded as a South Asian who was getting activated into the identity politics of the South Asian diaspora, but also as a filmmaker who had to learn that the definition of film resonates with what is happening in the contemporary ferment at the moment and how you have to respond to that. And that has always remained with me.

***Author:*** **That's incredible. The timing of that, obviously the things you can't predict, but having something like that ready at that moment.**

*Aashish Kumar:* Yeah, yeah. No, I remember coming, I was teaching in New Haven, Connecticut, at the time, and I remember coming down to Queens to Richmond Hill, which is one of the neighborhoods which is populated by a lot of people from the Sikh community. And they have a temple, a Sikh temple, which is called a gurdwara. And there's this old 70, 75-year-old Sikh gentleman with a white flowing beard, I mean the very image of a saint. We went to interview him, and that story was just so powerful that it sort of ripped the mask off of the stability that I thought that American society was all about rule of law, that when it came to when the chips were down, how would people react? And he was coming from the gurdwara after a prayer meeting and these guys jumped out of a pickup truck, and they had baseball bats and they did … they had nails studded into the baseball bat. So they were going around picking on people, and he happened to be the unlucky victim that day. So he crawled home half bloody, his daughter-in-law helped him … and that story happened just a few weeks before we went and interviewed him. That was very powerful that I really think I credit that experience of listening to these stories, developing a way of becoming a recorder, a witness to them that was very transformative for me.

***Author:*** **And amplifying them to the right ears and eyes. Yeah, absolutely. Was this your entry point and what do you consider your first paid or serious job?**.

*Aashish Kumar:* Yeah, yeah. So this was the project. So I realized that I had no track record of doing a project of that scope, of handling a subject that involved such a massive number of people and the impact on the community and so on. So I was learning what budgeting meant and very quickly because the funders … they had a limited pot of money and everything had to be done within that. And we said, just said yes, because I was so hungry to work on this project, I wanted to do it. It seemed exactly the kind of thing, the kind of story that I would want to tell. It had the elements of the community that I had some knowledge of and I would want to know more. So that would be the first big project that I got. And, of course, it meant it was from conception to delivery, so it was not one piece of it. I understood that very well that I would be responsible or we would be responsible for the entire project.

***Author:*** **What was the name of the organization?**

*Aashish Kumar:* At that time, this organization was being founded, it was called SAALT (South Asian Americans Leaders of Tomorrow). I don't know if they're still around. I believe they are, because this film was very formative in that organization coming into the center of South Asian politics at that time, because as you can imagine we had the ability to respond to the 9/11 events; we had the film ready by November of that year, and we were screening all throughout the country from the Southern Poverty Law Center to Chicago to LA at the Smithsonian at NYU, wherever was a need for stories to respond to the moment. So I think that was part of the organization's mandate to bring the South Asian community together and be able to respond to threats of racial violence and so on. And fortunately or unfortunately, we were part of that at the moment. Right?

***Author:*** **Picking up on the paid job and this starting point, we all tell students you've got to network, you've got to build a reel, you've got to build your skills. Do you feel like there was one particular thing that really helped you advance? Was it having these specific kinds of high-profile or really responsive documentaries, or was it something else?**

*Aashish Kumar:* Yeah, yeah, absolutely. I think it's very true that if you do work that impacts communities, and, of course, there is the artistic satisfaction part, you are all doing a combination of when you work in documentary, you are not just an artist. You are a public intellectual or public artist who's sharing something of value, entering into a discourse through that project. My work and the ability to produce something like that became known in the community. And it's interesting because I got a call a few years down after that film was finished from somebody in New Jersey who is to head a mental health organization called NAMI, National Alliance on Mental Illness. And she had reached out to people that she knew in the South Asian network and the executive producer of the Hate Crimes piece happened to be one of those people she reached out to. She immediately mentioned my name to her.

You can see that, of course, in the diaspora, you're not talking about a very, very large number of people, but there are a few filmmakers. And then once you have proven that you can commit to a project and you can see it through, and you're not just doing it because you are looking for it as a commission piece, that your involvement in the project far exceeds the remit. And that led to two other projects with NAMI.

I think I tell students all the time that whether it's a PA job, whether you're doing a one-day gig for somebody, you don't go in looking to just saying "How much money am I going to make?" Because if that's the outlook, then you're not going to get the impact because you are doing it because you can't wait to get paid for it. So yeah, I know that there's a lot of exploitation in our industry. There are a lot of underpaid gigs that's a lot of uncertainty around freelancing and so on. But it's also true that people remember who you worked with and how well you worked or how committed you were. And I think those things do matter, especially when you're producing a project, your commitment to seeing it through and how badly you wanted to get it finished or how badly you want to extend it.

I think, for me personally, the interesting growth in narrative techniques is not going to happen as much in what we call legacy media as it might in these very new plastic ways of storytelling that live on multiple devices that may have a counterpart in the legacy world, but they're doing more with it, they might be adding to, it might be extending the narrative. I'm very drawn to the idea of a living story where documentaries don't just have to be finished and then shipped and then you're done with it. But something that actually can be added, something can compliment, something that can be sort of a living history idea. And it's not easy to do that in the legacy media world, but these new ways of storytelling are certainly allowing for shorter but much more impactful ways in which stories can be told.

***Author:*** **You touched on this in a couple of your other questions, but in terms of your perspective as an editor, how do you feel it's unique?**

*Aashish Kumar:* [I] was working on a lot of … projects which involved traveling and interviewing multiple people. And my style of interviewing is somewhat in-depth, so I don't like to cut people off. I don't like to shape the responses to an editorial mandate. So I would edit these projects and there would be just such a wealth of stuff that never made it, and as any editor would attest to, and I started thinking about the efficiency of what I was doing and whether there was a way for these stories to have a different form. In which either editorially as well as structurally they might find the better use of the material or that use might be extendable as opposed to "I have only 30 minutes, I'm going to make a 30-minute film, and then everything else has to be in the bins."

So I was attracted by the gaming model where narratives can be an experience; a game of 20 minutes long or it can be two and a half hours long. Depending on how you were able to find those Easter eggs. And it is an expandable kind of accordion model of storytelling that compelled me to think about if somebody wanted to take a deep dive, they would not maybe be satisfied with just a 15-minute short, but they might want to explore it in other ways. Also, this idea of multi-perspective storytelling, oftentimes I found myself having to balance out or counter or do kind of montages of people's interviews that either supported or conflicted with or affirmed each other's narratives, but they had to live in the same space. I was thinking about a story at that time where giving space to just one person's story was more important as part of what the story demanded. I feel that this aspect of multi-vocality really became the driving principle behind Body Home World (BHW).

So in particular, I'll mention that I was working on a project, I still am actually, about LGBTQI stories involving a family and an LGBTQI-identifying family member. What I found in my research, and this is one aspect where the editorial and the structural decisions for that project was informed by the research that I did for the project, what I found is that both individuals, whether it was a family member or a queer person, were hungry for spaces that spoke to their story and their journey, irrespective of other people who are around them, but it centered them. I think it's false to say it was just their journey, but it centered them in their journey. And I struggled with the narrative forms that I had been working with at that point. I was saying "Oh, every time I cut from one family member to the queer person, I'm taking time away from that journey and I'm diluting, and also for the person that's watching it for whom I was making this film."

**Experience "Body, Home, World"**

Still images cannot adequately show the sound design, interactivity, and design of this story. To experience it fully, go to bodyhomeworld.com

So this idea of audience-centric structure of storytelling. I ended up deciding that I would create two channels of stories, and this became a multi-channel, if you may experience, where a parent who had their own journey would be able to speak just about that, and it'd be much more internal as opposed to referential … It was more about what they were feeling, and that became the heart of the story. Then I had to come up with a device that would address this multichannel thing, and that's where interactive story for me became a useful way where using modern media, for instance, the developments in coding on the internet, HTML5, WebGL … they opened the pathway for me to even conceptualize a storage for these stories, which would allow a navigation that wasn't overly complicated, but it was also a place for multi-path storytelling.

These stories are not 30-minute-long narratives, but they're shorter narratives that might total up to 30, 40 minutes, and you may not even finish the narrative completely. Just like in a game, you might just follow a queer person's journey, and that might be a ten-minute or a 15-minute short film that you have just watched.

I had to fit in new partnerships. I had to fit in new collaborators, and I had to figure out the entire process by which a project is structured, designed forward, and then the stories will live within that. But it had to be resonating with both. The stories weren't just going to be a little play button, it had to organically live within the design ecosystem. And I think that was a big learning for me – working with designers and illustrators who would draw from the stories, and the stories would draw from the design. It was, I would say almost like a new stream of editing and filmmaking.

***Author:*** **What's your software of choice?**

*Aashish Kumar:* Right now I am fully in the Adobe Creative Cloud universe. I use Premiere as my main editing tool. I use After Effects, it's just easier to stay within the Adobe system, and Adobe has developed both from the teaching point of view as well as from my personal point of view.

I live in these two divided worlds, my (academic) work is all Avid Media Composer. My school has historically committed to being an Avid school, and there were good reasons for that because many places, as you know, whether it's broadcast networks, whether it's big doc houses or even big reality and docuseries kind of places prefer the robustness of the Avid software. I think Adobe is more nimble and is able to respond to what's happening, thinking about cloud-based editing, thinking about collaborative editing. But Avid has for years dominated the post space and is still a calling card for a lot of people who are looking for editors.

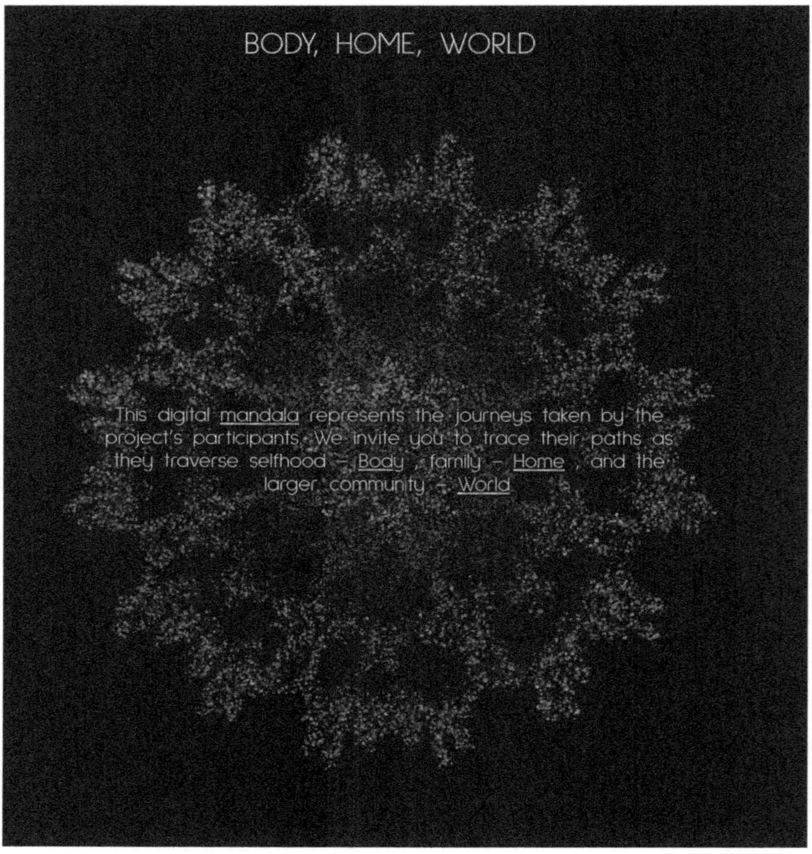


*Figure 11.2* The mandala that became a metaphor for the navigation in "Body, Home, World." Image credit: Aashish Kumar.

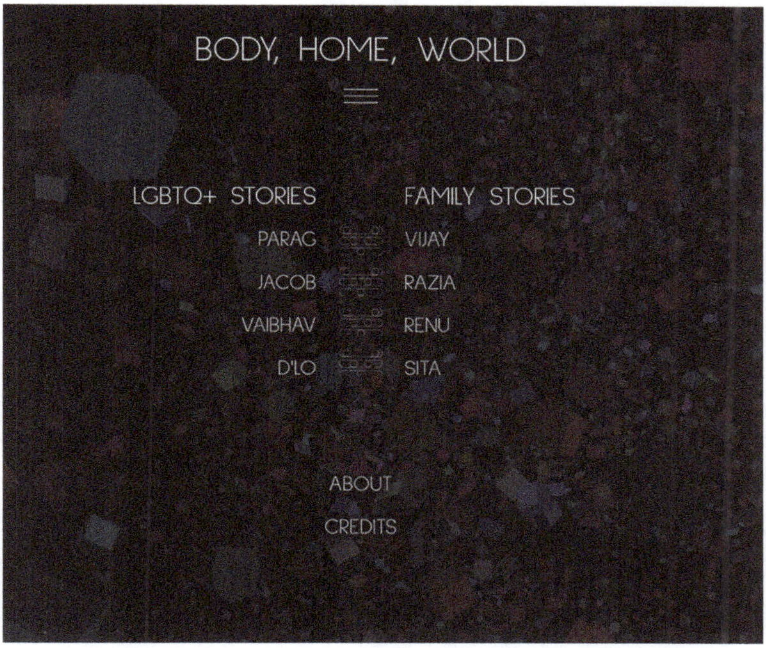


*Figure 11.3* The menu that allows viewers to travel into different parts of the "Body, Home, World" story. Image credit: Aashish Kumar.

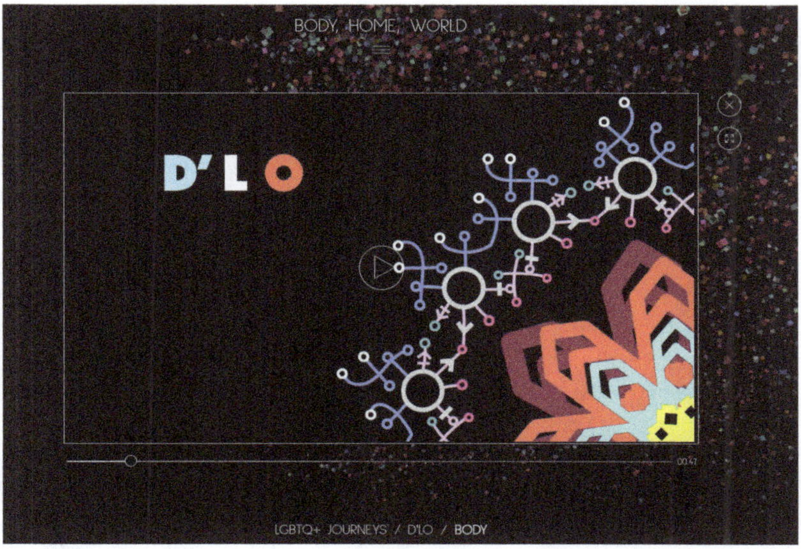


*Figure 11.4* Once a viewer chose a story, they were able to screen a short documentary segment of "Body, Home, World" story. Image credit: Aashish Kumar.

***Author:*** **What are some of your favorite scenes or do you have favorite scenes or favorite films that you like to refer to for editing and their style?**

*Aashish Kumar:* I think editorially, I'm kind of old school. I hearken back to times where I personally felt a revelation from watching something. Film has always been much more plastic in terms of technique. Television moves less radically and is much more traditional in repeating its formula. I remember watching "Homicide: Life on the Street," which was a show from the 1980s … and they used a certain style of sound editing where the dialogue of the next scene, not just the ambient sound, but the dialogue of the next scene would start permeating through an existing as the scene was ending. And I found that so profound because of how think about pieces of film as not spliced, but dovetailed. They're intermeshing and interlocking.

I would say, broadly speaking, I always think about editing styles that pay more attention, not just pay attention equally to how the film is moving longitudinally, but also latitudinally. What is happening across what you're listening to in the background, what the dialogue is doing, what the score is doing, and also what other images are doing in connection with the main story? Being a documentary maker, I love stories which allow us to think about more historical traditional ways of doing. For instance, simple things like we use a lot of archival material and documentaries, and there are always interesting ways in which people have presented archival footage. One of my most vivid memories is the film "Atomic I," which was made from the Freedom of Information Act or access to archival material that the filmmakers requested.

I think of "Strong Island" as one of my favorite documentary films that make such creative use of photographs that traditionally … So you see the person who is looking at the photographs, and it is not just a filmmaker who has scanned them and taken them to another place. So there's a very strong linkage between the person looking at the film and the viewer looking at these photographs with them. Those are a few that come to mind in the interactive world. My inspiration for the kind of stories that resulted in "Body Home World," was a Canadian series done by Kat Cizek from the National Film World of Canada, which was called "Highrise," was a five-year multi-part project that was funded – God bless tax-funded filmmaking – because that form of experimentation would not find a place in the American ecosystem. The Canadians pulled it off, and it is such a thoughtful, innovative, path-breaking series of films that unfortunately with the death of Flash, many parts of that project are no longer available to the wider public. I'm sure that in the way back machine there are screen grabs and so on, but that's one of the, is if you move one of the pieces out, it's like Jenga. It just falls apart.

***Author:*** **Do you have some go-to techniques in your own work? In your creative work, you have techniques that when you're putting things together, you just start to go to, you were talking about dovetailing, and do you find that just things pop up again and again?**

*Aashish Kumar:* I think for documentary makers, the historical … the bedrock of starting films that involve interviews is to always know everything that has been said and delve into that material, really become familiar with that. But it's not enough to just have those words because the story is not going to be told in just words. This is not radio. So figuring out the language that will accompany those words and doing so by spending time in the shooting process so that you can pre-visualize that style, that world that you want to create around the subject pays big dividends, if you have the time. If you have the budget, I would say push forward in the direction of not just thinking about the spoken word, but, so I'll give you an example. So I was in India recently filming with the activists in Assam who lived along, who spoke very fondly of this river that flowed near the city where she lived.

And people in Assam have a very strong relationship with this river. There are songs written about it. There are festivals that happen, there are fish markets all along it. And to me, I heard that phrase during the interview and I kind of filed it away, and I was going through the transcript and I saw that she mentions that "I'm like the Brahmaputra, flowing with it, changing with it." And that metaphor, that is a key, I think, for all filmmakers to find, if you are lucky enough that you participants or your subjects, however you refer to them, I prefer participants. [They've] given you something, but it's hidden somewhere. If you can find it, then it shapes. So I made sure that I filmed as many things around the Brahmaputra, whether it was a setting sun, whether it was people that live off of the river with fishermen, or whether it was simply cities that have grown alongside the Brahmaputra. And then you do this in a structured way, your audiences will pick up on the fact … I think enriching your work and infusing it with metaphors that have something to do with your character, not just your own imposition and your own kind of non-diegetic kind of insertion into the work. To me, that's very powerful.

***Author:*** **We talked a little bit about HTML5 and the death of Flash and different software. Are there tools or software or new developments that you're really excited about? (See Figure 11.1 for the gateway to "Body, Home, World," which mentions its web languages.)**

*Aashish Kumar:* Absolutely. So I saw a transition from tape-based editing to non-linear to the use of DV cam and digital video on tape to SD cards. And now I think the next era is cardless cloud-based editing. I think for large projects, it is really the solution that we have been waiting for. We just didn't know. And companies like LucidLink and Frame.io, and I'm sure there'll be many, many more that are allowing for quicker, not quicker than real time, but faster than the average upload speeds for other cloud-based services like Google Drive or OneDrive or what have you. They have figured out algorithms that allow for real-time access. So there's amazing developments. I mean, I saw a demo of LucidLink at NAB (National Association of Broadcasters) last year, and I couldn't believe that they were doing real-time editing off of the cloud. That opens up so many possibilities for collaborations throughout the globe as somebody who works with individuals in different countries, and we've always worried about how am I going to ship things to you?

Will I compress it? Will I do proxies? All these questions that didn't have a unified answer … I had students working on this project that we shot a lot of stuff for, and some of them were offsite. They were commuters. So they would shoot and the card was with them, but they were uploading footage to Frame.io from homes, and the story editors were able to look at them and the editor could take the selects and start working from them without us having to ship hard drives around. I think that piece is one piece of it, collaborative editing, something that I think needs to be handled very carefully. So Adobe has built it in there within using the cloud, Adobe Cloud and Premiere, the possibility of assistant editors and lead editors working on the same timeline and on the same project, and just updating changes by simply clicking a button. I think those advances are very exciting for post.

We cannot not mention AI the way it is changing the radical transformations that confine both from Generative AI, which needs to be thought of as different from AI that is … baked into systems such as color correction and sound enhancements and so on, which happen more passively without you having to type in prompts or amazing developments. We don't quite know where these things will settle because they're being added to updates every few months. But Generative AI, I think it's a whole different body of work that I think might even create a new type of, a new species of filmmaker who comes from that world, that process. So this notion of scripting a film through prompts, right? That's I think one way to think about prompts as the early script that may not have dialogue in it, but has descriptions, deep descriptions of scenes of moods and so on, and what that means for the industry of art designers and graphic people and filmmakers who are right now, will we see them being cleaved by this? Or will we see them using these tools as previsualization tools?

I mean, who knows what the answer to these questions are, but we are all sort of in this right now, and often when you're in something that is so nascent to jump to any conclusion, to build a fire and talk about the death of kings, I think it's too soon for that moment just with any technology. I think it'll evolve. Stories will triumph. I always believe that just because you're able to type a prompt doesn't mean that you have a desire for telling a story. People who have a desire for telling a story will stay with the story for a long period of time. They're not going to flirt with this idea of a quick two-minute shot that they were able to create with the prompt. So I think that's a well of it comes from a deeper place. It comes from a persistence, it comes from a tenacity.

*Author:* **What do you feel like are the biggest challenges in post-production now with all these developments? There's new challenges, so what do you see some of the big ones being?**

*Aashish Kumar:* So both of us, we deal with young people who are getting started and they don't quite know whether they want to be editors, they want to be storytellers, they want to be scriptwriters. Some of them know they are just tasting. I think the trickiest part is how to … because they've already done the indoctrination of … they've come into the world of reels and short palm cinema storytelling before they're going to go into long-form storytelling. And there are some examples. I mean, Quinta Brunson's "Abbott Elementary," began as reels on Instagram. I think sometimes understanding the connection between what the students have seen and the material that they're already bringing in and how to make that kind of dovetail, they might not even have an understanding of that.

It can be a double-edged sword because they're so used to that short-form storytelling, the quick and dirty form of filmmaking with a shaky camera or voice – it doesn't matter as long as you can get it out there, as long as people can respond to it; it's hard to really slow things down. For the learner to get them invested in composition, to have them think about what a two-minute-long piece might mean. I mean, two minutes seems long to some of my students because you've been restricted to a minute-long reel for Twitter or what have you. For TikTok, I think that's a challenge. Attention economy, we speak about that in terms of what students are doing in the classroom. It transfers to everything. It transfers to how they sit in front of a post-production or a project, write about it, think about it … The challenge as a professor … is I'm not immersed in that world as much as they are, and so how do I try to understand that sensibility and utilize that in my work so we are not just ignoring that world completely?

*Author:* **There has been a very traditional exclusion of women and people of color from especially the higher paid part of the film industry and industry in general. Has there been progress? How do you define progress? Do you see some initiatives making progress?**

*Aashish Kumar:* I'm hopeful. I'm more hopeful than I was ten years ago when there were no signs of the resistance, if you may call it that. I think fortunately or unfortunately, the death of

George Floyd prompted very across-the-board, unsustainable action … but … spasms of goodness that emerged during that time created some spaces. I think largely as one would've expected many of the traditional white-dominated spaces that felt that they had to do it, have run out of patience and have gone back to the old base. Where I do find hope is in places that set up projects at that time and are continuing with them. One that comes to mind is Rishi Rajani and his collaborator, Lena Waithe, who have set up a production company in Hollywood that has invested in hiring not just people who are traditionally established people in storytelling, but also seeding young people of color for their projects.

So they have entered into a partnership with Indeed and they fund ten filmmakers to scripts, and they make sure that they come to fruition and they have partnerships with festivals, prominent festivals like Tribeca and many other places where they're able to showcase the work of these creatives. Of course, one institution in a large sea of empathetic and sometimes hostile workplaces will not cut it. So the path is not straightforward. It's very uphill. But I do see shifts in some leaderships, whether or not the changes in leadership, for instance, the Netflix head of programming is a South Asian woman Bela Bajaria.

I have tried to do that in a small way in my own department. So we proposed a course called Color TV a few years ago, which centers on the work of creators of color. It's not just the old representation arguments like, "Oh, look what Hollywood has done and how bad it is and how bad people have been projected." Yes, that's part of the opening couple of lectures, but we move on to saying, "Well, if people of color were able to tell their stories, what stories would they tell and how are they bringing new aspects to how are they enriching the landscape of the stories that we do?" I think inculcating those types of traditions early into the curriculum and then staying with that within your program, convincing your colleagues that it's not just that one course where it needs to be ghettoized, it has to be across the curriculum.

We can't just teach queer studies in one course. We have to show queer films in the foundations of film. I think that's the fight that I think all of us who are invested in equity are fighting right now. I would not be … I think it's folly to expect that all of these changes will be easy because these canons have been in place for years, for decades, and to even shake open that canon and to kind of question the canon, is to invite ridicule. So you have to kind of be very resolute and be informed as to why you're presenting alternatives to them, even to your colleagues, because change is always tricky.

I tell them the students that are entering Hofstra … I think if you are in the classroom and if you're looking at your syllabus and you are not reflected in that, you should ask why are certain things absent and why are you not in it? Why are people like you not in that syllabus? And it's not easy for students to have the agency already to make those questions, bu' it's certainly important for us to wonder about that, what they must be thinking.

***Author:*** **We don't always think about safety in editing. And sometimes there's so much pressure and time schedules and unhealthy work environments. Do you feel like there are health impacts that people going into post-production careers should be thinking about?**

*Aashish Kumar:* Yeah, I mean, I think about a lot of the editing jobs are like working on the lighthouse – it's you and that flickering light. That's pretty much it. Of course, there's a reason why that space is important because the work is immersive and you really are in that tunnel. You are on that journey and it's hard to come in and out of it, but those long hours can be in addition to how much time we're spending on screens. Anyway, our necks are bent, our fingers are being used in different ways. I think the stresses that we are placing on the editor's bodies are different in the order of magnitude because of the way that we are using devices all the time in our lives.

I'm sure that we are seeing the detriment of what that might cause to the well-being of the average editor. As a young person, you're probably not thinking of it as much because you can just keep going and you can fuel it through all these coffee drinks and so on. But I think there's something about the impact of the way that we are spending time on screens and how the extension of that in the editor's life when we are looking at a screen, can be a multiplier than in the old times … If you think about the average person's use of cell phone, which is now easy for us to know, the phone tells us that you were looking at this phone for five hours yesterday, and if you're editing for another eight or six hours out of that time, that's the whole day that you've been looking at a screen. So that's scary.

***Author:*** **We are in a gig economy whether we like it or not, unless you're working for a broadcast outlet and even then it's often a gig or a short-term job. How do you recommend students entering this prepare to navigate and surf the uncertain tides of the gig economy?**

*Aashish Kumar:* Boy, yeah, they're already indoctrinated into thinking that that's the job they're going to have. So it's not as much of a shock because they see their alums out there. Talk about perma-lancing, which is a term that I detest with all of my viscera. Permanently being a freelancer … no prospect of benefits or in some cases maybe some benefits, but never having the certainty of a job. And I think those are the principles that a lot of people in our industry grow up with. They're also growing up with the idea that they will have to maintain not just one, but multiple revenues, and multiple ways of making a living. I think the nature of jobs has fragmented, as you mentioned, post houses that used to be a workplace. So you go in and you're doing a bunch of things. You might have been working on one project, then you might be moving on to another.

I think for our discipline, Hollywood has been globalized for the longest time. People don't talk about it enough. The money for Hollywood comes not from Hollywood alone, it comes from China, it's coming from India, it's coming from a lot of global investments, which means that they have a say in how people can be hired, what can be done to productions and so on. And that locus is shifting, and I don't think that our students know enough about global opportunities. Being in New York gives you this false sense that this is the be-all and end-all of what I must be looking to.

I and a few of the colleagues who have connections to international workplaces and are conversant with how much production work is going on in India, for instance; I mean, I walked into a color correction facility, room after room after room after room cubicles, just busy banging out everything from local soap operas to Netflix productions. It's insane. How does one compete in that marketplace? Because those are jobs that are being done, not just being shipped abroad, but they're happening in those locations. The production and the editing and the entire production is being done in those locations. So that model of globalization that we used to talk about where we will be farming work to other people, we'll be outsourcing, that's changed. So how can we become part of that? What are the internships and what are the relationships that a student in today's environment can avail? I think that I haven't cracked myself yet, but I'm interested because I see we are right now talking about doing a study abroad program for filmmakers in India and to that might be the first opportunity for our students to sample this big, big world. I mean this country that makes the most movies in the world, and there's so many production jobs and opportunities that can come out of that. So we'll see how that goes.

***Author:*** **Some people are of the school of pick a thing and specialize – be a colorist, be a sound engineer. Just do that one thing and then you'll get known that way. Other people are like, no, you're going to go from gig to gig and you want to have multiple skills. Where do you kind of rest on that scale?**

*Aashish Kumar:* I'm in the latter school of thought. I think pigeonholing oneself too early can be detrimental. Your skillset might quickly get outdated and you might have nothing to fall back on. If you're learning just one thing and trying to update just that thing, it might take you a while to re-skill. If you have multiple arrows in your quiver to use that metaphor, then of course it is more appealing because you can re-skill from one aspect while you still have something else to offer. Having said that, some students are very invested in drilling down and understanding and learning something and how it works. Those skills can last. Software skills on the other hand are much more rapidly in flux. So if you're a broadcast engineer, if you're somebody who wants to understand how cloud networks are working, how cloud storage is working, those skills are not going to be outdated very anytime soon.

But in the realm of software, people are updating things and they're looking for people that know the most latest version. I'm not going to knock the idea that skills are skills. If you know how to do color correction, whether you're working on DaVinci or whether you're working on another flavor, it's not going to change the nature of fundamentally what you do. But I'm speaking more to the idea that software options come up more frequently and new opportunities come up a lot. So if you have, for instance, the ability to do assistant editorial work and you have proven yourself, you should be willing to accept that. But if you already set your sites, then I'm just going to do one aspect of post-work and then keep looking for just those jobs. You're just fighting for a very small section, with very high-skill people, but there are a lot of them as well.

***Author:*** **And I love that idea of looking internationally and thinking about careers. We're in the United States, we think we'll ship out and bring back, and we don't think about ourselves as a labor market for other parts of the world.**

*Aashish Kumar:* Absolutely.

***Author:*** **Well, thank you. That was so in-depth.**

*Aashish Kumar:* I enjoyed this tremendously. Thank you for inviting me to this.

# 12 Interview: Allie Sultan and Ryan Rehnborg – "Incognita's Infamous Adventures"

## Bios

### *Allie Sultan: Editor, VFX Supervisor, Associate Professor*

Allie Sultan is a Media Arts Professor at Middle Tennessee State University (MTSU) and a filmmaker who works in both narrative and documentary modes. She is drawn to topics that involve youth identity, LGBT issues, and family dynamics. Her works have been screened in over 60 domestic and international film festivals. She earned a bachelor's degree in Recording Industries at MTSU, and an MFA from San Francisco State University, and has worked as a sound and picture editor for industry leaders such as ESPN, Berkeley Sound Artists, Zoetrope-Aubry Productions, Disney/Touchstone Pictures, and many other acclaimed studios. Her work in film and TV includes "Casanova" (Dir. Lasse Hallstrom), "Marie Antoinette" (Dir. Sofia Coppola) and "Feast of Love" (Dir. Robert Benton), as well as "Enchanted," "Spiderwick Chronicles," "Bonds on Bonds," and the Sundance award-winning documentary "The Devil and Daniel Johnston."

### *Ryan Rehnborg: Filmmaker, VFX Artist, Marketer*

*Ryan Rehnborg: Filmmaker, VFX Artist, Marketer* Ryan Rehnborg is an award-winning film and television producer with extensive post-production experience as an editor and a visual effects designer, a production manager sporting across-the-board technology proficiency from years working as a TV station engineer, and a video production expert with in-depth knowledge of every part of the process. An MTSU grad, his short films are screened at dozens of film festivals nationwide and streamed on Amazon Prime.

[You can view "Incognita's Infamous Adventures" on Amazon Prime and can see the behind-the-scenes at https://www.instagram.com/incognitaseries]

DOI: 10.4324/9781003473152-14

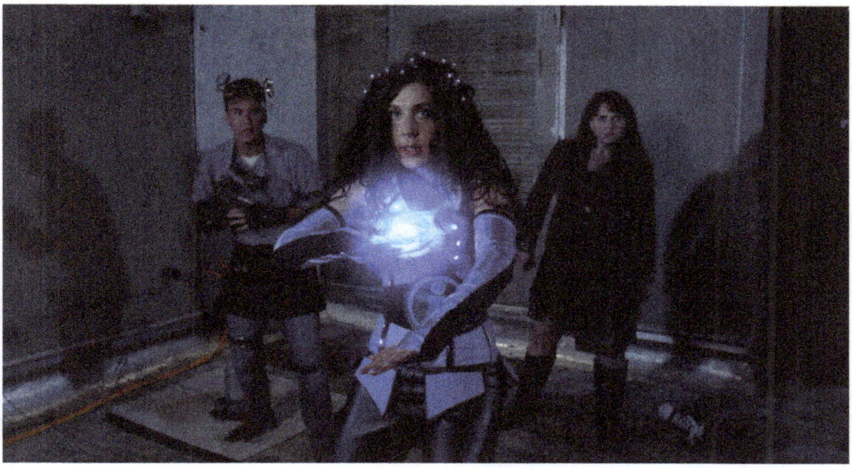

*Figure 12.1* Final composited still featuring Sarah Michele Bailey as Incognita, Darci Wantiez as Connie, and Tyler Evick as Buddy. Image credit: Chris Hollo and Ryan Rehnborg.

***Summary — "Incognita's Infamous Adventures"***

A four-part superhero musical series on Amazon.

> Anna Jane Pazeski has hit a slump in her superhero career. Eliminated from Superhero Idol, she and her sidekick, Connie, take desk jobs working for tyrannical Ms. Witz. But everything changes when handsome Adam fills the empty cubicle next to A.J.'s. Strangely, Adam's arrival coincides with that of the cunning supervillain, Baddio, and his sidekick, Buddy. Can A.J. and Connie save Big Pond City?

Directed by Allie Sultan. Written by Sarah Michele Bailey. Produced by Christopher Bailey and Allie Sultan. Cinematography by Chris Hollo. Edited by Sarah Michele Bailey and Allie Sultan. Starring Sarah Michelle Bailey, Christopher Bailey, Darci Wantiez, Tyler Evict, and Carla Christina Contreras. [https://www.imdb.com/title/tt9820580/fullcredits/?ref_=tt_cl_sm]

***Interview Selects***

Listen to the full interview and view the complete transcript on the associate website for this book. *Author's note: These interview excerpts were lightly edited for clarity.*

***Author:*** **What are your primary roles in the film industry and then do you have other roles in addition to those?**

*Allie Sultan:* I have two parts of myself in the film industry: me as a film worker and me as a filmmaker. I went to San Francisco State University for an MFA in cinema and spent my time there working in post-production. After graduation, I did a lot of work in sound editing, including working with Michael Kirchberg, a sound supervisor in San Francisco. He was one of the first people to give me a paid job, which was as an apprentice sound editor on "Casanova" (2005) with Heath Ledger. That job led to my joining IATSE Local 700.

From there, I worked as an editor on reality television for ESPN and as a visual effects editor at Tippett Studio in Berkeley, California. I bounced around between sound and picture editing but always made my own films on the side. That has always been my primary drive – not just to be a film worker, but to be a filmmaker.

Along the way, I've also taught, and I'm currently a film professor. In fact, I'm going up for full professor today and submitting my materials by 11:59 PM! I teach filmmaking to the next generation of media-makers and storytellers, and I love that work equally.

Over the past ten years, I've focused less on freelancing and more on teaching and making my own work. So, I guess I'm a bit all over the place, but it all ties back to my passion for storytelling.

*Ryan Rehnborg:* In the narrative film area, visual effects supervisor is probably my primary role and editor as well. In terms of my day-to-day, I work as a video producer for an in-house marketing agency. So I do a lot of the same things … heavy on the video editing and I get to incorporate my visual effects chops in there occasionally. But then when I'm working on projects like "Incognita" or other feature projects or music video projects, I'm a lot of times doing the editing and visual effects for those.

***Author:*** **How did you get your start in filmmaking or storytelling in general if you did something before film? You mentioned that you both did musical theater, so you got the storytelling bug early, but how did you get your start in film and media? The next question is what was your first paid or serious job? If you want, you can answer those together.**

*Allie Sultan:* I started working backstage building sets my freshman year of high school – building staircases, using table saws and power tools. I ended up doing sound for theater, where I saw the power of what I was doing to contribute to the storytelling happening on stage. That was my first job ever.

*Ryan Rehnborg:* I was maybe nine when a relative brought a camera to a family gathering. I realized, "Oh my gosh, people can have cameras and do this themselves." I was obsessed. I saved up for the cheapest camera and just never stopped making films. My first editing setup was two VCRs, one feeding into the other.

*Allie Sultan:* My first job out of school was an internship at Berkeley Sound Artists with Jim LeBrecht. He's probably the best sound designer for documentary film in the industry. He's a genius and he's worked with so many amazing filmmakers like Bing Lou on "Minding the Gap." … He taught me the power of sound design in documentary film. So I worked with him initially as an assistant sound editor, editing dialogue on a student project that was very low budget, so he couldn't pay his regular dialogue editor, and I just loved him and wanted to learn everything from him. So I stayed and made him coffee, I wouldn't go away. And so he decided to start paying me a regular salary, but to just cut dialogue, do some Foley, and that's actually how I learned ProTools on the job with him. I had learned Sonic Solutions in school, which again is like you learn the software, you're going to go learn something else in the industry, so just learn the technique behind it.

But all that to say Jim is amazing, and he ended up making his own film with Nicole Newnham called "Crip Camp" that got picked up by the Obamas and was nominated for an Oscar for Best Documentary, but lost to "My Octopus Teacher." But Jim is a big disability rights activist now. He's directing his first narrative feature, I hear; I'm just thrilled. And he's since retired from sound editing, but super cool. He got his start in theater too at the Berkeley rep as the sound designer for theater. So there's something about us theater people; we know emotion because we could see it in the audience in real time. Maybe that's when we bring that to filmmaking, we're anticipating how the audience will react more in tune with it.

*Ryan Rehnborg:* My first paid gig was making a green-screen music video for a band. They had built this aluminum foil spaceship with practical effects, and I wanted to make the space itself look as real as possible. I used NASA images, which are in the public domain, and learned on an iMac in the library. It was campy, but I poured everything into making it amazing.

***Author:*** **Which of your credits in post or visual effects or any other role are you most excited by and proud of?**

*Allie Sultan:* Beyond "Incognita"? I mean "Incognita's Infamous Adventures" was an eight-year project that brought together so many different people. Ryan was a student in the program I teach in, but he graduated before I got there and it was so cool to meet Ryan and work with him on this, but also our co-producers, Sarah and Christopher Bailey, were just really incredible at bringing a whole bunch of people together. So I think making "Incognita" was one of my favorite experiences, like being on set with everyone and then the editing process and then COVID hit right as we locked in the final edit and Ryan happened to be there just in time to save us.

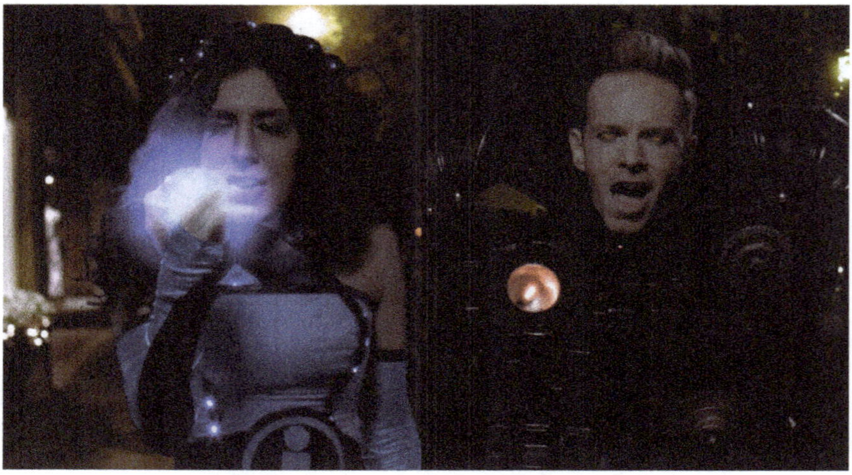

*Figure 12.2* Final composited still featuring Sarah Michele Bailey as Incognita and Christopher Bailey as Baddio. Image credit: Chris Hollo and Ryan Rehnborg.

*Ryan Rehnborg:* Alright, so I'm going to be predictable because hands down "Incognita's Infamous Adventures" is my proudest work. I have it at the top of my website. It's just … it's the coolest project I've ever worked on and the amount of storytelling we got to do through the post-production process was really unique and engaging … [In other jobs] just making visual effects to order … kind of like a visual effects barista, is sometimes the way you feel, but for "Incognita" it was really getting to do the art side of it and come up with ways to complete the story and grow the world through the visual effects. So definitely that's my proudest accomplishment.

I got connected to "Incognita" through Carla Christina Contreras and that the project where I first got to work with her directly was a project that I produced in a weekend called "Watch the Skies." It was post-apocalyptic Nashville that was the premise that I came to the script with. And doing that, it was a fun way to bring storytelling more into the visual effects. I was really thinking back to the original "Planet of the Apes" movies and when I first saw that as a kid, and saw that shot with the Statue of Liberty, and just how simple that matte painting work is but at the same time how iconic and impactful; I was trying to do some of the same things but with my hometown of Nashville. And so doing that was another beautiful moment in the artwork that I've been able to do.

*Allie Sultan:* I want to second something that Ryan mentioned – the fact that Ryan, you really created a lot of these worlds. I remember "Incognita," and I think you went so above and beyond with that. I was the director of that project, and my job was to take what was inside Sarah's brain and put it on the screen. She had this idea about a crystal ball

**Box 12.1 Want more on Incognito's VFX?**

The team behind "Incognita's Infamous Adventures" put all their work on IG! Check out their channel @incognitaseries for videos, BTS stills, and stories showing how they did their VFX.

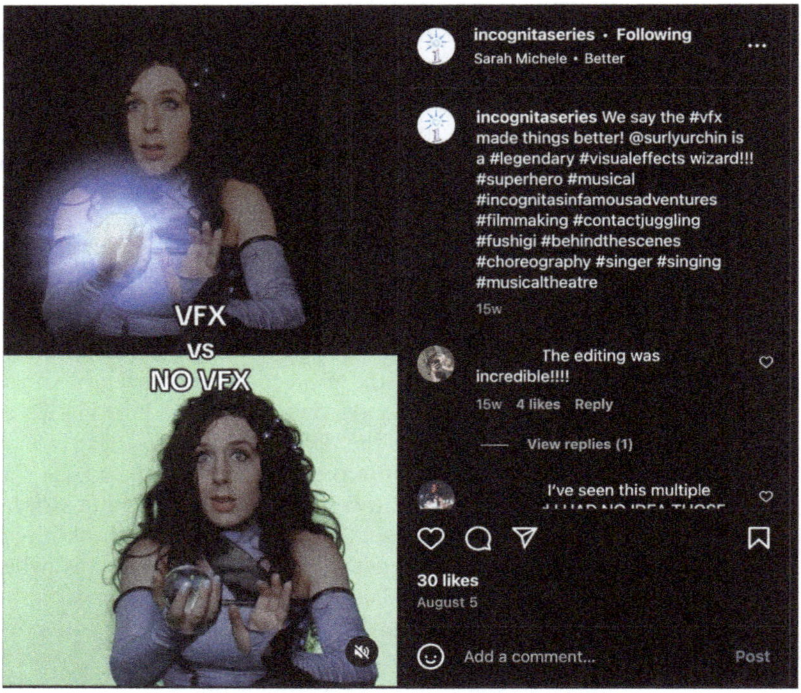


*Figure 12.3* Still from Instagram @Incognitaseries. Image features Sarah Michele Bailey as Incognita. Image credit: Chris Hollo, Ryan Rehnborg, and Sarah Michele Bailey.

as part of her character, and Sarah and I had talked about how the ball had powers when she touched it. But what does that look like?

We also created an entire city based on Nashville called Big Pond City, and we had no idea what that looked like either. So we were like, "Ryan, make something." I think I talked to Ryan about the character – honestly, I don't even know what I told you, Ryan – but you created an entire world and the magic to make it happen.

There are some scenes in this movie where we filmed over three different years for the same scene. Some of those were thanks to Ryan. Remember? Some of it was shot in a studio with a black curtain, and the rest was shot on a green screen. And yet you can't tell it was pieced together from three different years. We had no money; we were an independent production. Ryan not only created the world but made it seamless – which I thought was incredible, especially for $60,000, which is what it cost us to make a 70-minute feature-length film.

Collaboration is pretty fun. I mean, Ryan was on the set of "Incognita" not only as the visual effects supervisor and we would talk about "How is this going to work all the way through the pipeline?" because we're on a green-screen set right now. "What's possible?" "What framing should we film this with to make sure he has got enough room in post to make it fit?" But also, Ryan was the camera operator on a lot of days of the shoot, but we all have multiple hats and the credits can be kind of ridiculous in that case because we're all multi-skilled and why not let each other shine in whatever ways. Sarah even helped edit and doing some of the visual effects.

Last day of filming … we had to fix all the problems that we had created for ourselves in production. We were on set at 3 am, and people's hair is, because it's humid, it's like a hundred degrees at night in August and everyone's melting. So we had to make people look better.

*Ryan Rehnborg:* It does relate to how I ended up in visual effects – the green-screen pickup plan early on. I think, even in 2017, Sarah was looking at and very concerned about the shooting schedule. She was wondering, "I don't know how these things are going to come together," especially a couple of shoots in. It was like, how are we going to get all these people together? We're missing X, Y, Z shots from these shoots, and it's hard to make that all come together. I'm not sure where our coverage is on X, Y, Z scenes. I was like, okay, so here's a piece of experience that I don't know if I should be recommending, but when I started college I was already working on this enormous project that I had set for myself. There were so many things I hadn't learned about filmmaking, and I shot it all in one month. It was basically a feature-length project, much like "Incognita," in that it was four episodes, but if you put the four episodes together, it would make a feature-length film. It made more sense that way because the first episode was way longer than the others.

I shot it all in one month, and shortly thereafter I started taking my first film class and found out all the things I had done wrong. I was like, "Oh my gosh, what am I going to do?" I was also exploring After Effects for the first time. I had taught myself Premiere and Final Cut leading up to that, but I had never done After Effects before. I was sitting on the IMAX computers at MTSU, which had the Adobe Creative Suite, and I started teaching myself After Effects. I thought, "Maybe there are things I can do in here to fix this in post." But then I started realizing how daunting that was, and I couldn't get everyone back together for an entire additional month of shooting.

I was like, "I'll just have one day and bring all these people in and shoot on a green screen." I figured out how to key in backgrounds and stuff like that, so we could grab frames from other things and use them as backgrounds. That was something I did to fix my early student film. I just said, "Hey, if you want to set up pickups – we didn't have a particular studio, we were thinking about shooting some stuff at MTSU – just plan to do that, and we can cover a lot of things by grabbing plates and other elements."

Obviously, by then, I had several years to learn and become more sophisticated in how I approached visual effects. But I did kind of dig that hole for us by suggesting that there might be a way to fix all the logistical stuff with visual effects.

That's really why I started learning and teaching myself visual effects. I never took a visual effects class, but I wanted to make the stuff I was creating and make it the best it could be, even though I didn't have a lot of resources. So I started doing that. When I was working with everyone on "Incognita," I was prescribing some of those methods. I definitely don't love the "fix it in post" mentality, but the growth through the tools of post-production and being resourceful in how we met those limitations – visual effects became one of the tools I worked hard to put in my tool belt. So, that was how I was approaching it or recommending it to Sarah:

"Hey, maybe this is a way to overcome the fact that we don't have a budget and can't shoot everything, but we do have a way to make some of these things possible that might not be easy to shoot or reshoot."

*Author:* **So Ryan, I have a feeling if I ask you what's your software of choice you're not going to say one, you're going to have a list. So what is your software of choice and what do you recommend students should be coming out of school knowing?**

*Ryan Rehnborg:* Wow, that kind of depends on the student, of course, and what you're going into, but if you're focused on editing, I still feel there is a certain amount of visual effects software that is always kind of necessary. For me, that's After Effects, and I'd also say After Effects and Blender are still necessities for editors, especially now that more and more editors are being asked to handle primary motion graphics. If there are visual effects, people often group that together with editing. I think it's all kind of connected. So, I would say that's a great path to go.

I've never really invested time in learning paid three-dimensional modeling software when Blender was available. I've had Blender since college, and I think it's a wonderful resource. The fact that it's out there and available to anyone for free is magnificent. On the other hand, if I were to go back and relearn everything, I would definitely include Fusion in that. So, learning Resolve and Fusion again would be part of my path, because the fact that Blender is out there and available to me to make

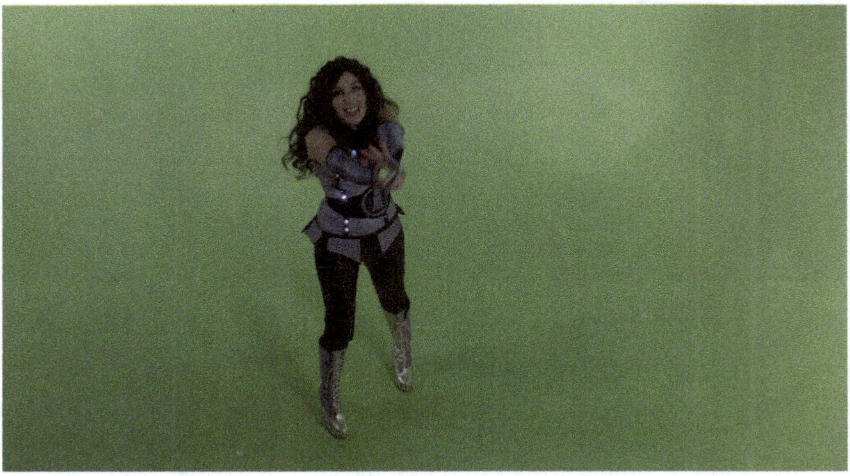

*Figure 12.4* Green-screen production still, before compositing, featuring Sarah Michele Bailey as Incognita. Image credit: Chris Hollo and Ryan Rehnborg.

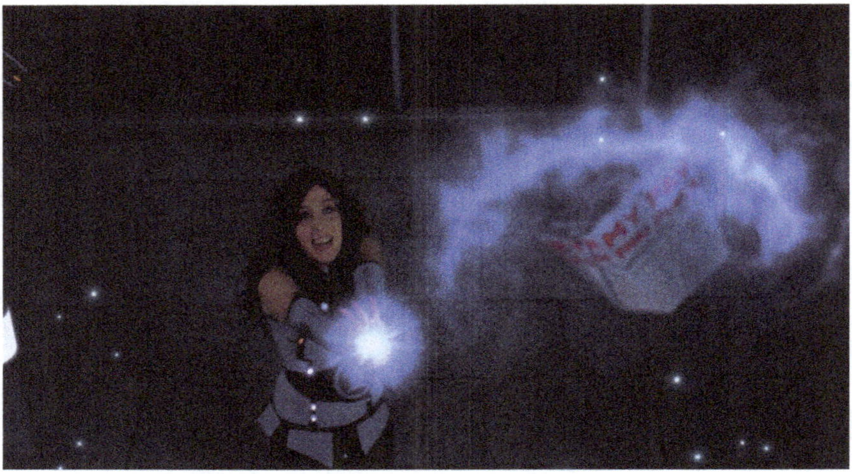

*Figure 12.5* Green-screen production still, after compositing, featuring Sarah Michele Bailey as Incognita. Image credit: Chris Hollo and Ryan Rehnborg.

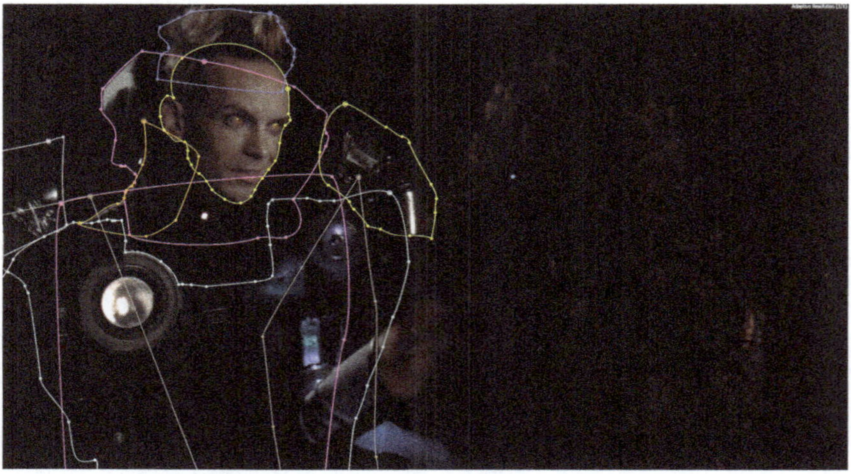

*Figure 12.6* Rotoscope frame, featuring Christopher Bailey as Baddio. Image credit: Chris Hollo and Ryan Rehnborg.

things possible without having to pay for a subscription or something like that is amazing. The fact that Resolve and Fusion can do professional-grade work on their free versions is wonderful.

So I'd definitely suggest learning Resolve and Fusion to anyone out there, whether you're learning as an editor or as a visual effects person. I don't really venture outside of those too much, but there's one thing I've been working hard to add to my arsenal:the Unreal Engine. It's everywhere right now, but I don't think it's going anywhere. It's definitely been hugely popular in the last few years, starting with its use in "The Mandalorian" and expanding everywhere. It really changes the game for what kind of vision you can realize, whether through in-camera visual effects.

***Author:*** **I knew you'd have a detailed answer. Do you have a favorite if you were just going to open your computer and be in one software all day? What would that be?**

*Ryan Rehnborg:* Gosh, I guess I'd be in After Effects all day. For "Incognita" and almost anything else I do, I'm using a plugin to do three dimensional more expansively inside After Effects. So Element 3D is what I use for that – it's its own little software inside After Effects. So yeah, probably that. But it would be painful not to be able to round-trip to Premiere if I were stuck in just one platform. There are a lot of things I do much faster in Premiere, especially when it comes to timelines versus the intense, densely populated compositions I create in After Effects.

***Author:*** **Allie, what is your favorite software?**

*Allie Sultan:* Well, I'm just bitter. I'm bitter because, in audio, I was a sound editor, and ProTools has pretty much been consistently used in the industry, so you learn it, you spend time with it, and it becomes a tool you like to use. I also work with tools I like and get comfortable with, so I'm not afraid of technological changes. When Apple dumped Final Cut Pro in favor of a more consumer-friendly version, which has since evolved, I was mad. Then I had to learn Premiere and Avid. We had to hire people just to make our Avid systems run, and I can't even get Avid to run on my MacBook Pro because of the licensing thing. I just feel like we should all start teaching DaVinci Resolve. That's exciting to me, but also, there's a bigger learning curve, and my time is limited. Especially, I'll just say it, as a single mom, I don't have the time to learn every single new piece of software.

*Ryan Rehnborg:* No, I will second that, Allie, in terms of that complaint, especially with the way the industry is so specific about software requirements. It's just like, who out there is looking for cinematographers with experience with specific cameras? Cinematography is a craft – you learn the technical functions, and then you can use that knowledge across any camera. It should be approached the same way, in my opinion, for editing. You learn the technical skills and then apply them across whatever software, as opposed to how much searching goes on for someone who uses a particular program. It's like, even if it's not my primary program, I'll use my editing skills because I'm an editor first. I'll know what to do, and I can figure out which buttons to push. Usually, a quick reset of the shortcuts to something I'm more familiar with is all I need to switch back and forth.

# 13 Interview: Carla Gutiérrez – "FRIDA"

## Bio

***Carla Gutiérrez: ACE, Director and Editor***

Carla Gutiérrez is an Emmy- and ACE Eddie-nominated documentary filmmaker. Her directorial debut "FRIDA," about iconic Mexican painter Frida Kahlo, premiered at Sundance 2024 where it won the prestigious Jonathan Oppenheim Award for Best Editing. Among Carla's many masterfully edited films are the Oscar-nominated films "RBG," about Supreme Court Justice Ruth Bader Ginsburg; "Julia," about renowned chef, and television personality Julia Child (Telluride, Toronto Film Festivals, CNN Films); and "Pray Away" (Tribeca, Telluride, Netflix Original). Carla's work has received awards at Sundance, Tribeca, Berlinale, Outfest, the Critic's Choice Awards, the National Board of Review Awards, and the DuPont Columbia Awards. ["FRIDA" can be streamed on Amazon Prime.]

***Summary — "FRIDA"***

> '"FRIDA" is an intimately raw and magical journey through the life, mind, and heart of iconic artist Frida Kahlo. Told through her own words for the very first time – drawn from her diary, revealing letters, essays, and print interviews – and brought vividly to life by lyrical animation inspired by her unforgettable artwork. A cacophony of rich archival sights, music, and journal entries joyfully brought to life, we become immersed in Frida's interior world, fears, arduous relationships, and events that drove her indelible artistic creations. Gutiérrez vibrantly guides us through Frida's complex relationship to her own work, navigating the tension between art as commerce and painting for pleasure and self-knowledge. With reverence, thoughtfulness, and the color of pure emotion, FRIDA invites us to get to know one of the greatest artists of the 20th century in a completely new way.'
>
> (Description from the Sundance 2024 Film Festival listing.)

DOI: 10.4324/9781003473152-15

**Interview Selects**

Listen to the full interview and view the complete transcript on the associated website for this book. *Author's note: These interview excerpts have been lightly edited for clarity and brevity.*

*Author:* **Could you introduce yourself with your primary role in the film industry and if you have any additional roles?**

*Carla Gutiérrez:* My name is Carla Gutiérrez. I would identify myself as a Latina immigrant, and I have been in this industry since 2004, so it's been a while. And I have been working as an editor for most of those years. And I just finished my directorial debut, which I also edited, which is "FRIDA." So yeah, so I've had a long career and I'm well known as an editor, and now I'm coming into the same space as a director.

*Author:* **So exciting. Which of your credits, whether as an editor or a director, do you feel most excited by and proud of?**

*Carla Gutiérrez:* With directing, it was really the story of Frida that pulled me into that role. I wasn't really thinking … I want to direct, I was mostly motivated by "I have to make this film and I think I'm the right person to do it." I'm kind of surprised that it hasn't been made this way. So there was a certain urgency, even though her story had been told many times before, but in different ways. I think now that I've had the experience of both directing and editing a film … I set up the structure of my team to be able to support that dual role for me. I really enjoyed it. So I want to be able to continue to do that, but I don't think I can direct solely; I want to be very involved in building the narrative as an editor or just really being very involved in the editing process. I think more than maybe other directors would be.

*Author:* **Yeah. One thing I do want to mention in this book is how many directors are involved in the editing process, for example, the Coen Brothers always did their own editing, but they used fake names for it**.

*Carla Gutiérrez:* It's really interesting to see, in the documentary landscape, how editors make that transition. Some directors stop editing altogether, but the experience we gain from understanding what the story is – or being able to write the story in the edit room – gives editors a really strong sense of storytelling. It also provides a deep understanding and control over the possibilities of a narrative in film.

So a lot of the editors who have made that leap to directing are incredibly strong directors. It's exciting to see how that knowledge transfers so beautifully into guiding a film from the very beginning.

***Author:*** **Yeah, in the documentary world I feel like people started doing it out of necessity, but in the fiction world I never understood why they wouldn't credit themselves, but maybe that's just a thing that's changing slowly.**

*Carla Gutiérrez:* I mean, it's also about the collaboration. I've never really had experience editing fiction, but I think there's a confidence and decisiveness that we, as documentary editors, need to have. We can't be afraid to try very different things because we're essentially writing the film in the edit. Some of the most famous fiction editors started their careers in documentaries, and I think that there is something there with their talent. It's like not being scared to really change things up and not follow a script, because we don't really have a script. So we're really following our instincts and making big-picture decisions from the very beginning.

***Author:*** **What is your favorite part of post-production?**

*Carla Gutiérrez:* I tell people to really concentrate on learning how to do storytelling really well because having that if I can say this … I love to talk about the metaphor of pushing my chair and being able to have a big picture of the story. Because the form, the style that you choose, the approach that you choose, even the rhythm of the edit needs to lift up what you're trying to say, what is at the core of your story and how your narrative is going to be built.

And if that can be done, always leaning into the emotional narrative and not necessarily the informational narrative. Especially for documentaries, that's really hard to learn and very few people do it really well and continuously do it over and over with each of their films, like either as directors or editors. So for me, that's at the center of the process. And for me, form or technique has to just follow what is the heart of the film. So learning how to tell the story that is at the heart of the film is what's really hard. And also what is the most enjoyable and the most challenging, but it's delicious. The challenge, the mental challenge and the creative challenge of not being able to see a film … for a long time. And trusting the process and trusting that you're going to get there. It is a challenge. It is really hard, but that's the most yummiest of it all.

***Author:*** **That order out of chaos and finding that, I like how you said how the form, you don't kind of come in with this idea of what the film will be. You look for the heart of it and then figure out your form of it.**

*Carla Gutiérrez:* I think if people come in kind of stuck with the style of the film, but haven't thought about how that style connects to the theme of the film or what is the film about? For example, with "FRIDA," obviously it's about an iconic artist. It is about a figure that a lot of us know pretty well. Many of us know really well. But the theme for the film, and we talked about it from the very beginning … the film ultimately is about a woman who is experiencing normal things that a lot of women experience in our lifetime, who chooses not to contain her voice. She decisively has the courage to express her voice freely. And sometimes that expression is problematic. Sometimes that expression is a little fraught, but it's always very honest and it's always very open. And so that was the central theme of our film.

***Author:*** **Another aspect of this book is to provide career guidance to people entering the film industry, mostly students, but also professionals trying to navigate careers. I'd like to provide some examples of what people's entry points were. How did you get your start in filmmaking? Did you do something before making films?**

*Carla Gutiérrez:* So I got into filmmaking really pretty late. I was 27 and I got into filmmaking through film school. Also, I think as a Latina immigrant education has always been a very secure access point for me to get into different spaces that sometimes it's hard to get into if you don't have connections or you don't have a lot of knowledge about those things. So for me, film school made sense, but I mean, for a lot of people it is a huge expense.

But that was my entryway and that worked really well. And that's when I decided that I loved editing during grad school, but I went to a school that trained you for everything back then. No streaming platforms. It was mostly independent work, so they really trained you to be a one-person band if you needed to do your own camera work, do your own sound work … if you needed to do your own directing, producing, and then editing.

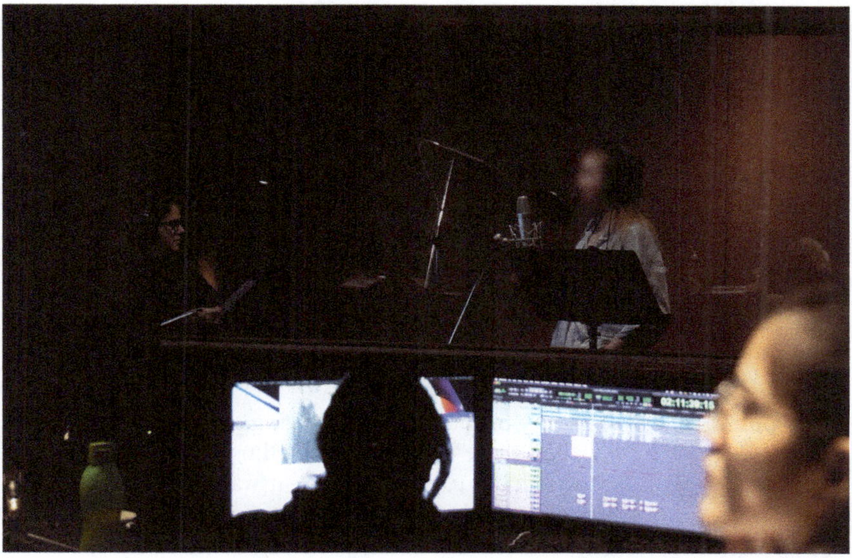

*Figure 13.1* Carla Gutiérrez directing an actor in voice recording. Image credit: Adrián Gutiérrez.

I started translating things for work as I was finishing film school. And then I became … they gave me the credit of second editor, which I don't think I've ever seen before or after. So I assisted, but then I edited a couple of scenes in the film. So that was my first job. And I just want to say that being bilingual was … it gave me a big window of opportunity when people looked for bilingual editors, it was kind of both an opportunity, but also for a long time I was kind of pigeonholed in only hearing about those types of jobs.

***Author:*** **Were there other things that helped you build your career after you got that first job?**

*Carla Gutiérrez:* I started … I founded an organization that unfortunately I'm not involved with it or I really can't be involved with it anymore, but it's called BIPOC Documentary Editors (BIPOC is "Black, Indigenous, and People of Color"). It's a database and an initiative I started with editor David Teague, and it's still very much alive. They're doing a lot of amazing things. And it was to encourage the industry to look outside of the networks because it's so much word of mouth that you just get recommended by the same people, and a lot of times it's mostly white filmmakers recommending white editors. And so we wanted to create a database so that people can just expand their circles and their networks and make an effort to do so and to hire more diverse editing teams.

***Author:*** **You kind of touched on hiring, and since remote editing is so possible now, and some people are telling me they have these global teams and you don't have to be in New York and hire an editor in New York, so you can sit side by side. You can hire someone in Bombay or London. Since you just mentioned hiring, could you weigh in on your experience or how you see remote work and that kind of affecting hiring?**

*Carla Gutiérrez:* [Remote work] affects both hiring, but also it affects the way that we're learning storytelling a lot. Because that first job that I told you about, it was with a very experienced editor who became my mentor, and I learned a lot from that experience in film school … it was very intense and you had to have thick skin, and I learned a lot about my own voice as a filmmaker. But I was making short films. And in that first job I learned how to tackle a narrative arc for a feature film, which is a whole different monster. The peaks and valleys of drama for 90 … 100 minutes is just a different thing. So mentorship was really important for me then, and mentorship is really effective when it is mentorship while you're making something. Not only having meetings, not only doing the networking where you're having meetings and asking people how they got this job or asking people for a recommendation.

It's really learning the craft and learning how to be a storyteller. It's not easy. And I'm learning continuously by looking at other people's films. I love, love, love going to screenings because I'm able to see behind the scenes whether coming against what are the issues that they have, how are they working with the themes and the narratives of the film? And that's just kind of like a lesson when you see other people's process and you also see how hard it is for everybody. So that's what we're losing with some of the remote stuff that is happening. We're losing that personal contact for the assistant editor to be able to be in the room where the story is being discussed. If you give an assistant editor something to cut, how do they know how that scene is going to fit into the larger picture, the larger story?

They're going to cut that scene and it might not make any sense in what we're trying to say. So I feel like that's one of the downfalls of remote because apprenticeship is not as normal anymore and people are getting stuck with just the technical aspects of it. And even with, I mean at the same time in "FRIDA," we did a lot of remote work, but mostly the core team was in New York. It was important for me to get together. I hired a supervising editor. I had a very creative producer.

***Author:*** **I heard, in another interview, you spoke about hiring animators in Mexico for "FRIDA."**

*Carla Gutiérrez:* It was important for me to get together and my supervising editor, David Teague, the guy that I did the database with, if you look at his credits, he's just incredible.

I would say he's one of the best storyteller minds in our community. That was just such a treat, especially because I knew that I needed to work in collaboration with somebody else, especially if I was going to both direct and edit at the same time. He became instrumental in finding the voice of the film. My producer also was really involved in the creative aspects, the story.

But the work was happening in different places. Our composer was in LA and I mean, that's the beauty of remote. It has its limitations for some of the collaboration that is beautiful to do in person, but it also allows you to be able to work with talent that is not near you. And that was really important to me to be able to pull in talent from Mexico or Mexican talent that was anywhere in the country. Our composer is from Michoacán (Mexico). He lives in LA and that's the beauty of remote, to be able to just share, not only be able to talk in virtual calls, but also just share work so quickly. It's just so fluid now. So it's exciting, but we need to be aware of what are we losing if we don't come together.

***Author:*** **You mentioned being in film school and finding your voice. How would you articulate your voice in filmmaking? What is your particular perspective?**

*Carla Gutiérrez:* I think that there's a rhythm to things that I like. I think really learning how to be true to myself and finding my voice in terms of confidence, not being scared to make big decisions and not being scared and being okay and being trusting with the process. To be able to fail, because that is the process. The process is a continuous failure. Until you have the shape of a film, right? Like you're

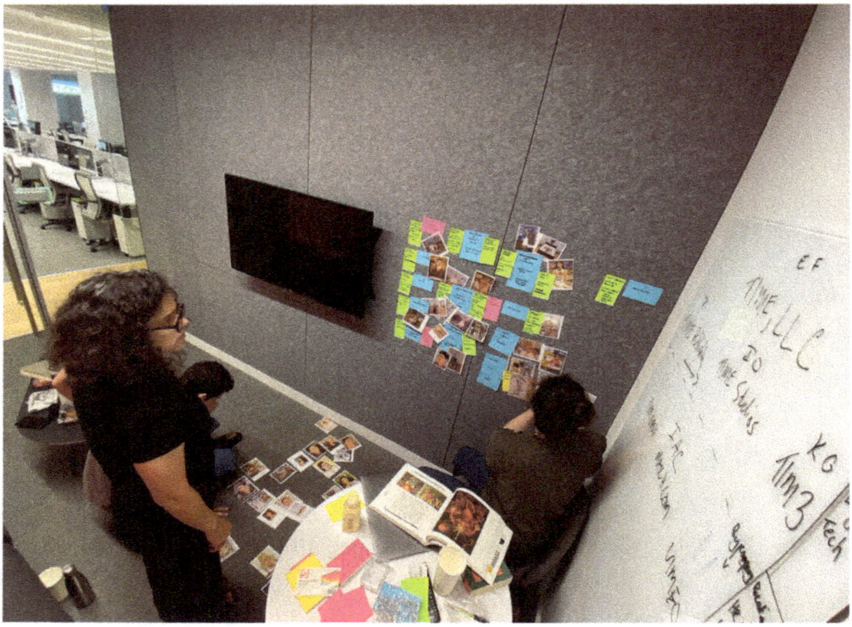

*Figure 13.2* Carla Gutiérrez and team sorting out the story in "FRIDA." Image credit: Paula Ospina.

learning a lesson every time you have a version of the film, you're learning a big lesson. You have to be decisive. You have to decide that scene is only going to be about one thing, because if you're stuck with, "Oh my God, everything that happened that day is important," then that's where films kind of get lost in themselves, right? They're not focused.

***Author:*** **How do you find music? Do you tend to work with a composer or do you ever find yourself doing stock tracks and just buying them? Or do you do stock tracks and then take that to a composer?**

*Carla Gutiérrez:* Yeah, I usually do temp music … because sound to me is really important in the edit, and sound very much changes the way that we experience time, how time moves when we're seeing something. So, for example, I always cut archival with sound effects. I can never just only have the video and say, "Oh, the sound team will add stuff." Because I know that once you add layers of sound, and depending on what decisions – if you want to go abstract, poetic, or very literal to what you're seeing – sound just kind of changes the experience that we have in terms of the rhythm of how things move and how time moves. So I start cutting with music right away if that's something that I want to try for a scene or not. Sometimes I have to be careful not to use music as a crutch.

And then with temp music, it's difficult. With "FRIDA," it took us a while to find something that kind of got toward what we wanted to try out with the composer. And then the composition was very different from our temp music, but it just kind of gave us some ideas … So with temp music, you never get everything that you will get with composed music. It's very different, but you can at least get a little bit of rhythm and a little bit of emotional mood and maybe a little bit of the texture that you're going for. So for FRIDA, we used a lot of temp music that didn't work at all, and we found some temp music that was working a little bit better. And then we started working with the composer kind of early on, with a couple of cues, just to be able to get the voice. And then he worked really fast for the rest of the film, but we already knew that we got it with those two cues, and we worked those two cues for a long time. For us, the music in that film was another voice of "FRIDA," and it just kind of took us a while to really capture her voice with the music as well.

***Author:*** **Are there developments that you're excited about?**

*Carla Gutiérrez:* Well … you have to be careful with all the AI staff, and all the technical staff … but it is exciting to see the technical advancements being used creatively. If I see a film that I know has a foundation of really understanding the story, being ethical with both the story and the subjects, and then they're using technology in really interesting creative ways, that's really exciting to me. I mean, there is technology now that can actually separate audio from archival. So, for example, when you have archival from the news and you have a broadcaster talking, you can actually separate the background noise from the person talking. That's amazing. So you can even just play with the background noise, with the actual background noise of that image, stuff like that. I mean, God, I wish I had that when we were working with "RBG" to be able to get her voice away from some of the background that we had. So that's exciting.

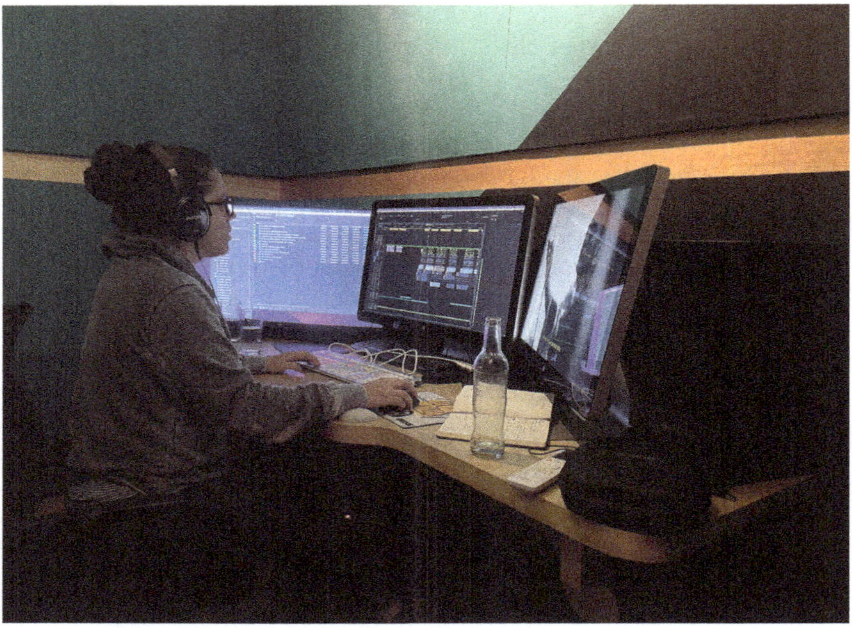

*Figure 13.3* Carla Gutiérrez editing "FRIDA." Image credit: Paula Ospina.

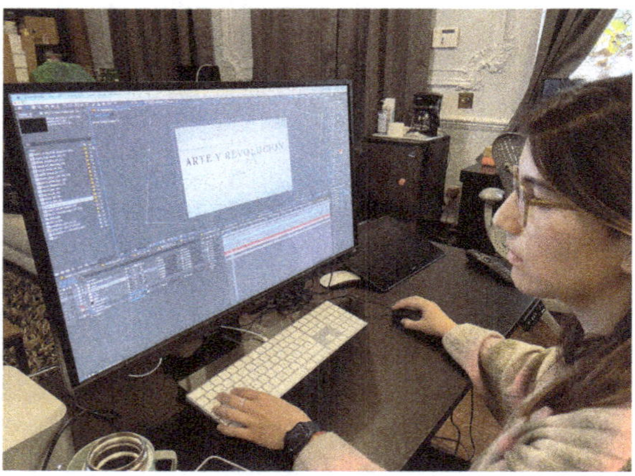

*Figure 13.4* Art director and animator Renata Galindo, working on "FRIDA." Image credit: Paula Ospina.

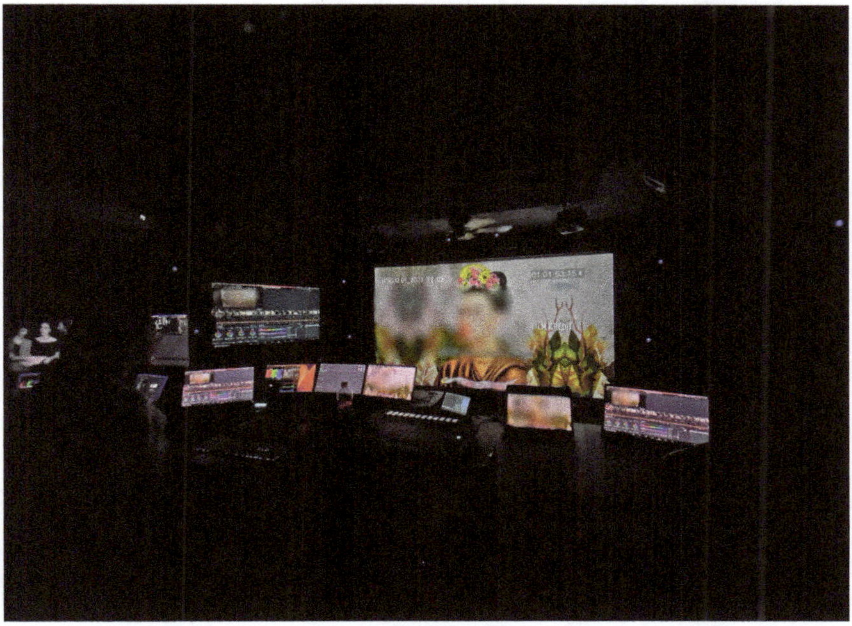

*Figure 13.5* Final matchback in the DaVinci studio on "FRIDA." Image credit: Paula Ospina.

I mean, we didn't use [GenAI] in "FRIDA" at all, but I've found that, for example, there are people recreating voiceovers from writing material. And that's what we did with "FRIDA." We took writing materials, we took her words from her writings. There's no voice of her recorded, but we just chose to do it through actors. And we also use other people's voices through actors as well, so to make everything equal and the same. But I know that people are recreating if they have a recording of somebody, but most of their words are in writing. They're using GenAI to make those writings alive in voiceover, and they still use actors to be able to get some kind of emotional performance. But then they use GenAI to get the texture of the person's voice, to get to the person's actual voice, to make it sound like their actual voice. And I think that as long as we are … really forward with the information that this is what we're presenting to you. I think that that's a super interesting creative way of using it. I don't know if

I would do a first cut. That's what I'm a little nervous about, doing a first cut just with AI.

*Author:* **It seems like there's two schools of thought. One is to focus and become a specialist, and you do this one thing and then you get known, and then people come to you. Other people is to diversify. Know a whole bunch of things. Both schools of thought probably are valid, but where do you have a side?**

*Carla Gutiérrez:* Think we pigeonhole people too and too much. I would trust an editor that has done an amazing archival film to edit a verité film in a second. Because what is important again – the story. What is the narrative foundation of a film? And then you figured out how to use the form, the tools that you have to be able to tell that heartfelt story. That's what I saw. I mean, when I was doing the Latino films, it was all verité, archival, anything. It was getting pigeonholed in a subject matter of [films] in Spanish. Then I did "RBG," and all I was hearing about was archival films. And I am going to see how that affects me as a director as well. I have something that I really want to do that is a verité film. It's like a competition film. Very different from "FRIDA."

I mean … the first time I really worked with animation with Frida. I've done a lot of graphics, but this was animation. It was a different form. Still. I knew what I wanted to say in those scenes, and that's what informed the way that I treated this new form that I was playing with. So a lot of people come and tell me like, wow, I didn't realize archival is that hard. And it's like, well, it's because most people think of archival as this band-aid, that whatever the interview is telling you, you're showing with archival. And no, it's a tool for story. And so you have to look at it like that. So I do not believe in being specialized in one thing or another. I think that you just need to learn how to tell a story really well, and then the style and form will follow.

*Author:* **We don't think about safety in the editing room, but health and mental health are being discussed a lot in film. And editing rooms are known for intense pressure and working under these super intense deadlines. How do you protect your mental health and energy and your health in general when you're on an edit?**

*Carla Gutiérrez:* There is the aspect of [the type] the footage that you're dealing with, which is a potential mental health issue if you're dealing with trauma or pretty intense violence in the footage. So that's one aspect of it. I've found, throughout my career, and I've dealt with a lot of bloody images, unfortunately, in a very intense political context. And I found that what helped me the most was to know that the production team and the director had done really sound work in researching, and really understanding the context of the story. I felt really safe if I had that support to understand that world and that story. And it made me feel secure about making creative decisions that were ethical. Sometimes people think about research and knowledge as, "Oh, that's going to make a really boring film because we need to include all this stuff." For me, it's very different … it's like once you have a really strong foundation of understanding what the story is, and also the context of that story, then you can make very confident decisions.

Even that happened with "FRIDA" a lot … every decision is based on research. And then you can really truly lean into the emotional journey of this story. So for me, it's creative freedom. I feel really safe navigating a very difficult subject matter because I know that [the] people are doing it in very ethical and very grounded [way]. They've done their homework. So that's an aspect related to mental health; I always found when I felt really safe with the team, I felt that I could navigate and I could interact with that footage [in a way that I] knew that I was doing justice to the story, and that made me stronger in terms of dealing with that type of footage.

The other aspect is the mental health and the physical health of just the process of editing and filmmaking. And that's something that I've had to learn the hard way, and I don't think I've learned my lessons yet. Because editors come in every eight months, every ten months, maybe every year … they come into a film that is the one film that the directors have been living with for many years. So in a way, it's like you're coming into a birth and you're a doula. But this is the one kid at this point. This is the one birth, this is the one baby that they're birthing. So for them this is the entire world.

And so sometimes as an editor, the project demands a lot of hours from you, and they're emotionally also intense based on the subject matter or they're just mentally incredibly intense. I think that you need to set boundaries for that because it doesn't make the work more productive. It is their baby, they want to make the deadline, and so you have to navigate that. It's really intense for them, but you really need to take care of yourself. And there's been moments in my career where I was just like, I'm just putting myself physically through too much and mentally through too much, and I need to set some boundaries so I can be a better editor and I can help them better. But psychologically, you're also dealing with a team where sometimes the intensity can be … like, fire … and you've done this a few times. We'll get it done, we'll have a film finished. So that's something that I'm still kind of learning. And obviously when I was both directing and editing, I put that pressure on myself. So it was a very intense process for me. So yeah, it's something that I need to figure it out better.

***Author:*** **It's hard to shut off. It's hard to be like, "Okay, it's 5 o'clock, I'm going home."**

*Carla Gutiérrez:* Yeah, it is really hard. The one thing that I have gained from experience is knowing that we can get there. Because sometimes it's a first-time director or early in your career as an editor, you don't trust the process. And the process is there's so many ups and downs … now I know that we've done our homework. We'll get there and there's kind of a pressure off my shoulders because just like, we'll make it happen. We're a good team. We're going to make it happen. And everybody needs to chill a little bit, including me, and we'll get done.

***Author:*** **I like that. That's a good editing motto. Everyone needs to chill a little bit**.

*Carla Gutiérrez:* And dance a little bit. Have some jokes, laugh, laugh, laugh, laugh, laugh. Love it. Yeah, it's a lot of pressure. So I hope this makes sense.

***Author:*** **It does – thank you!**

# 14 Interview: Zeb Achonu – "White Nanny Black Child"

## Bio

***Zeb Achonu: BFE, Editor, Documentary and Fiction***

London-based Zeb Achonu started her career on a BBC Post-Production Trainee scheme, where she learned cross-genre skills from some of the best in the business. She works across various styles, editing documentaries, factual entertainment, drama, children's entertainment, and music. Recent projects have included feature documentary "White Nanny Black Child," Netflix four-part documentary series "Ladies First: A Story of Women in Hip Hop," and "Jimmy Akingbola: Handle With Care" following acclaimed actor Jimmy Akingbola as he tells his own story about growing up in the care system in England, while exploring themes including identity, mental health, and cultural connection for ITV, and "Queens of Rap," a 60-minute single documentary for Channel 4. She mentors, speaks on panels about her path, choices and career, and regularly engages with young people starting out in the industry. Among many other honors, she was a selected participant in Berlinale Talents 2024 and one of Edinburgh TV Festival's Ones to Watch 2020. ["White Nanny Black Child" is streaming on Netflix UK and available from Together Films.]

## Summary — "White Nanny Black Child"

"White Nanny Black Child," a feature documentary directed by Andy Mundy-Castle, is about a group of adults finding solace in sharing their experiences of growing up as children of Black Nigerian immigrants who were fostered by white British families. Between 1955 and 1995, over 70,000 West African children were fostered by white Britons, in a practice known as "farming." Many individuals then had to live, often in silence, with the long-lasting impact of this controversial official policy. Nine of those raised this way were invited to a workshop retreat, under professional guidance, to discuss their experiences. Each takes turns delving into their past, revealing the

DOI: 10.4324/9781003473152-16

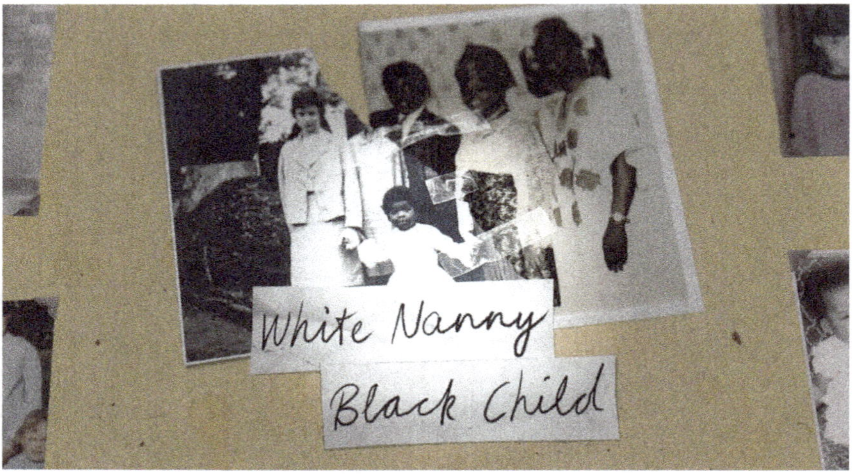


*Figure 14.1* Title image from "White Nanny Black Child." Image credit: Courtesy of Doc Hearts.

confusion and trauma of dealing with such change at a young age. For many, this marks the first time they have had the opportunity to connect with people who have shared a similar childhood. "White Nanny Black Child" presents a personal, moving, and sometimes unsettling meditation on identity, belonging, and the nature of family.

***Interview Selects***

Listen to the full interview and view the complete transcript on the associate website for this book. *Author's note: These interview excerpts were lightly edited for clarity.*

*Author:* **Would you be so kind as to introduce yourself and share your primary role in the film industry?**

*Zeb Achonu:* My name is Zeb Achonu and I'm an editor and an occasional editing consultant as well.

*Author:* **Do you do other roles beyond that?**

*Zeb Achonu:* I don't direct. I've recently been getting a little bit involved in executive producing for very small things, but it's kind of more the advice side of it than the hiring and organizing side of it. But mostly I always focus on the editing and the edit. Consulting is something I'm just getting into really. It's where I see myself going as I get older, wiser.

*Author:* **Correct me if I'm wrong, but I think you were on a couple of boards too, is that right?**

*Zeb Achonu:* I was, yes. I've kind of pulled back on those a bit because my editing has been so all-consuming, which is great, and my family has been always all-consuming. I was on the board for Women in Film and TV UK for four years, and that was amazing. Absolutely all the love for that organization, and for all the women in that organization. And then I also was an associate governor for the British Film Editors Guild, which I then took on the running of the subcommittees for the diversity division and the parents' and careers' divisions as well. So yeah, it's really important to me. That part of the industry I find so fascinating, but I just also had to pull back about a year ago. Yeah, my editing, I needed a few years of that being the priority.

***Author:*** **Which of your credits as an editor are you most proud of? Most excited by?**

*Zeb Achonu:* This varies quite a lot because of the different points in my career they represent. So I mean, I could go back to when I worked on continuing drama UK soap EastEnders, which was such a big goal for me. So that was a massive highlight. All the women in hip-hop documentaries I've done. So I did "Queens of Rap" for Channel 4 … so that's all me. And then I was involved in the "Ladies First" four-part Netflix documentary, but more recently I think the obvious one is "White Nanny Black Child" … because that won the BAFTA and because it was such an experience and such a journey, such an important film to make and luckily was received so well as well. So that's my current credit, and obviously my most exciting.

***Author:*** **What is your favorite aspect of post-production?**

*Zeb Achonu:* So I think my favorite has to be the general creative outlet that it gives me with the collaboration and I guess being able to be creative in collaboration. I really, really, really enjoy that. And the crafting of stories … I mostly work in documentary and some drama, but mostly docs and it sounds so obvious to say I just really love storytelling, but it's just so true. I really enjoy hearing someone's story or discovering someone's story and finding a way to craft that to make it really valuable for other people as well. And to find elements of their stories that touch people that you just hadn't really considered. Just the way they come out. I think everybody is so fascinating and it's just really amazing to be part of getting their stories onto screen.

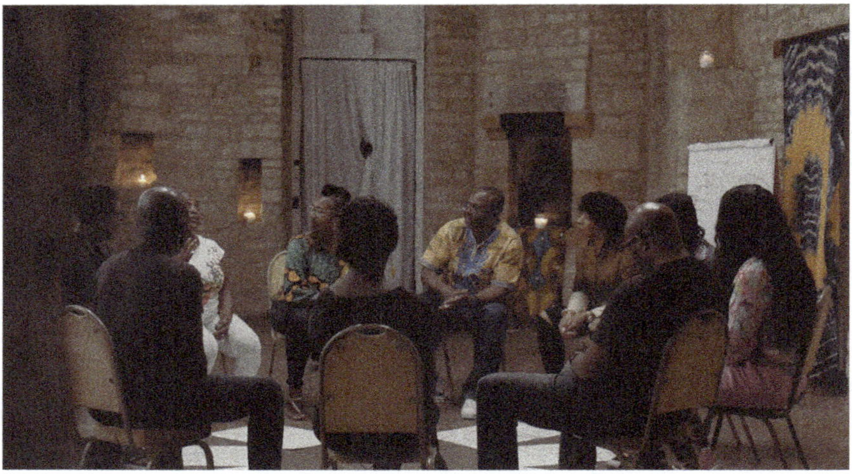

*Figure 14.2* Group session with participants in "White Nanny Black Child." Image credit: Courtesy of Doc Hearts.

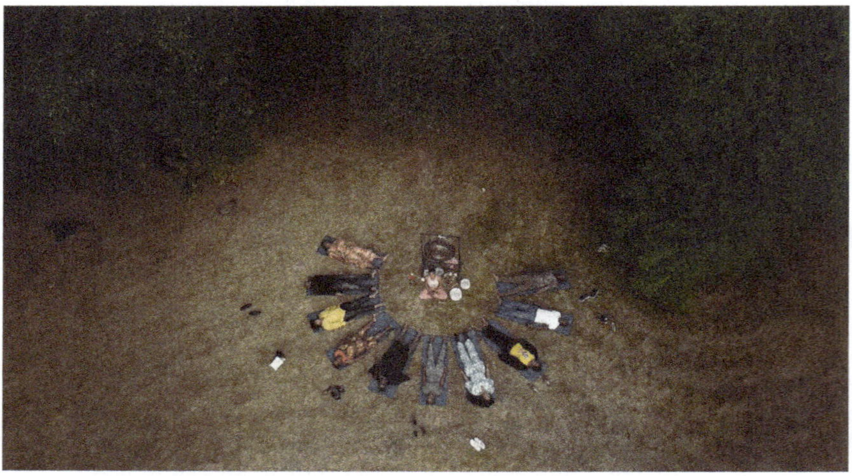

*Figure 14.3* Overhead shot of a sound bath session with participants in "White Nanny Black Child." Image credit: Courtesy of Doc Hearts.

***Author:*** **What's your least favorite aspect of post?**

*Zeb Achonu:* Without a doubt, schedules. Schedules getting shorter and shorter. Tighter schedules, really long days. It's been like that since I started my career, and I only realized that that was something I need to put boundaries around after I had kids.

Something that I think we should all be thinking about, but it took me a good 16 years before I went, actually you don't have to work 18-hour days and get back in again at 7 am the next morning to do the same. Budgets are … I don't know if budgets are getting smaller, but we're being squeezed for more, and so our schedules get tighter, our days get longer, and so it becomes really antisocial and that feeling of burnout is always present and you don't want to do that. You want to be creative, but you want to give, give, give because you love what you're doing and you love crafting. So yeah, definitely just more, I'd say more hours in the day or just less hours of work expected in the day.

***Author:*** **I've seen a few interviews with you talking about your start in film and media, and I wonder if you just tell that story here and if you had a storytelling career before film and media too, if there was something preceding that got you started.**

*Zeb Achonu:* Before I got into film and TV, I had visions of becoming a pop star. That was going to be my life. I grew up watching Madonna and I was going to become her or Brittany or Beyonce or whoever I followed after that. And it didn't happen. I ended up here. I was in bands, I was in choirs, I toured with my own band and I did that. And then I sort of fell into post-production. I had done creative arts at university, I had experience of editing, but I didn't know I had experience of editing. I was just making videos to go with my songs. And so when a job came up at the BBC trainee program, I applied for it not really knowing what post-production meant. I just thought I could work in sound there. And I actually thought the "post" part meant I'd be in a post room and I'd be sorting out letters or parcels or something, but it was in the right direction. And then the more I looked into it, I was like, this sounds really interesting. I can do sound mixing and I can cable up bands and things like that. And then I started the job and after a bit it worked out quite quickly.

And over the years just sort of followed a path toward picture editing, editing videos, and haven't really looked back since. I just discovered that I had a skill for it and I really, really loved it, which was … I mean, I had a lot of people telling me that I didn't have the temperament for it and I wasn't the right sort of person for it because I was too interested in sound and music. I was too interested in having a good time. Going out in daylight. This was in the time when edits were pretty much always in windowless basement rooms. And I enjoyed daylight and dancing and having fun with my friends. And apparently that wasn't an editor's lot, but luckily that seems to have changed over the years. And here I am.

***Author:*** **I see you have a window in your room …**

*Zeb Achonu:* It had to be really dark, and you always have to have perfect viewing conditions. But I don't know anyone who … unless you're at the cinema and you've paid for the experience, it is very rare to have that … perfect viewing room. I watch TV on my phone. The closest I get is watching it on a phone while my children are falling asleep so that I'm in the room watching my stuff while I'm trying to convince them that it's time to go to bed. But that's about the dark as it gets.

***Author:*** **What was your first paid serious job in the business?**

*Zeb Achonu:* I was in the BBC Post-Production Trainee apprenticeship scheme. And it was a full-time job, but it was learning on the job. And so that was great. And then I guess when it got serious, when I started editing seriously, I was still within the BBC because I stayed with them for nine years making children's programs. So I would make a lot of the preschool UK Children's Channel programs and cut the sort of bedtime stories that were read by celebrities every evening at children's bedtimes. And so that was my beginning, and it would be sort of sound and music and rostrums images, putting those together and then moving from there into slightly older children's programs like *Blue Peter* and I can't remember the names of anything, but children's programs about science and things like that where you'd be putting little packages together of journeys that the presenters had taken or experiments that people had done.

Yeah, and I think it was around that time that I took an interview and became a proper or a named editor, and that was it. I was like, "Well, I'm not an assistant anymore. I'm an editor now and this is my job and I think this is me." Yeah. But I mean, again, while that was all, that was my proper serious work, but I don't think even I took it seriously for another … it was about 16 years in when I took it seriously and when actually this is the job that I want to do and this is the job that I love. And that was because I had done, I'd been a participant on a mentoring scheme and suddenly something switched in my brain and I suddenly said, "Wow, this job that I have," which was always second place to being a pop star, suddenly this job had been paying my bills.

And someone said, "Yeah, but what do you want to do? What do you want to work on? You don't just have to do everything that comes." And it was then I took stock of what I enjoyed, what I really liked, the kind of programs I wanted to make and told people, because no one ever tells you if you don't tell people they don't know what you want to do. Suddenly I was telling people where I wanted to work and getting those roles, and that's when it became serious for me. That's when I was like, "Oh, now actually I'm an editor. This is my job and I'm going to carry on." So yeah, that was probably about 16 years into my career.

***Author:*** **So for you going from those early BBC programs into getting that first paid job, what do you feel like was the most helpful?**

*Zeb Achonu:* I think that our industry is without a doubt, whether we like it or not, is run on who [you know] and also who you can get to know. And so the networking side of things is huge and it's always been huge. And I used to say, "Oh, I hate networking, I hate it." Which everybody says, until again, on one of those mentoring schemes, someone pointed out, you are just getting to meet new friends. And if you go in with that mindset, it is a lot easier depending on where it is. It can still be awful walking into a huge room of people you don't know. But when you're just making new friends, the ones that you like, you'll chat to and then you get to work with your friends rather than forcing yourself on someone that you just cannot vibe with. But you're going to have to spend three months in a room with or nine months in a room with. So that's always been quite good. So I find networking has been really, really useful and making sure the industry's so different to when I started.

There's no trainee schemes in that same way. So many of us work remotely, which is it means we lose the opportunity to train people on-site. I can't have someone in shadowing me as often, which is a huge loss because it's so important not just to see what buttons I press but to see how I communicate with my clients, that kind of customer service, all of that comes into it. And so we've lost that. So now I think it's so important to find a community or a network that will tell you about opportunities that who know what it is that you want to do.

There's also the argument that you should cut as much as you can or edit as often as possible and all those things are true. But for me, I think the networking and finding out who's doing what and who you might want to get to know,

I guess talking – as you can tell – I love talking. So just trying to meet people that you are interested in. And obviously since lockdown, we've all been online a lot more. And people I know from the British Film Editors Guild have become a lot more active. Never used to speak. I didn't know any, I knew their names, but I didn't know them until lockdown; the British Film Editors Guild and I were involved in some US Zooms as well. People would come together and have conversations. And so you sort of learn that the editors that you looked up to were human and you could actually send them a message on Twitter or Instagram or whatever, and they would more often than not respond.

So the community became closer. And it does also mean that if I see something I'm really interested in and I check the credits and I think, "Oh, that's such and such an editor, I'll drop 'em a line." And if they're in my area, I might try and meet them for coffee or just tell them what I thought because who doesn't love praise, but just trying to make those connections or just learn who they are and see what other work they've done so I can get some inspiration from the way that they work. And so I think it's all those things. I think it's network, it's reaching out to your peers and it's really studying the art of the people that you admire.

***Author:*** **What's your favorite software? What do you use every day? What do you feel like students should learn?**

*Zeb Achonu:* I'm an Avid girl, always have been and always will be. It was the first software that I learned, I probably used iMovie or things like that, but actually knowing or thinking I knew I also used Final Cut Pro, but only up to version 7. I loved it; I haven't tried X or 10 or whatever it's called. Premiere is my other go-to. I do believe that editing is more than the software obviously. I think it is what's in you and your storytelling, and I think what you get through experience. You do have to learn the software first to get that experience. But I'm happy to flip between Avid and Premiere. I find that in the UK the TV industry is very much Avid still. The documentaries, the feature documentary industry tends to be a mixture of Premiere and Avid. All the work I've done in the States has been on Premiere.

***Author:*** **How is your perspective in this industry unique? How do you believe it's unique?**

*Zeb Achonu:* I think when it comes to telling the stories, I dunno if this is unique, but I think I very much sit on the fence. I'm not sure if I'm supposed to. I like things to be very fair and balanced, and I've always been that way in the same way as I don't strictly want to only do docs. I want to do drama as well. I want to be open to everything. If I'm making a documentary, I'm really keen on it. They're not supposed to be biased one way or another. And I'm very keen to be like we are documenting what we know. Even if I have come to something with some sort of preconceived notion of what the story is going to be, if actually that's not there, my job is to document what is there.

My job is to sit on that fence and say, well, this side thinks this and this thinks [that]. And to give the viewer a chance to make their own decision based on this. Obviously I'm a bit harsher with certain politics and things that are going on in the world, but I think with my work, I like to sit in the middle. I don't want to come in and know what's right and what's wrong. And it's the same way if I'm reviewing someone else's work, I know a lot of people who will come in when they're consulting and be like, this is wrong because X, Y, Z. And I'm like, "Oh, I don't understand why you've done this, but it's your story." So you need to help me understand your story rather than me coming in and too that's wrong because that's not my opinion.

***Author:*** **What are some of your favorite scenes or favorite films that you love for their editing?**

*Zeb Achonu:* Let me think. I really enjoyed "Landscapers," which was a three or four-part TV drama. And because it had a very documentary quality to it … Anything with or about music as well just has my heart every time. And I think that comes from … I believe that music is in all of us all the time. You got, it's always around, it's a soundtrack to our lives, so our memories, it gives us a feeling. So it doesn't have to even be a film about music. If the music is done well, you just go along with it. Of course, everything flies from my brain as soon as I try and pin it down. I grew up loving "Ferris Bueller's Day Off." That's what I normally say. It's my favorite film because then nobody asks me any more questions about it because it seems so obvious.

***Author:*** **I just want to touch on AI a little bit more. I have a love–hate relationship. I love what it does for my transcripts. But it also really scares me. What's your take on GenAI? Do you feel like it's going to take our jobs? How do you use it?**

*Zeb Achonu:* The script sync stuff, I think that's brilliant, thankfully. And I think all of the AI promos and films I've seen are a little bit weird and a little bit soulless, and I'm hoping that we can cling to … the fact that there's something missing. But what scares me about that is that silent films used to scare people, and now we can watch them and be like [shrugs]. Michael Jackson's "Thriller" had me hiding behind my aunt's sofa. My kids wouldn't even flinch now if they saw it. We change, our minds change. And that I think scares me about AI is that when I watch an AI advert or promo, I'm like, that's weird. Their face was wrong. There's no soul. But will my kids feel that or will their kids feel that?

I do think we have to work out how to work with it. The industry will keep changing, and I have to stay really positive about the fact that it will change and we will find ways to change with it. I keep reading, again, Instagram. I keep reading the stuff where people are like, I wish that instead of being in all the creative stuff and leaving me to do the dishes and the cleaning, I wish AI could do the dishes and the cleaning so that I could explore my time being creative. That's what we need to work out, how to use it. Can it do the stuff that no one wants to do? But equally, the stuff that no one wants to do is the stuff that trains you to get to this point. The stuff I spent two years doing … copying from Digi-Betas to VHS. Nobody wants to do that, but I now have in-depth knowledge about how Digi-Betas work. Nobody uses them anymore, but I have in-depth knowledge about this stuff.

***Author:*** **Everybody in this book who's being interviewed is also a parent. But how do you balance that? How can you have a home life? Personal time? And feel safe? Can you talk about maintaining your health and well-being?**

*Zeb Achonu:* Yeah. I mean, I think I mentioned earlier at the beginning, I did all of that stuff and unfortunately it took until I had kids before, I had to go "I can't do this" … I say we shouldn't need to have a reason. You should be allowed [to leave]. I mean, I've talked on training programs where they've told me that they teach the students that you basically have to give up your life to work in this industry, that you won't have a partner. That's how it is. And I'm like, it's rubbish. And then someone told me I'm a unicorn because you don't have people who have kids and do all this. What I can say is it is not easy.

I'm just very stubborn. [After child #1] I did go back to work. We get a lot more time off, although I'm freelance. So I went back after three months for a day and realized I wasn't ready. And I walked off the job and said, I can't do it. And then, because I have a supportive network, I came from the BBC, so there's a lot of people I see around the industry who know me. So I went back, but I was still expressing milk from my breasts every day in toilets and shopping center toilets and hiding with a breast pump. Crazy. So when I had [child #2], I knew that that wasn't the world for me. So I went in and spoke to someone on a reception desk in the building. I went in and said, listen, I need to express milk. Where do I go? And she was like ... it was a woman ... and she said, come, I'll get your pass. Here's a room, with the velvet sofa and a fridge. This is for you whenever you want. I was like, "Oh, it's that easy." And so I started telling other women, "Oh, if when you have a baby, this is available, you just have to ask." And then by the time I had [child #3] I think I'd read [the book] *Lean In*, I was a bit more about "ask for what you want."

I have an awful lot of support. I have an after-school nanny for four days. My partner also works in the industry, so we are a nightmare at planning. We never know where we're going to be. So I mostly work from home so that I can be here when people are around. I make sure that I get out for walks, I take breaks, and I work with teams that understand.

When I was pregnant with [child #2], I did a great flexible freelance contract for a year where I was with another mom. And between us, she did two days, I did three days, then we'd switch the next week. If someone was sick or the kid was sick, we'd cover. And it worked seamlessly for the company. They loved it because there was always someone who knew what was [going on]. That suite never needed filling because we had it covered. But it took a forward-thinking company. I think it happens more and more now. But yeah, it is really hard and you have to be really quite stubborn and determined. But there's an awful lot of people doing it, and there is a lot of support out there.

*Author:* **How are some of the assistant editors that you are working with, how are they balancing the gig economy? How are they navigating that? And how did you navigate it? What advice would you have in that regard?**

*Zeb achonu:* I think it's really difficult. I think a lot of people are balancing it … they're signed up to ten agencies at the same time and trying to do that stuff or trying to get in with post houses. But since post houses are shutting down all over the place, it's not easy. And so it's really hard to say have a backup because not everybody does. I mean, in my mind, this was my backup. I was going to be a pop star and I became this instead. So that was my backup. And my mom always instilled in me, even when I wanted to be a pop star, "Well, you're still going to study physics and this and that because just in case, just in case you need something else."

And so I think it's that. And I do think being involved in knowing the conversations that are going on in the industry, knowing what's happening, just that you can stay ahead of the game where possible, but it is really hard to have any advice except from finding your community and making those networks. Really finding friends in the industry that you can trust to let you know if something's happening … to keep spirits up in this because we need a creative outlet. So making sure you have that creative outlet to try and keep positive about it. But that sounds terrible. It's a really hard time at the moment. And so I think it's just finding out where you fit in the whole scheme of things. There might be something else that you're interested in that you're better suited to, that you'll have a better chance of getting into. But like I said, I thought I was going to work in sound. It turned out, I do pictures and sound now. My partner was a camera op for years and then discovered lighting, and he's a gaffer now. It's that sort of finding out there are things that you'd never heard of. There are roles that you'd never heard of that you might be better suited to.

Be ready to change direction. I mean, some people really like that. They know what they want to do from day one and they go and do it. I really didn't, and everyone told me you can't be a jack of all trades and a master of none. And I was like, "Why not? Why not?" I dunno what I want to do. I've never known what I want to do. I still don't. That's why I don't want to let go of drama. I don't know, in two or three years time, I might say that's it done. I don't want to tell people's stories anymore. I don't want to do only drama. I want to do something else. But I just think it's really important for me as someone who feels quite creative to follow my interests and follow the direction that I want to go in. And the same way I spent years making programs, just because those programs paid me, I enjoyed them and I learned from everything, but I wasn't particularly discerning about the subjects or whatever. Whereas now, I mean, it's different. I'm in a different time and position in my career, but I do now sort of go, "What's it about? What's the deal on the table? Who am I working with?" And I want to put all those things in. What's going to sustain me? Am I going to be interested? I can take less money if it's going to fascinate me for a while, and if it's not and there's nothing else on the table, then give me more money and I'll stick around.

I want to follow my heart and my interests and my gut. It is very important to follow my gut all the time. But yeah, I mean, I think it's important not to just be really flippant with it though. If you want to follow something, head down, work out what it is, get a deep interest in it, learn everything you can. But actually if something else sort of sparkles over there, go and find out about that as well. We've got it all at our fingertips these days.

***Author:*** **Thank you so much!**

# Part 3

# The Industry

# 15 Looking Back to Look Forward

## What Can We Learn from the First Filmmakers?

This chapter addresses the reclaiming and restoration of acclaimed early filmmakers whose contributions to the industry are undeniable and extensive. While both featured filmmakers are directors, they also both edited their films or worked very closely with editors. This chapter will help readers see a broader and more accurate portrayal of "filmmaking" so they can see themselves as part of this industry.

### *15A Alice Guy-Blaché, Director, Writer*

Alice Guy-Blaché (1873–1968) is considered to be the world's first narrative filmmaker. Not the first woman filmmaker, but the first filmmaker who applied fictional techniques to moving images. Her story is extensive and, now, becoming well-documented. Here are a few highlights. Guy-Blaché worked as a secretary at the Gaumont Film Company in Paris at a time when camera technology was first being developed. Learning the craft while working on Gaumont's productions, she started to understand directing, story, screenwriting, location, acting, and the business of filmmaking. She was given the opportunity to direct and in 1896 she made "La Fée aux Choux" (The Cabbage Fairy). This one-minute film depicts a fairy finding babies under cabbage leaves. It is available to stream online through a quick internet search.

Guy-Blaché became a leader in the French film industry and developed a robust body of work. She also learned to apply various techniques and special effects. Post-production in the very early days of film was a very short phase, and these were silent films, which limited post-production primarily to editing, montage, color, and titling.

Guy-Blaché's films were popular. She writes in her memoir how the success of *La Fée aux Choux* allowed her a budget, equipment, and the opportunity to try again. She was instrumental in carving out what the emerging film industry could be, and what films could do. She herself was involved in developing special effects techniques, colorizing films for a greater sense of

DOI: 10.4324/9781003473152-18

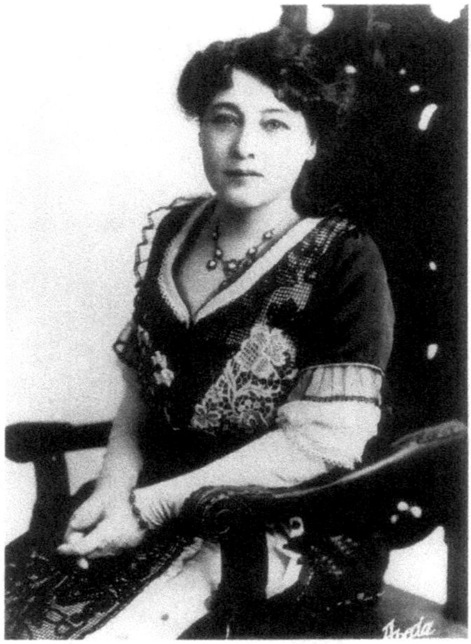

*Figure 15.1* Alice Guy-Blaché portrait. Image credit: Public domain.

story, and credited with filming the first sync-sound film, using the chronograph, or a disk-based audio recording system patented by French inventor Léon Gaumont in 1902.

**Special effects**: Specific to post-production, because the actual post process was so limited, the early filmmakers developed many in-camera special effect techniques. In her memoir, Guy-Blaché talks about the effects that she learned while working at Gaumont:

> "It was there, thanks to the goodwill of my little acting troop and the advice and lessons of Frédéric Dillaye (technical adviser to the Gaumont establishment and author of excellent books on art photography), to the experiences gained day by day that we discovered many little tricks such as:
>
> - **Films turned in reverse**, permitting one to take a house falling down and then reconstructed as if by magic, a person falling from a roof and jumping up spontaneously, a greedy client at the bakery finding his bill too high giving back intact the swallowed cakes.
> - **Films slowed down or accelerated by a turn of the handle**, transforming peaceful passersby into creatures seized by frenzy or, on the contrary, sleepwalking.

- **Stops** permitting one to displace an object which in projection would seem to be animated by a supernatural life stupefying an archaeologist when his precious mummy plays in the laboratory (Example: La Momie)
- **Double exposures**.
- **Fade outs**, used for visions and dreams."

**Colorizing films**: Guy-Blaché also writes about how films in the early days were colorized, primarily by women who worked in post-production.

> "Many of our films were colored. Two workers, installed at tables for them like those that serve today for montage, jewelers' glass at the eye, would comb with fine brushes and transparent colors the images in which the actors were lilliputian. Imagine the care and patience necessary for this work when one considers the enlargement these images sustained upon projection. This early procedure was followed by that of cutting three ribbons to serve as stencils for mechanical coloration. This decoupage was made with the aid of a cutting pen, "le stedik," and required the same care, and same dexterity as that earlier process."

**Sync-sound film in 1900:**

Guy-Blaché's synchronized Café–Concerts were innovations that predated the film most often credited as the first sync-sound film, "The Jazz Singer," by 20 years.

> "In his memoirs Léon Gaumont says that after obtaining the first film he was obsessed by the desire to give the images sound color and depth. this was the chronograph, first talking picture, a French invention … It was not the talking picture as you know it. The voice of the artist (singer, speaker), the music for the dance were recorded in the studio. The actors then rehearsed their roles until they obtained a perfect synchronization with the phonographic recording. Then the cinematographic record was taken. The two instruments (photo and phono) were united by an electric contrivance which assured their synchronization.
>
> I was charged with the cinematographic part of the repertoire and thus filmed the Mante sisters, very fashionable popular dancers at the time; Rose Caron of the Opéra, with her singing class."

There is far, more to say about Alice Guy-Blaché and her prolific work, including that she opened one of the first film studios in the New York City area, Solax Studios, in 1910 in Flushing, Queens. Their first year was a commercial success, and in 1912 she bought a studio building for Solax in Fort Lee, New Jersey, and moved the operations there. Guy-Blaché owned and ran

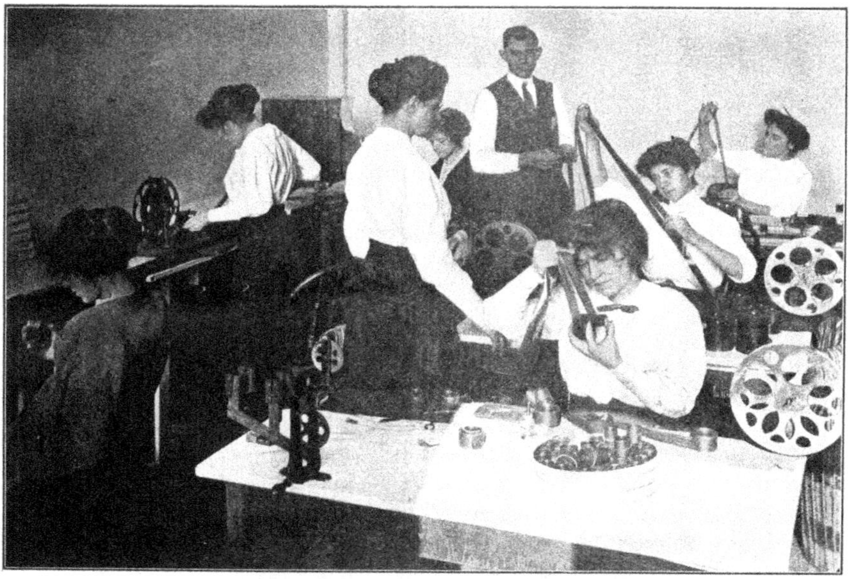

A Corner of the Assembling and Joining Room at the Philadelphia Studio of the Lubin Company.

*Figure 15.2* Women editing film at the Philadelphia studio of the Lubin Company, called "assembling and joining." 1914. Image credit: Public domain.

Solax with her husband, Herbert. They were among the most prominent film companies in the world at the time, and Guy-Blaché, as creative director, made films that pushed social norms, including a 1906 film, "The Consequences of Feminism," in which male and female characters exchanged roles, portraying women drinking and reading newspapers in cafés while men iron, sew, and tend children. A few years later, Guy-Blaché made "A Fool And His Money" (1912), which featured an African-American cast, among the first films to do so. She also spread the storytelling techniques she developed in France, which had resulted in making her work popular with American filmmakers. In her memoir, Guy-Blaché shares that when her production company started working in the US, the camera operators did not know how to do the kinds of special techniques she created, so she had to teach them.

Guy-Blaché had a prolific and multifaceted career, directing, producing, or supervising over 1,000 films before she left Hollywood to return to France. She lectured at Columbia University and developed relationships with film historians to ensure her work was preserved. Her work and films are finally starting to be included in retrospectives and at silent film events. Biographies about her are starting to become more widespread. Her legacy is starting to gain much-deserved attention. But much more is needed to pass along the wisdom and creativity of one of the founders of the film industry to emerging filmmakers today.

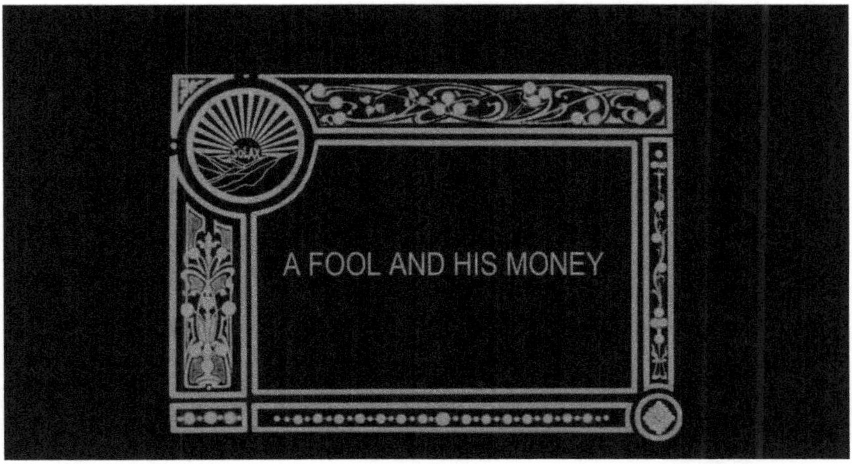


*Figure 15.3* The title graphic from "A Fool and His Money," 1912. Image credit: Public domain.

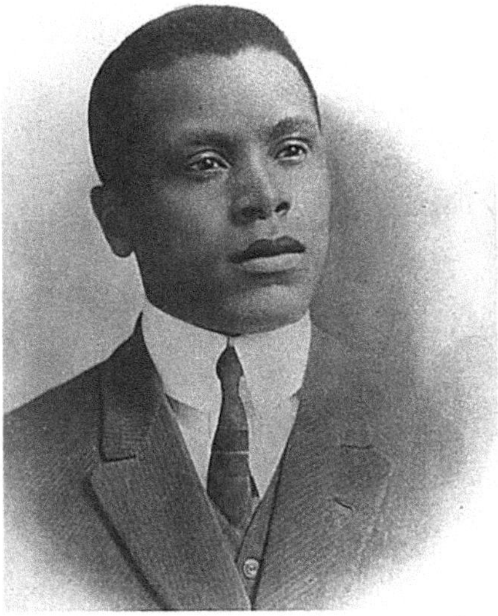

*Figure 15.4* Portait, Oscar Micheaux. Image credit: Public domain.

For more on the work and life of Alice Guy-Blaché, the Women Film Pioneers Project (www.wfpp.columbia.edu) is an excellent starting point to continue learning. There are also many books and documentaries about her work, including a memoir by Anthony Slide and written with Guy-Blaché's daughter, Simone Blaché, and daughter-in-law, Roberta Blaché, based on an autobiography that Guy-Blaché wrote herself when she realized she was being excluded from historical records of the film industry. The citations and additional resources have more information on these books, and they are easily available online.

### *15B Oscar Micheaux*

Oscar Micheaux (1884–1951), born in Metropolis, Illinois, was a filmmaker, author, businessman, farmer, and producer. Over the course of his career, he made 40-plus films, an astonishing amount as these productions were self-funded. He also wrote and self-published several novels. As one of the first Black filmmakers in the United States, Micheaux broke boundaries to make his films, which had all-Black casts and were made for Black audiences. One of the methods he used to pay for his films was to work with Black theaters and theaters in Black neighbourhoods, to secure advances to then make his films. Micheaux worked with people who have become film legends: one of his actors was Paul Robeson in his first role. One of his camera people was Haskell Wexler, who later won an Academy Award for Cinematography and was well-known for supporting socially conscious films.

Micheaux's body of films shows a engaged filmmaker who did not shy away from complex stories and layered topics, including racism and segregation. His films often looked at the struggles of farmers and educated Black people. Accounts of his work also note that he recreated story tropes that were popular from studio films for white audiences, including romances and crime stories, which Micheaux customized for Black audiences.

Micheaux's most noted film is the 1920 "Within Our Gates," considered to be a response to the racist storyline and characterizations in "The Birth of a Nation" (1919, D.W. Griffith). Micheaux used a story construction to refute the bald racism of "The Birth of a Nation," which uses the rape of a white woman by a Black man as a central story plot. In response, in "Within Our Gates" Micheaux portrayed the reverse: a Black woman is the target of an attempted rape by a white man. Micheaux has been quoted as saying that truth was his inspiration for this story reversal, and shows how he used his storytelling and business skills to create a counterpoint and alternative cultural narrative to "The Birth of a Nation."

In terms of post-production, which was a very expensive part of the filmmaking process in the early 1900s, Micheaux faced a unique challenge: censorship. As an author, his novels were considered very successful, however he self-published them, which meant he avoided a crucial step for his books: getting them through gatekeepers. But he could not avoid gatekeepers in filmmaking. In *Oscar Micheaux: The Great and Only: The Life of America's First Black Filmmaker*, his challenges with censors were both unique and expected:

> "Last but not least was the matter of censorship, Micheaux knew little about this side of the film business. As a self-published novelist, he had never confronted even a publisher's professional judgment, never mind the biases and whims of a white censor. He couldn't have guessed how much censorship would color his career. Several states and many individual cities had all-white censorship boards that officially licensed film showings, [a business associate] warned Micheaux. That added to costs. Fees had to be paid, sometimes palms had to be greased; it was all par for the course if the film was ultimately approved. But race pictures (this was the term used at the time for films made for Black audiences) rarely passed without some problems everywhere in America, but especially in the Deep South, race pictures were scrutinized for every conceivable violation, any inference that defied the prevailing social order. In some parts of the south, anything Black people did on screen would be greeted as an affront by local White authorities."

Finding ways to navigate through these censors, Micheaux got his films screened. One example is his 1922 film, "The Dungeon," which met with strict censorship when he sent it to New York State. The censor board denied approval for the exhibition, based on perceived issues with the storyline. In 1924, he radically re-edited his film "Body and Soul" in order for it to pass the censors. Norman Studios, which today is a Florida-based online musuem, but was one of the nation's first studios producing "race films" has an online exhibit about Micheaux's work. It states:

> [P]roblems with censors, as recent scholarship has revealed, continued throughout his career. The Dungeon (1922), for instance, was disapproved for exhibition in New York State "on the basis that it was inhuman, immoral, and would tend to incite crime"; in particular, the censors seemed disturbed by the portrayals of a woman being exploited by a man and enticed by a drug fiend. (Those same censors, however, failed to remark on the film's important subplot involving political hypocrisy, in which a corrupt Black politician works against the interest of his people in order to be elected to Congress.) *Body and Soul required rather radical editing before it received approval in New York: Micheaux ultimately reduced the film from nine reels to five, added new title cards, and altered the theme by deflecting some of the villainy of the minister to other characters.*
>
> (Emphasis added)

Contemporary filmmakers, imagine this: the last step of your film, before being aired by Netflix, broadcasting, or screening at a film festival, is that you must run your work by a censor board. They have the power to change your story and cut the film to half the length. You pay the additional costs to complete these edits (if they can be called that). You might also have to pay fees and bribes.

The talent and drive that Micheaux brought to his work were enormous. To make self-funded feature films in the era he did, then to have to re-edit the films based on individual state censors, required enormous resilience and an exemplary desire to contribute to culture and his community. It also shows how the already complex process of film post-production was made even more complicated and full of obstacles for Micheaux. His understanding of story, shaping a film in a way to get it to audiences, and business skills resulted in a well-deserved national reputation and a sizable body of work.

Micheaux's films are being recovered and can be found through internet searches, in university archives, and in a growing number of festivals and events. His contributions were so significant that, in 1986, partially due to pressure from contemporary filmmakers, the Directors Guild of America posthumously presented Micheaux with the DGA's Golden Jubilee Special Award, along with Fellini and Kurosawa. He was also given a star on the Hollywood Walk of Fame. Norman Studios is an excellent starting point for anyone who wants to learn more about Micheaux's work (www.normanstudios.org).

# 16 Emerging Issues in the Edit Room

## Film is an Ever-Evolving Field – How Do You Think It Should Evolve?

In previous chapters, interviews with many contemporary editors show how they work in their respective film, media, or television production. Because the world of filmmaking is constantly evolving, one goal for this text is to include this professional diversity, covering fiction films, documentary, interactive, broadcast, and international productions, so that readers can combine their technical learning with the creative application of that learning. Another goal is to address the damaging narratives of exclusion that do not recognize the many women and people of color working in film today, nor in previous eras, and to help readers find ways to see how people of all identities have not only participated in film- and media-making but been some of its most important innovators.

Most of the previous chapters were a look *around*, at many editors and post-production professionals and at the practices and protocols of the craft that emerging filmmakers need to learn. The last one, Chapter 15, was a look *back*, at how early filmmakers contributed to post-production in unique ways.

This chapter is set up for you, the reader, to look *forward*, to see what contemporary post-production careers look like, and to understand some of the pathways you might take in your work and career. By design, it is brief and asks you to continue building on what others have started: ways to align together, support ongoing progress, and find pathways for sustainable and collaborative careers.

If you are still in school, this chapter hopefully will provide you with some insights that you can learn from, and some pointers to the kinds of experiences you should try to have while you still have the freedom of being a student. If you are out of school, and already in the professional world, hopefully the following chapters will help you focus on specific next steps you can take to advance to where you want to go, and to figure out where that is, if you are unsure.

DOI: 10.4324/9781003473152-19

## Why Are Equity and Diversity Initiatives an Issue for Editors and Others in Post-production?

While most post-production students will dive fully into the technology of editing, it is important to consider what is involved beyond the technology of computers and software. Consider that filmmaking is a series of many decisions, with post-production being the final stage in which many prior decisions can be changed, but the decisions made in post-production cannot be changed or undone (at least not without re-editing the entire film). Post-production is also where deadlines loom for every stage, and incredible pressure might be placed on an editor or editing team, particularly in television production, which is driven by fast turnaround and a need to feed a content pipeline.

It can be overwhelming to make the dozens of decisions needed for a high-quality film or television show. Often there are competing opinions of what works best. In a pressure-filled, deadline-driven, demanding workflow, editors and editing teams are often challenged to maintain respect for the story, the characters, and also their own health and well-being. In such an environment, it can be difficult to see the way to new and creative approaches to storytelling. It can also be difficult for people to begin their careers and create a strong professional reel. It is an even greater challenge to create equitable work practices and foster an environment welcoming to diverse creative professionals, when your mandate and job is to meet tight deadlines and protect the integrity of the director's vision. One way to address these competing needs is to look at how to balance them and weave them into the entire process, to include professional practices that protect the editor's health, support new voices in the editing room, and model practices for sustainable careers in editing.

In this chapter, we will explore some of the ways in which film and television industries are beginning to evolve and address issues of diversity, equity, and inclusion in the editing room. This chapter intentionally looks more broadly than the technical aspects of post-production, as diversity in one part of the film team often affects what happens in another area. This means that a director or producer who has been supported by a network understands how inclusive and supportive practices in the editing room benefit everyone, or even benefited from a program to welcome diverse voices, is more likely to include them in their own productions. It also explores resources and methods focused on fostering diversity in the editing room as well as throughout filmmaking.

## Equity Finally Gets a Spotlight

The film and television industries have long faced increasing pressure to address longstanding issues of equity and inclusion. At the same time, growing awareness among many women and people of color working in film and television about their desired opportunities has led to multiple, varied initiatives to address equity, promote inclusive practices, and create more opportunities for sustainable careers. These initiatives have been led by artists, by industry organizations ranging from traditional unions to new professional affiliation groups, and by universities, studios, and streaming services. Collectively, while many of these are still in the early stages, they are already producing results that merit ongoing resources and attention.

### *A Brief Backstory*

These initiatives must address historical practices and deeply embedded roots of exclusion. For decades, mainstream film and television industries paid little attention to diversity on screen or behind the camera. The vast majority of television characters were predominantly white, which contributed to limited perspectives and limited stories being told in popular media. Film studios were no better, and film industry leaders often expressed a belief that white characters spoke to universal stories, while actors that were Latino, Black, Asian, Native/Indigenous, and/or LGBTQI would only appeal to those respective audiences. They referred to audiences outside of a white suburban norm as "niche" audiences or sometimes as "ethnic" or "urban" audiences. Many of the types of stories labeled "niche" include sizable demographics that cross lines of race, ethnicity, and economics, such as single moms, divorced families, immigrants, varied religions, and dozens of other demographics. Today, film and television industries are finally producing stories about multiple so-called niche communities – and enjoying popular and commercial success because of it.

This welcome evolution in diversity and representation on film and television screens has an impact on the editing room. Historically, editors, who are responsible for creating meaning by the way they assemble footage, were also predominantly white and male. This resulted in only bringing certain perspectives and experience to inform the countless decisions that create meaning in editing. Under-representation in the editing room perpetuated systemic inequalities and reinforced harmful stereotypes on screen by the simple fact that editors from one particular demographic do not always have the personal or cultural background to tell stories authentically and might make choices that perpetuate incorrect narratives about a particular group of people.

Under-representation in editing rooms also influences which shots make it on screen and which ones are left on the cutting room floor. Editors can weigh scenes toward certain characters through the kinds of reaction shots they would cut to (as discussed in previous chapters). They can create characters with depth and backstory through simple editing choices like lingering longer on a reaction shot or choosing a certain type of framing. A few simple choices in the timeline can present the same character or story as a caricature, a stereotype, or a fully understood person.

**Initiatives for Evolution and Progress**

Changing today's editing rooms builds on long-fought initiatives to create more diverse on-screen representation going back to the 1970s and earlier. Multiple groups, including Black, Latinx, Asian, Native/Indigenous, immigrants, women, and members of the LGBTQ+ community, conducted campaigns, wrote articles, and made their voices heard in expressing the need for change. After many years of building coalitions of support, these efforts successfully influenced directors, producers, showrunners, and writers to create more diverse on-screen characterizations. Often, this was accomplished by filmmakers from these communities writing and producing their own stories, at least to the extent possible given the economics of producing films and television shows.

Editing played a key role in these efforts because it is a time-consuming and expensive phase and also because it is the final phase. With the particularly important role editors play in creating and ensuring authentic characterizations, ensuring that there is diversity in the editing room is one of the most effective, pragmatic, and immediate ways to ensure relevant diversity in the stories shown in mainstream films and television shows, as well as in other types of media from advertising to music videos to YouTube channels. Directors who wished to have a certain specific look or feel to their films – to take control of the narrative – did their own editing, often using a pseudonym. Steven Soderbergh has edited over a dozen films and TV shows under the name Mary Ann Bernard (his mother's name). The Coen Brothers edit their films under the name Roderick Jaynes, sometimes in collaboration with Tricia Cooke, Ethan Coen's wife. Many A-list directors have edited some or all of their films, including David Lynch, Alfonso Cuarón, Akira Kurosawa, Gus Van Sant, Robert Rodriguez, Steve James, and Frederick Wiseman. This is relevant for authentic representation as the film industry has always had leaders who know what they want, and know they are the best person to cut together a film's story, but this dual role is, for some reason, considered something that needed to be a secret. As more directors share that they do their own editing, and some editors navigate the pathway to becoming a director (like Carla Gutiérrez and Allie Sultan), and end-to-end filmmakers (like Aashish Kumar), this normalizes the sharing of two of the most important roles in story creation. It also normalizes that directors who have a certain specific vision, including a particular type of representation, not only can, but should, stay very involved with their film's editing process.

For this reason, contemporary initiatives for diversity in the film and television industry include creating pathways for people to find careers as directors, editors, and in other filmmaking roles. The initiatives are also increasingly included in their content practices for their participants to maintain sustainable careers. For a creative industry to truly reflect its audience, its artists and professionals need to share a sense of commonality with that audience. Editors who have deep cultural competency and understand how to portray cultural values on the screen will inherently create different types of stories. They are also less likely to rely on harmful stereotypes and biases in the final creative products and to more accurately and deeply represent the experiences of diverse communities.

## Measuring Change

Measuring progress in diversity initiatives is a challenge for any industry, and in filmmaking, there are a handful of ways to evaluate change. These metrics might include the number of films featuring diverse casts and storylines, the range of those films' budgets, and the diversity of above-the-line crew such as showrunners, directors, and producers. Metrics can also look at the diversity of the entire below-the-line creative crew, even down to creating apprentice roles for robust on-the-job training. In post-production, diversity can be measured in the decision-making roles such as lead editors and commissioning editors, as well as in specialized fields like sound designers, colorists, animators, composers, and even the subtitlers and captioners. Awards within the industry are other measures of change, as are mentorship programs. Any industry that is trying to improve its inclusivity also needs to look at entry points, including university-based ones as well as broader points of entry from community colleges, certificate programs, and entry-level jobs that lead to professional training. Historically, the entry point for filmmaking was apprenticeship programs, and there are strong arguments that all studios, streamers, production companies, and broadcasters can bring these back or amplify existing programs.

There is still a long way to go before the film industry can truly claim to be equitable and inclusive, and as educators, filmmakers, and students we might consider how these important career paths for those entering the field can and should continue to evolve. By the time you read this book, hopefully, there will be even more progress through the programs outlined below – and new ones – for people entering the industry.

## Defining the Problems

As the industry evolves to become more reflective of a diverse world, it started efforts to define the problems and created many important initiatives. Highlights from two recent industry surveys about diversity in filmmaking and in post-production, listed below, serve as important benchmarks. There are many other surveys and groups starting to set baselines for measure progress on some of the most deeply entrenched issues in film and media industries. It will be interesting to see the progress from these baseline surveys, in, say, a decade from now. But it will be more interesting to see how the industry can start developing paths to success for upcoming generations starting right now.

### *2021 Editors Guild Demographics and Workplace Survey Report*

A 2021 report from the Editors Guild showed that an astoundingly high number of editors – 76 percent – believe discrimination is often or sometimes present in the workplace. The survey also detailed race and gender demographics – 68.5 percent of the Editors Guild members were white, and 67.7 percent were male. Guild members are the highest-paid portion of the post-production industry, and this benchmark shows significant room for improvement. (Find out more at www.cinemontage.org/mpeg-diversity.)

### *2022 Hollywood Diversity Report*

A UCLA study on diversity in Hollywood entertainment industries, backed by Netflix, Hulu, Disney, the Hollywood Foreign Press Association, and the Latino Film Institute presents annual detailed statistics charting diversity in scripted television. The 2022 report shows improvement for people of color and women in key creative roles like writer and director, from previous years. This indicates that, while under-representation continues to be an ongoing problem, consistent efforts do pay off. For example, in 2020–2021, there was an uptick in creators of color for scripted television shows, as well as improved representation in diverse casting, although many of these shows did not have budgets that compared to those of white male counterparts. (Find out more at www.socialsciences.ucla.edu/hollywood-diversity-report-2022.)

## Strategies and Initiatives for Diverse and Inclusive Creative Workplaces

Many strategies and initiatives are being employed in film and television to create a more inclusive and equitable film and television industry. While there is still much to be done, the progress that has been made is encouraging and points toward a future where diversity and inclusion are valued, celebrated, and supported throughout media industries.

Studies like those mentioned above are just one method and serve as important benchmarks for future progress. After movements like #MeToo and #OscarsSoWhite brought the need for these initiatives into a very public and intense light, knowing measurements like the metrics indicated above is a welcome concrete starting point. For an industry that refused to acknowledge the need for diversity measures to finally start participating in regular annual surveys is meaningful progress, even if what those surveys reveal is the need for much more progress. Participating in studies leads to more tangible programs, like mentorship and targeted outreach efforts, which leads to an increasing diversity of show creators and producers. Showrunners who value these programs are more likely to open doors to hire editors, cinematographers, and other crew from diverse professional and personal networks.

One significant barrier to diversity efforts, which is unique to film, television, and media production, is that many jobs are freelance or done on time-limited contracts for the duration of a show or production. In larger industries with full-time regular employment, like broadcast television, it is possible to institute hiring policies managed by human resource departments, and to begin outreach and recruitment campaigns. In film and most types of television and streaming content, the show is contracted out to a production company, which then hires freelance professionals or uses their own regular team, who might be staff or might work on a project-by-project basis. In this type of decentralized, freelance economy, it is a challenge to create overarching hiring policies. But it is not impossible.

One powerful solution is that A-list stars have started executive producing their films and television shows, and requiring they get the final cut. Many also include "*equity riders*" in their contracts, which are agreements about the equity practices of the production. By doing so, the most visible leaders in film – the A-list actors – can ensure a means to open doors for a diverse cast and crew. If they are an executive producer, they also can ensure their creative vision is realized. Another solution is a new professional role of a "*Diversity Coordinator*," who takes on the task of working with directors and producers to create more inclusive sets. Similarly, some studio heads are hiring diversity consultants to work with their leadership and human resource departments. Just two national organizations working in this capacity are Color of Change, which has a Hollywood program, and Harness, founded by a trio including actress America Ferrera, which works for greater Latinx inclusion.

## Health, Happiness, and Productivity – Maintain a Balance When Under a Deadline

The COVID-19 pandemic affected film and television in countless profound ways. Particularly as the world looked to streaming services and television as a way to escape, the "pipeline," or the massive stream of continually scheduled content populating streaming services, broadcast channels, and social media, was made significantly harder to produce as people stopped traveling. With production sets enforcing extremely strict health requirements, it simply became harder to find people who were healthy and could work. Even as vaccinations started to become more common, the residual impact of the COVID-19 restrictions refocused the industry on the need to protect the personal health of film and television workers in multiple ways.

Another health-related issue is the growing awareness of the need for measures to support positive mental health and well-being in the workplace. For film and television editors, this means creating schedules and practices that make sense. These professionals work long hours with tight deadlines, leading to stress, burnout, and other negative effects on their health and productivity. In response, there have been a number of initiatives and resources aimed at supporting television editors and helping them maintain their health, happiness, and productivity when under a deadline. Please take a look at the full interviews with the four editors, each of whom addresses how they maintain physical and mental health, from the amount of screen time and sitting in cramped chairs to edit, to the intense pressures of deadlines, and the toll that it takes to watch all the raw footage for films that have violence, human rights abuses, and other material that is necessary to make documentaries revealing major social and cultural issues.

The industry is starting to see tangible signs of support for the health of creative professionals. The first step is speaking up, and in 2021 the US Editors Guild of the International Alliance of Theatrical Stage Employees (IATSE) voted against ratifying a new contract because they wanted better working conditions. As the union that is the bargaining entity for major studios, including Netflix, Amazon, Walt Disney Studios, Apple, and Warner Bros, a strike by IATSE members would have stopped production on hundreds of film and television shows. The sticking points were schedules, turnaround times for shows, required time-off periods, and wages – all perennial labor issues that were heightened in this case due to this negotiation happening during the most chaotic days of the pandemic's lockdown. After months of negotiation, a strike was averted, and the IATSE leadership celebrated a contract that mandated adequate rest and stiff financial penalties for violations of the new agreement. While these are still difficult to enforce, having a union contract that codifies safety and reasonable working hours is a strong backdrop. More importantly, it starts a conversation and sets a precedent for the next round of contract negotiations (which take place every three years).

In addition, a growing focus by employers on promoting work-life balance and flexible working arrangements has reached some film and television post-production offices. Many production companies and studios offer telecommuting options, flexible hours, and other benefits designed to help editors manage their workload and reduce stress. These initiatives have been welcomed by many editors, who appreciate the increased flexibility and support for their mental and physical health. Other tangible initiatives include previously unheard offerings like the "EditFest Wellness Room," a designated space at the national EditFest conference which offered attendees a place to take a break from the hustle and bustle of the event and engage in yoga, meditation, mindfulness exercises, massage therapy, and other wellness treatments. While this won't impact every editor's daily work, initiatives like having a "Wellness Room" start to introduce these ideas to people engaged in the industry, as many editors operate under a work ethic that emphasizes productivity, or hyper-productivity, and not balance and sustainability.

The importance of mental health and well-being in the workplace has led to an awareness about health, and even some strong, concrete initiatives like those negotiated by the IATSE contract. An important evolution for the film and television industries is to continue to promote the health and well-being of post-production professionals who work in dark rooms alone for long hours. As new filmmakers enter their careers, maintaining personal standards of health while also balancing a strong work ethic will be a key factor in creating a more sustainable and supportive editing profession.

## Networks and Connections

There is an unprecedented number of organizations, entry-level programs for studios and broadcasters, and job sites for hiring diverse creative professionals. These are constantly growing and often created by just a handful of motivated individuals with crowd-sourced content. As many of the filmmakers noted in their interviews, developing a professional network was crucial in their emerging years, and continues to be one of the most important ways to have a sustainable career. The author is based in New York City, and many of these are US-based groups, however there are similar groups around the world. Search through LinkedIn, Facebook, other social media, and industry press and announcements to connect with groups wherever you live. Or, start your own networking group. Many film schools are developing ties with industry initiatives to create paths to careers. The groups listed below are a small handful, and readers can research their specific industry or local area for relevant opportunities and community networks.

Sites for job listings, professional organizations, and networking:

- Across The Cut.
- Asian American Documentary Network.
- BIPOC Doc Editors.
- Black In Post.
- Black Women Animate.
- Brown Girls Doc Mafia.
- Film Fatales.
- Free The Work.
- Meetup.com – this website for forming groups has many place-based filmmaking meetups.
- Many different women in film groups, based by region and city.

Studio-based employment programs:

- CBS Directing Initiative.
- Disney General Entertainment Content Directing Program.
- HBO Access Programs.
- NBCU New Mexico Directors Initiative.
- NBCU TV Female Forward.
- NBCU TV Directors Program.
- Paramount ViewFinder Emerging Directors Program.
- Sony Pictures Television Diverse Directors Program.

## Part 4

# Appendixes

Activities, Charts, and Supplemental Materials

# Appendix 1

## Story Forms

What is your film's destination? This list attempts to detail the most common forms along with different types of content within those forms. No doubt there are a few forms that are not listed, or maybe even new forms that have emerged since the publication of this book.

Take a close look at all these various forms – when you read the types, do they ring a bell? Do you start to see the many small pieces that make up a media environment? Something like "sports programming," which is one of the largest media sectors, has multiple forms within it. Television does as well, as does social media.

Notice also that standard lengths for all forms are not included. The ones listed might even not be as precise as they were in traditional media. Duration by media form used to be extremely rigid, however, that is one of the many things that has changed, even within the most traditional types of media. Fiction films used to be 90 to 120 minutes, and now 250 minutes or more is quite common. Some media has stayed precisely the same for others, such as mainstream broadcast programs at 52 or 56 minutes for a non-fiction hour and 44 minutes for a scripted hour. Other categories, specifically social media, vary widely in terms of duration, and there are no explicit standards but simply people trying new things and seeing how long an audience's attention will hold.

*Table A.1* Media Forms

| *Form* | *Type of content* | *Typical Runtimes (if empty, it is because there is no typical timeframe)* |
|---|---|---|
| **Television** | Feature scripted | 44 mins |
| | Episodic, scripted, hour and half-hour | 44 or 22 mins |
| | Episodic non-fiction series, news/talk | 22, 44, 52, or 56 mins |
| | Episodic non-fiction, late night | 40 mins |
| | Feature documentary | 52 or 56 mins |
| | Segment, news or documentary | 3 to 7 mins |
| | Sports programming, live events and commentary | |

(*Continued*)

*Table A.1* (Continued)

| | | |
|---|---|---|
| | Sports programming, specials not related to live sports, like background documentaries | |
| | Sports programming, specials for live sports, like short segments on athlete's backgrounds for major sporting events | |
| | Sports programming, multiple segments in varying lengths, for example analysis, predictions, play-by-play, and historical segments | |
| | Sports podcasts | |
| | Advertising | 30 or 60 seconds |
| **Theatrical** | Feature films | 75 to 200+ mins |
| | Trailers | 1–2 mins |
| | Advertisements | 30 seconds |
| | Documentary | 75 to 120 minutes |
| **Streaming** | Features (one-offs) | Ranges from 60 mins to 180 mins |
| | Episodic, limited | Generally 45 mins per episode, 4–8 episodes |
| | Episodic, series | |
| | Interactive/choose your own ending | |
| **Social media** | YouTube channels | |
| | YouTube versions of television shows listed above | |
| | YouTube live stream | |
| | Instagram content | |
| | Instagram stories | |
| | Instagram live | |
| | TikTok | |
| | Facebook content | |
| | Facebook, live stream | |
| | X content | |
| | Other social media | |
| **Festivals** | Feature films | |
| | Short films | |
| | Installation, VR, and new forms of film and media | |
| **Museums** | Installations | |
| | Specials, like background stories | |
| | Kiosk content | |
| **Radio** | Podcasts, commentary and news | |
| | Live or daily series | |
| | Podcasts, drama and fiction | |
| | Broadcast radio | |
| **Other content** | Music videos | |
| | Advertising | |
| | Virtual Reality | |
| **Online media** | Interactive websites (not social media) | |

# Appendix 2

## Ocean University Sample "Introductory Briefing"

This is a sample of the kind of varied, factual and emotional information you might receive as an editor. It includes facts, ambitions, characters, goals, emotional entanglements, visual footage, and other types of information you might receive. This is styled like a documentary, but as you read through it you will see how it could also be a fiction film, web series, reality show, or another type of media form. For the exercises below, you are free to choose any genre you like.

For the purposes of this book I will use the story as an example and there are several class activities that refer back to this. The idea is to get used to cutting to story form and "killing your darlings" – aka the film and media industry's term for letting go of what you want or like in the raw material in order to create the best story possible.

**Meet the Swim Team at Ocean University**

1. Ocean University is a small university with an enthusiastic swim team. They just won a national championship.
2. There are 25 students who went to nationals from the men's and women's swim teams.
3. SAM won the national diving competition, the first ever time the university won a diving medal.
4. ALI came in second in the 100-meter butterfly, also a first medal.
5. The rest of the team performed well, and just by placing at nationals they all made their personal best times in the pool. Plus they had an excellent bonding experience.
6. The swimming pool where the team practices is a gorgeous, Olympic-sized pool on the grounds of Ocean University, and so beautiful and well-appointed it is often rented out for professional competitions.
7. Ali is the youngest member of the team, and attending college on an athletic scholarship.

8 Sam is the oldest member of the team, and will graduate this year, and does not know what she wants to do.
9 There are five couples on the team, and most of the team knows they are dating but the coaches do not know.
10 The competitions that rent out Ocean University's pool can provide students with internship and apprentice programs, as a way to get training in being a professional swim coach after college.
11 COACH AMY has been with the team for 40 years, and this is the first time she has gone to nationals. She means well but after 40 years of coaching, she really does not have a lot of new ideas. Her team grumbles that all she does is yell at them to "swim as hard as possible" and then spends most of practice on her phone looking at social media.
12 ASSISTANT COACH HAROLD has only two years on the team. He has a wife, a new baby, a new mortgage, and makes about half of what Coach Amy makes.
13 When Assistant Coach Harold joined the team he started new training programs, videotaping the athletes and helping them learn by watching and critiquing their own performances, and bringing a science- and evidence-based approach to team workouts.
14 Ali is friendly with everyone, close with both coaches, and never misses a practice.
15 Coach Amy is close friends with the President of Ocean University, and she attends all the events with alumni. She is a graduate of Ocean University.
16 Sam is close with Assistant Coach Harold, and has some issues with Coach Amy. Sam almost quit the team last year because she does not believe that Coach Amy supports the team members enough, but the rest of the team convinced Sam to come back for one more year.
17 Sam is particularly close to her teammate TREVOR. They are friends but not dating, but Trevor has had a secret crush on Sam for two years, but has never acted on it.
18 Trevor has been dating Ali's older sister, NASMEEN, who is also on the team, for two months.
19 Nasmeen has been on the team as long as Sam, but has never won a national medal.
20 Sam's mother, MOLLY, comes to as many swim meets as she can, and has supported Sam for her entire life of going to swim practice, meets, coaching, and provided every single thing Sam needs to be an excellent swimmer.
21 Ali and Nasmeen's parents, Pratibha and Liam, come to every single swim meet. Neither of them went to college, yet they are accountants who have a small business together and considered very successful.
22 PRATIBHA, LIAM, Molly, and all the other parents and the coaches often socialize together (Ocean University is in a small town).

23 The student couples that are dating could be kicked off the team if Coach Amy finds out. There is a strict policy against dating other team members. It has been around as long as Coach Amy, and no one is sure about the reason for it, but no one can ask Coach Amy because she is by the book and does not like questions.
24 By winning two medals at nationals, the team improved the university's overall national rankings. An alumni, MS. LOLA JACKSON, was very excited to hear about the win and the improved rank, and made a large donation to the school to support more athletics.
25 By winning a gold medal, Sam will have great career opportunities open to her, and might be able to compete professionally.
26 By winning silver, Ali has ensured that his scholarship will continue.
27 Molly has been sick, bedridden for the past three months, and does not have a good prognosis.
28 Nasmeen taught Ali to swim and she wants to be a swim coach. She helps all the other swimmers with advice on training and their strokes, has read everything about being a professional swimmer, and treasures a photo of her with Michael Phelps at a youth swim camp.
29 Molly attended nationals and watched her daughter win. It was the last swim meet she attended before she fell ill.
30 Optional: add a wild card fact (students, make something up)

## Now What?

As you can in the list above, there are many directions, tangents, and behind-the-scenes stories for the Ocean University Swim Team. Your task is to tell the best story. What is irrelevant? Who is irrelevant? What are the most important facts? How do you decide?

## Class Activity 4 (repeated here from Chapter 4)

### *Paper Edit: Find As Many Stories As You Can*

Review the "Ocean University Sample "Introductory Briefing" and read this overview of 30 facts, details, relationships, and other information about a totally fictional swim team at a made-up university. This list represents the types of complex and layered information you will find as you edit a story.

### *Activity*

Break the class into groups or have students work individually. Each will do a "paper edit," which is a written cut of the story. There are limits on the number of facts that the student(s) can use, emulating the time-limited nature of media. They must choose their story. How many versions can you get to?

1 Decide if you will work in groups or have each student do this individually.
2 Break into the groups or work on your own, and create your story. Who is your main character? Who is left on your cutting-room floor? Pick a storyline and choose the facts that follow it through to the end.
3 Because all types of media have to fit the story into a specific time frame, you are limited to using only a portion of the information listed. A good ratio would be using 30 percent of the provided information, meaning each student or group can choose a maximum of *nine facts* to create their story. Clarify with your class how much of the information they can use, typically 20 percent to no more than 50 percent (for an episodic).
4 Once the groups or students have created their own versions, have them share their story with the class.
5 Add the options below to further challenge the class.

   - Add a *genre* or *audience* to focus the storytelling.
   - Assign each group or student a particular audience or genre.
   - Fictional versions include: a dramatic series, a coming-of-age film, a horror movie (you might need to use an extra wild card), a rom-com, a sit-com, and other genres.
   - Non-fiction versions could include crafting the story for: Ocean University's annual fundraising gala, a documentary on a sports network about young people aiming for competitive sports careers, to be used in training programs for swim coaches, a tell-all feature documentary on the challenges of being a student athlete, a reality television show, and more.
   - Specific audiences could include versions for: other student athletes, parents of student athletes, owners of professional sports leagues, alumni of Ocean University, people who watch the Olympics, and other audiences.

6 Share your stories – Each group or student shares their versions of the story.
7 Reflection – Use the class discussion or a written reflection assignment to address how each story followed a certain perspective, and how the class saw opinion and possibly even bias play out in the storytelling process.

A few questions for the class discussion:

- Were there characters no one wanted to follow? Why?
- Were there characters everyone liked? Why?
- Were there people listed who seemed completely irrelevant, and others who seemed to have only a tiny amount of information but seemed to play a larger role?

- Was there one version of this story that most people gravitated toward? Why?
- What gaps and flaws did the class encounter in this process? What information did they feel they needed more of to fully tell the story? Where were they guessing? What was not on screen?
- If they were going to film this, what added information would they seek?
- What influence did time pressure have (if there was a time limit?)
- What tools would have helped sort out their story?

# Appendix 3
## Class Activity: Editor and Story Choices

When you ask your friends if they want to see a movie, and they say, "Which movie?," the typical answer is the actor or the director. "The new Bong Joon-ho film." Or, "the one with Greta Gerwig acting in it." Unfortunately, it is unlikely someone will ever say "the one edited by so-and-so." The same is largely true for cinematographers, although there are cinephiles who *might* say they want to see the newest film shot by Emmanuel Lubezki or Roger Deakins. But, for the most part, viewing audiences identify films by director or actors not editors or other crew. Almost all the other roles, from editing and cinematography to production design, costumes, visual effects, special effects, sound design, and scoring … these are invisible arts. Or at least, invisible to audiences even if they are well-known among industry professionals.

As filmmakers, we learn to be invisible – you should not see the cut. You should not be aware of the camera movements, or lack of them. You should look at a production design and believe it to be real. This is what film and media is: the art of creating very believable illusions. And many filmmakers are quite happy with this, as we tend to be craftspeople who enjoy the collaboration of artistry more than we crave public attention. In fact, our crafts are made more magical because we have the protection of an invisible curtain keeping the edit suites and sets from public view. Too much information on how a film is made, for example, like seeing a shot before it is green screened, and the magic falls away.

In this exercise, we will pull back the invisible curtain and look at who edits television, documentaries, and feature films, and the choices they made along the way.

For this to work, you will need to find an interview with an editor or editing team. Make sure you find a detailed one that goes beyond basic promotion of the movie, to a description of how they did the editing. A few resources to get started are listed below, all of which share conversations with editors of contemporary films, television shows, documentaries, and series:

- *The Manhattan Edit Workshop* has an extensive library of video interviews with editors on its YouTube channel.
- *The Art of the Cut*, a podcast and YouTube channel, is another robust collection.
- *Editfest*, the annual conference of the American Cinema Editors (ACE), has several interviews on their website.
- Search through YouTube for film festivals, museums, and art centers dedicated to the moving image, and other related channels for more interviews, as there are a great many of these institutions that post their in-depth interviews on their channels.
- Review the notes and citations for this book, which list many other resources.

## Class Activity

1. Start with either a) a film of your choice, or b) searching for an editor. You are looking for an interview with an editor about how they cut the film, and need to have access to the full film as well. If you start with the film, you may need to have a few choices in order to find one that you can match back to an interview.
2. Listen to the interview while scrolling through the film.
3. Watch for image cuts while they describe what they did. You may want to turn the film's sound off while watching for image.
4. Listen for sound choices while they describe what they did. You may want to look away to hear the film and not watch it.
5. Reflect, based on their commentary: how was the film made? Do they list other story directions they considered but rejected? Do they discuss their process of creation? Detail what each editor did to elevate the film's story.
6. This reflection can be written or in a class discussion.

### *Example*

"Lawrence of Arabia" includes one of the most famous cuts in all of film history. In the scene, Lawrence, an intelligence officer in the British military, is ordered to go to the Arabian Peninsula. He is in the office of the diplomat who is sending him on this mission. Lawrence bends over to light the diplomat's cigarette. As a way to take his character to a different time and place, when Lawrence blows out the match, the film cuts to the desert at sunrise, with an airy "whoosh" reminiscent of desert breezes. It is a match cut and a sound bridge, and an elegant way to transport the viewer from the office to the desert, which is Lawrence's next chapter. It is by many accounts the most famous cut in film history.

According to Anne Coates, the editor of "Lawrence of Arabia," it was also a happy accident. In an interview with the *Manhattan Edit Workshop*, Coates describes how the cut was supposed to be a dissolve. In those days, editing on celluloid, the dissolves were indicated in a work print by a grease pencil mark on the film. During a test screening of that sequence, the scene was shown with the hard cut that ended up in the film. Coates explains:

> We were in film in those days, so I wonder if we would have seen it the way we did if we were on digital like today. Because I would have done the dissolve in the machine and we would have never seen it as a direct cut. Because it was film, it was cut together with the old chinagraph marks on it. And we saw this, we took it in the theater to run the whole sequence, and we saw this cut together like that. And David and I both, almost at the same moment, looked at each other and said "that's a wonderful cut."

Coates goes on the say how they kept a long duration clip of the desert sunrise in the scene, in which the audio is soft wind that eventually transitions to the film score. She was concerned the sunrise shot with minimal audio was too long. The editing team tried cutting it down but they felt it did not work, and they returned it to a long clip with the score coming in after several seconds.

This long duration clip acts as a kind of story beat and "white space" or a way to provide the audience time to absorb the transition and follow Lawrence's emotional journey. The audience remains in the story for a moment, catching up to the transitions of time and geography, and when the score rises with the next cut, it brings the audience back to the story and ready to move ahead.

# Appendix 4

## Class Activity: Create and Edit a Story

This activity is meant to be done in writing, in a class workshop, to understand the inherent challenges in making films, and also how directors, writers, and editors all make deliberate choices. This is meant to provide the show of clarity needed for the story to elevate, and how different teams will tell different stories for different venues. Perhaps the class starts with the included sample list, for the most neutral experience, and then creates their own list with someone or something they know and care a lot about, to see how the editing experience is different when you are familiar with the subject.

### Activity

Start with the basics most fundamental aspect of editing – creating a story for a certain length.

#### *Challenge*

Understand how perspective, theme, director's goal, distribution outlet, and other elements influence the story:

#### *Process*

If you are using the sample *Swim Team: Ocean University Sample "Introductory Briefing,"* which includes facts, quotes, emotional experiences, and other relevant aspects that you might capture if you were going out with a camera, then skip to the "Create Your Story" section.

- **Create Your Own Introductory Briefing**
  - Create your own Introductory Briefing like the one in the sample by listing facts and experiences, from the who, what, where, when, and why, to the human complications like rivalries, crushes, hopes, dreams,

ambitions, jealousies, and virtually anything that you think might be relevant or interesting. The more ridiculous or secret the facts are, the more your different versions will be exciting and revealing. Controversial facts could result in some very good dramas.

- Your list should have at least 20 items on it for this exercise to work properly.
- Start with a person, place, situation, or process. This can be done together as a class, or the instructor can provide these to students. Or student teams can create their own introductory briefings, then switch and edit each other's scenarios.
- Decide your level of neutrality and controversy. This exercise can get more heated and intense with controversial figures, although it will also yield more insights into storytelling. Also consider things that a lot of people have heard about but few know that much about, and how much the facts of the story are controversial themselves, such as someone winning a race (fairly observable and uncontroversial, as it is possible to see who crossed the finish line first) versus someone winning a dance or comedy contest (these are harder to know who won, as this is more subjective and opinion-based).
- Write your Introductory Briefing as a list in a common place in the class (a blackboard, dry erase board, or large sheets of paper) or create a shared document online. What matters is that everyone can see the full list as you will all be referring to the same information.

- **Create Your Story**

  - Divide the class into teams. This is important, as people will have different perspectives and the team will need to come to some kind of agreement.
  - Give each team a "fact limit" of how many of the listed facts and experiences they can include in their final story. For example, if you have 20 facts and experience, give each team a maximum of using 30 percent, or just six of the listed facts and experiences.
  - Get ready, get set, and have your teams start telling their stories.
  - Each team must agree on what they feel is the best story they can tell, who the main character(s) are, and what is most compelling about the story.
  - Each team must give their story a name. No untitled stories.
  - Strongly recommended: Once the class has had time to review the Introductory Briefing, add a time limit to complete this to make it more exciting. This is best done as a lightning round style class exercise with time for all groups to share their stories. The time limit should reflect the real-life pressure to tell a story in a limited amount of time, for example perhaps a range from 10 to 20 minutes.

- Have each group share their version of the story. Note how each team used different characters, story arcs, or other material, or if everyone was drawn to similar material.
- Have the teams share how they chose their particular storyline. How did they decide what was most important? Were there creative differences? How did they resolve those differences? Did they feel a desire to be more creative or add to the story?

- **Optional**
    - Add a "wild card" for each team, particularly if using the options below.
    - Add a genre to guide decision-making. For example, each group creates a version for reality TV, horror, romance, coming-of-age, broadcast news, comedy, doomsday apocalyptic, science-fiction, social justice, educational, etc., versions.
    - Alternatively, assign groups to make versions of this story for common media outlets. For example, one group is assigned to make a theatrical version, another will do the mainstream news version, others will do versions for documentary, sports television, TikTok, Instagram, YouTube, and so on.

# Appendix 5

## Daily Logs and Naming Conventions

"How do you sort through all the footage? And how do you keep track of it?" I am asked this question so many aspiring documentary-makers that it begs its own section. Recently, while traveling, I shared a cab with a young filmmaker. He had just finished filming a motorcycle road trip through Italy and Southeast Europe for a documentary about a photographer whose subject was fathers and sons. Together they had traveled for a few weeks by motorcycle, with the photographer looking for willing participants and the filmmaker getting it all down. He had piles of video footage along with amazing photographs, and a wonderful adventure behind it all. So, now what? When he learned I was a documentary filmmaker he said this was his first documentary and asked my advice on sorting through the giant pile of footage in his camera bag.

This is a typical scenario with which every filmmaker, or at least the documentary ones, must sympathize. *Film first, figure it out later, right*? I certainly had those moments, and really wish someone had told me how to name my files when I was starting out, as it would have saved an enormous amount of time.

Fiction film has its own challenges in logging and naming footage, but fiction films are made scene by scene, and footage will adhere to a script structure. Therefore the naming and organizing is built into the process: follow the script – Scene 01, Scene 02 – and add in camera angles. Documentary, on the other hand, may occasionally follow a scripted process, but many are filmed out of the kind of passion and adventure described above. Filming is done during very long filming days, most often without the benefit of specific crew to offload and sort the footage on set. Adventure and passion are wonderful as a basis for a film, however in the editing room, methodical, clear organization will win every time over a more adventurous approach to organizing your files.

This guide helps to understand how to sort and name footage, starting with fiction film, and then applying those practices to documentary.

**Fiction Logs and Naming**

Design a systematic format as described in Chapter 1. The naming convention needs to be easy to understand and something all team can follow. For a large team, you may need to create a manual or cheat sheet. Common structures include:

- Project name.
- Scene number.
- Take number.
- Type of shot.
- Character.
- Camera identifier.

For example, something like "ProjectName_SceneNumber_TakeNumber_CameraID" can work well. For your footage it will look like this: "Dune2_S04_T07_CamB.mov"

Other metadata can further refine the naming convention, like:

- Date of the shoot, in "YYMMDD" format, or "Dune2_S04_T07_CamB_240301.mov"
- Character names, or "Dune2_S04_T07_Chani_240301.mov"

**Documentary Logs and Naming**

For a documentary project, which might take several years to film or use large amounts of archival material, naming your footage is absolutely essential to manage the complex array of data. Some productions create a database and attach images and clip summaries in order to track footage.

The naming convention above can work for all footage, but documentary has some expanded categories to address the needs of those projects:

- Use location or event instead of scene.
- Use type of shot instead of takes, for example, WS, OTS, establishing, long take.
- Characters.
- Camera identifier.
- For archival material, indicate which archive.

An example might be "Project_Date_LocationCode_Character," as in: "Swim_240301_Paris_Ali" and "Swim_240715_Oregon_Ali"

When relevant, add descriptive tags, camera information, and camera angles like:

"Swim_240301_Paris_Ali_overhead-drone" and
"Swim_240301_Paris_Ali-Interview"
If you had two cameras you add that as well:
"Swim_240301_Paris_Ali-Interview_CamB"

If this starts to make for some very long file names for your team, you can find abbreviations and codes that work as well, however for many people this type of "natural language" naming makes the most sense to simplify the naming convention.

# Appendix 6

## Post-Production Workflow Guide

**Organize and Ingest:**

- Raw footage.
- Create a naming convention and file structure for all film assets.
- Rename, transcode, back up on RAID drive and/or separate drives.
- Bring footage into your editing system.
- If you are starting post during production, continue to name, organize, and ingest footage.
- *Milestone #1: Project set up.*

**[1] ORGANIZE AND INGEST**

Raw footage

Create a naming convention and file structure for all film assets.

Rename, transcode, back up on RAID drive and/or separate drives.

Bring footage into editing system.

If you are starting post during production, continue to name, organize, and ingest daily footage.

**Milestone #1: Project set up.**

**Editing – Beginning:**

- Log and transcribe.
- Sort into bins/folders. Tag, code, and log using the NLE tools.
- Selects of interviews, best takes, and other key footage.
- String-out scenes, by script or other categories (for example, a documentary might string-out scenes for specific events and for each character).
- Optional: create one timeline per scene. Create "reels" or acts with your timelines and break the film into smaller chunks. Start placing scenes onto reels, so you can watch them in sequence but still have them separated.
  - Note: This is an option to help reshuffle the film, if you have a scene at the film's midpoint, and want to move it up to the beginning, it is far easier to do if they are already separated by individual timelines.
- Continue the edit: trim, shape, tighten, and delete.
- Remember to frequently "save as" and make new copies of your project file.
- Music: some people use temp music at this point, and others start cutting to the final music. A few teams use no music until the end. This is entirely up to the project's needs and the type of music. An original score might start at this point, some stock clips might wait until later.
- Sound editing may also begin at this point, working on dialog and adding in effects.
- Visual effects may also begin at this point, depending on their complexity.
- *Milestone #2: Rough cut.*

**[2] EDIT —BEGIN**

Log and transcribe

Sort into bins/folders. Tag, code, and log using the NLE tools.

Selects of interviews, best takes, and other key footage.

String-out scenes, by scripted scene number, characters, date of filming, and other categories.

OPTIONAL: create one timeline per scene or otherwise break the film into smaller chunks in your timelines.

Using nesting or grouping, structure scenes into reels and acts so you can watch them in sequence but still have them separated in timelines.

Continue the edit: move scenes around, trim, shape, tighten, and delete.

MUSIC: Many editors start using temp music at this point. Others start working on the original score and it evolves with the cut. Depending on the project's needs and the type of music start planning and cutting to your music.

Sound editing/design also begins at this point, particularly dialog editing and sound effects.

Visual effects and graphics may also begin at this point, depending on their complexity.

**Milestone #2: Rough cut.**

**Editing – Middle:**

- When you feel you have a solid rough cut, take a break. Go outside, get some air and exercise. Get some sleep! Your film will be there when you get back, and you need to recharge your batteries. Also important is the need to freshen your eyes and ears, as you have been staring at this film for a long time. In order to finalize it, and really make it sing, you need to have some space then come back to it.
- With the director and producers, find a few trusted, smart, honest people to show your rough film. They ideally should be outsiders to the film as you want to see how it lands with people who do not know the story. Also show to the crew and possibly actors and participants.
- Listen. Be prepared for feedback, ask for constructive critiques, and listen very carefully. Being defensive at this point will not help the film. If you find yourself wanting or needing to explain a scene, or the overall story, refrain. If you need to explain something likely it is not clear to the audience and you should take note. Remember, this stage of feedback is your best friend; it is the best way to gauge if the film is working, and is done to improve it before it goes to a much wider audience.
- Take notes. If five people tell you the same thing about scene – it is too long, too short, doesn't make sense, it is perfect – then you should probably listen to that. If five people all have different reactions to a scene, then it is your call, with the director, on how to proceed. Take a lot of very specific notes, and try to understand why someone might say a certain thing. If you have a target audience, make sure you have feedback from members of that target audience.
- Discuss with the team what you will do to finalize the cut.
- *Milestone #3: Feedback notes, ready for revision.*

**[3] EDIT —MIDDLE**

Take a break! When you have a solid rough cut, take a break. Go outside, get some air, exercise, and sleep! Your film will be there when you get back, and you need to recharge your batteries to return to the cut with fresh eyes and ears.

Find viewers. With the director and producers, find a few trusted, smart, honest people to show your rough film. They ideally should be "new eyes" as you want to see how it lands with people who were not involved with filming or editing.

Listen. Be prepared for feedback, ask for constructive critiques, and listen very carefully. Anonymous notes might be a good option. Avoid being defensive and try to take it all in.

Create a process you trust. Trusting your revision process is important, so you can proceed feeling you have made the best film possible.This stage of feedback is your protection! The goal is to gauge if the film is working, catch weak areas, and improve them before the film goes to a wider audience.

Consider each note of feedback. If you find yourself wanting or needing to explain a scene, or the overall story, refrain. If you need to explain something likely it is not clear to the audience and your energy is better used figuring out what you can do creatively to fix this story element.

Evaluate notes. If five people tell you the same thing about scene — it is too long, too short, it makes no sense, or it is perfect — then you probably should listen to that. If there are widely different reactions to a scene, it means the editor, director, and producer(s) need to decide how to proceed

Refine notes to finalize all revisions.Try to understand why someone might have said a certain thing. Can you correct it? If you have a target audience, make sure you have feedback from members of that audience.

Plan. Discuss with the team what edits and revision you will make to finalize the cut.

**Milestone #3: Clear plan for revision.**

**Editing – End:**

- With notes in hand, return to the editing suite. Some of your notes will likely be very straightforward. Others will be very complex. It is best to tackle the complex ones first, as sometimes fixing the complex problems takes care of the simple ones. In any case, figure out an order so you don't start re-editing the film completely.
- Revise the film. Continue the process: feedback, rest revision. Feedback, rest, revision.
- Music: If you have been using temp music, this is the point where you will replace it.
- *Milestone #4: Picture lock.*

**[4] EDIT —END**

↓

With notes in hand, return to the editing suite. Some of your notes/revisions will likely be very straightforward. Others will be very complex.

↓

Create a plan and delegate revsions. Assign some things, like revisions of graphics, to one team member, and other things, like replacing dialog or finding new shots, to others.

↓

Set deadlines and structure for each set of revisions so you can have a finalizating plan.

↓

Tackle the complex notes first. Sometimes fixing the complex problems takes care of the simple ones. You also simply need to give complex issues more time.

↓

Continue the process as needed: Feedback, rest, revision. Feedback, rest, revision.

↓

MUSIC: If you are still using temp music, replace it with the final score and/or songs.

↓

**Milestone #4: Picture lock.**

**Visual Effects and Graphics:**

- Final compositing of green screen, rotoscoping, and other visual effects.
- All final graphics and titles.

**Sound Design:**

- The sound designer adds ambience, re-records certain clips, and adds sound effect.
- The sound editor finalizes all the dialog editing.
- Final music: Adding the final score and/or songs.
- *Milestone #5: Final cut.*
- Sound master: With the sound design, editing, and music completed, the sound master mixes down all the tracks.

**Color:**

- Color correction and fixing image issues.
- Color grading, if you are creating a certain look.

**Matchback:**

- Matching the sound master back to the color-graded image master.
- *Milestone #5: Matchback.*

## [5] FINISHING STEPS

| Color | Visual Effects | Sound master |
|---|---|---|
| Final color grade | Final compositing of green screen, rotoscoping, and other visual effects | Final sfx, ambiance, any dialog rerecording or ADR. |
| All color and image corrections | All final graphics and titles | When sound design, editing, and music are complete, the sound is mastered and mixed down. |
| **Delivery of color corrected master** | **Delivery of all final vfx** | **Delivery of audio master** |

**All masters reassembled in timeline**

*Whew! Rest, relax. You are matchback!*

**Milestone #5: Matchback.**

**Captions and Subtitles:**

- Captions are swiftly becoming a standard part of delivery. Subtitles are still optional for some productions however are quite common. They will be done at this step and synced to the final film.
- Your caption or subtitle delivery might be in any of several formats: scc,. vtt, formatted. srt, unformatted. srt, or something else.
- *Milestone #6: Captions and subtitles.*

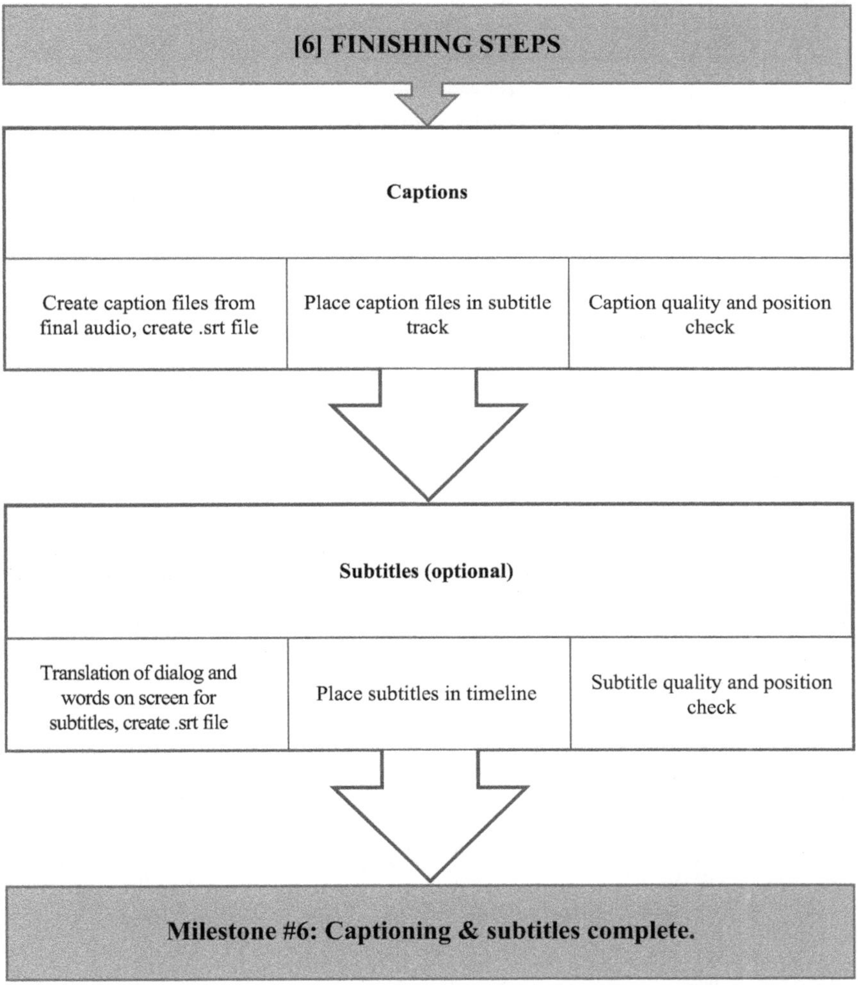

**Exhibition Screeners and Delivery:**

- Exporting out the DCP and other exhibition versions.
- Managing the upload or hard copy delivery of the final package of exhibition screener and other assets.
- *Milestone #7: Exhibition screeners created and Milestone #8: Delivery.*

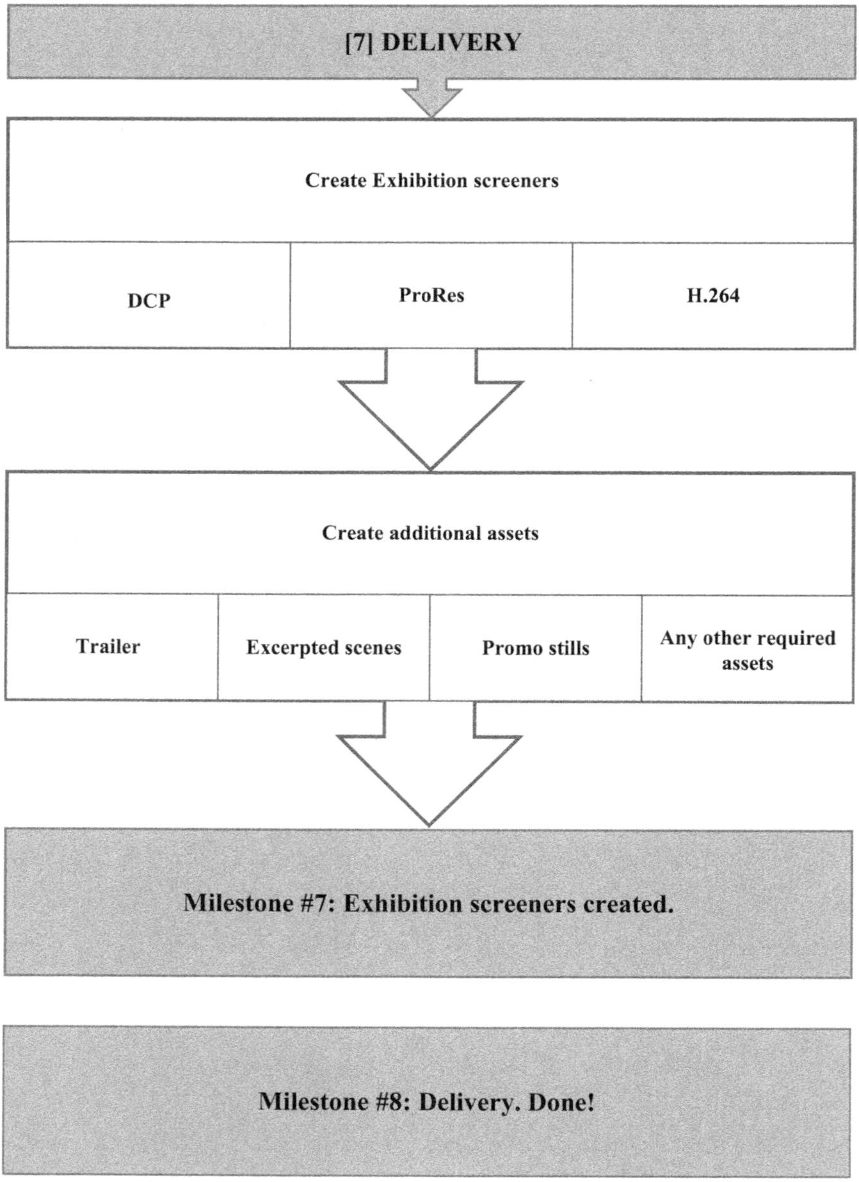

# Appendix 7

## Post-Production Guide by Form

### Delivery Packages

Delivery packages vary by form and target audience. While your project may vary, this is an overview of which types of deliverables will be expected by each media form.

| | *Theatrical* | *Broadcast TV* | *Streaming* | *Festival* | *Interactive* | *Museum or institution* | *Social Media* |
|---|---|---|---|---|---|---|---|
| Full film, DCP | X | | | X | | | |
| Full Film, ProRes or other high resolution form | X | X | X | | X | X | |
| Full Film, H.264 or other low resolution | X | X | X | | | X | X |
| Selected scenes for promotion | X | X | X | X | X | Maybe | X |
| Trailer(s) | X | X | X | X | X | X | X |
| Textless version of feature film | Maybe | Maybe | Maybe | | | | |
| Music-less version of the feature film | Maybe | Maybe | Maybe | | | | |
| Versions for texting/ Whatsapp sharing | | | | | X | | X |
| Closed Captions | | X | X | X | Maybe | X | |
| Subtitles | | | X | | Maybe | | |
| Open captions | Maybe | | | Maybe | | Probably | |

## International Delivery Considerations

Delivery to audiences outside of your same language and culture, for example, a UK-based production to an audience in Africa, for example, might require many other steps. The obvious one is subtitling, and whether those subtitles are burned into the image or need to be turned on through a closed captions option.

Less obvious additional delivery steps include promotional clips or teasers of the film in a way the audience can watch based on cultural realities. If people do not have the same level of access to streaming content because of limited bandwidth, or they might watch on phones as opposed to laptops, you have to consider how to deliver so the film is viewable readily by your intended audience. In his interview, Aashish Kumar talks about how he created micro-scenes, or very short shareable scenes, to share "Body, Home, World" accessibly with audiences who might first view snippets of the film on a text or WhatsApp chat. That required a very low-resolution version even of a short snippet in order to be viewable on the types of bandwidth and cell phone plans that are common among his specific audience group. Then, using those micro-scenes to start connecting with audiences, audiences could see screenings of the full project through a hosted event at a community center.

## Textless Versions

An additional delivery step might be a version of your film with no text on screen. This typically is required for broadcast or theatrical international screening. Your team will remove all the text elements on screen - not the ones baked into the image, but your graphics, inter titles, and relevant lower thirds - for translation. That way, the text will be replaced in the language of the subtitles, reducing the amount of words on screen.

## "No Music" Version

Another potential delivery step might be a version of your film with no mixed in music. This is for cutting a trailer and having the option to use any dialog or sound design elements without the score/music mixed in. In some unusual instances, music also might be changed for international distribution, depending on rights acquisition. For example if a song was licensed for distribution in the U.S. but not in the U.K. or Mexico, the music might need to be replaced for international broadcast in those countries.

# Appendix 8

## What Are We Going to Do About AI? Use It? Fear It?

At the time of writing of this book, Artificial Intelligence (AI) has already become a normal everyday tool. From text suggestions in emails to color correction on your Instagram posts or smartphone photos, AI tools have been helping consumers, whether they knew it or not, for many years, in a form called "assistive AI." Now, the bigger, badder cousin has emerged: Generative AI (GenAI). The "generative" name distinguishes it from assistive AI, as GenAI, at a minimum, creates words, images, and audio following on existing media and language in it's data bank. But GenAI goes far beyond that: it creates compelling narratives, writes poetry, and generates very believable voices and faces, all created through simple prompts from a user.

All types of AI are moving much faster than human speed. By the time you read this book, the entire preceding paragraph might be totally out of date! One of the most extraordinary characteristics of GenAI is the speed at which it develops. The implications for the film and media industry are profound. Within the last few years, GenAI-created voices, modeled on famous actors, have also generated high-profile lawsuits because permission to mimic that particular actor's voice were not obtained. The challenges are from far more than one person or one lawsuit – many actors and public figures are publicly and legally objecting to being recreated without consent. Yet, there are many instances of "deep fakes," or using someone's voice and face to create a fake story or encounter. By the time you read this book there may be hundreds or thousands of legal means trying to prevent the worst aspects of AI. There might also be legal precedents about using GenAI and consequences for violations. Or, there might be attempts at legal protections but not many tangible means to enforce them! Enforcing legal consequences for even flagrant violations of consent in using GenAI is one of biggest challenges around AI in general and GenAI in particular.

In the meantime, the film and media world are being impacted enormously. And starting to develop practices and policies around GenAI. AI and GenAI already play a role in the day-to-day life of filmmaking teams. These range from benign tasks like transcribing audio files, some aspects of color correction, cutting selects reels from transcripts, creating translations, subtitles, and captions, and even ethical use of GenAI to create stories. GenAI has already become the editor's little helper. The implications of GenAI on these tasks has more to do with labor markets, budgets, and workflows than ethics. For many of these tasks, GenAI is a digital tool that expedites work, at very low or no cost. While some film industry veterans express valid concerns about the impact of GenAI tools on jobs and wages, is hard to see the difference between GenAI helping you transcribe or color correct, and any other digital tools like an app to rename files or auto-tag clips in a bin.

But there are also less-benign aspects to GenAI. It goes far beyond a mere tool and has the power to create entirely believable and convincing media pieces. Combine this with an internet full of trolls and bots, persistent fake news, and constant pressure to create more content on smaller budgets, a very dangerous scenario has also emerged. What does an editor do when confronted with the option or request to create something with GenAI? Perhaps just a scene or two, or one audio clip, to fill a gap in a piece. What damage would it do? The ability to recreate voices became one of the first public discussions about the ethical use of GenAI: should a director be able to recreate the voice of an actor who had passed away, perhaps to fill in a role or even as an entirely new film? Who had rights to that actor's voice? The family? The manager? Will an actor need a manager after they pass away to manage their GenAI voice career? The answers have been murky, varied, and personal.

One of the first creative uses of GenAI involves the iconic voice of Darth Vader, created by actor James Earl Jones. In a pioneering incident of using GenAI in filmmaking, Jones had given permission to Skywalker Sound and a company called Respeecher to use GenAI to recreate the classic, highly unique, and utterly recognizable voice of Darth Vader. This GenAI version of Jones' voice appeared on the Disney+ series "Obi-Wan Kenobi." This authorized use of GenAI shows the promise and hopes – it can help actors extend their careers in countless ways and support the industry in even more ways. It also shows the enormous potential for misuse, exploitation, and an infinite range of legal and ethical issues. Not all actors are open to GenAI and such uses were one of the core points at the heart of the 2023 SAG-AFTRA strike which brought the US film industry to a near-standstill for months. Just one example is another Star Wars-related lawsuit, in which Lucasfilm resurrected the likeness of actor Peter Cushing for "Rogue One: A Star Wars Story," in a new film made over 20 years after Cushing passed away. Unlike Jones, Cushing did not have the opportunity to give permission as GenAI did not exist when he was alive. The lawsuit centers on this posthumous use of someone's likeness, who controls the intellectual property of someone who has long since passed away, and how contracts signed before GenAI existed should be interpreted.

This two cases show the entire universe of GenAI hopes, possibilities, dangers, and complications. At time of writing this book these are developing faster than the profession can keep up with them. In addition to creating legal precedent, which are lengthy cases that are settled on a one-by-one basis and may or may not help the rest of the film and media fields, there are other initiatives. One of these is the creation of guidelines for using GenAI in films, documentaries, news, and other media. Guidelines are not laws: they are suggestions of best practices that are meant to support professionals in their work.

Mixing the opportunities and ease of GenAI with the pressure to create more content, faster, on increasingly smaller budgets creates a dangerous recipe. Several scenarios are becoming common. For example, an actor, performer, or expert is not available, but a media piece needs their input. GenAI can recreate their voice, convincingly, and the actor/expert might even be able to license their voice and/or likeness as an additional income stream. Or, a producer wants to experiment with a new technology and see what they can create, ranging from experimental media forms to mock documentaries, to test the limits of a new type tool and new form of performance. Most common, a post-production team is on a tight deadline to produce content, and a human voiceover actor will require a minimum of 12 hours, while GenAI will require a maximum of 12 minutes. These scenarios beg for guidance to ensure ethical use of a new tool that has both exciting aspects along with darker and more sinister uses.

Some film and media professional organizations are developing written standards and best practices for GenAI. One such document is the Archival Producers Alliance (APA) "Best Practices for Use of Generative AI in Documentaries" which was endorsed by more than 40 established organizations, film festivals, and leading production companies working in non-fiction film. Among their many excellent recommendations, is to consider using GenAI in ways that preserve the connection of truth. Audiences for documentary and non-fiction expect to be shown true, authentic content. Using GenAI in ways that undermine this expectation is not any different than it would be to hire actors to perform and call it a documentary, or to otherwise knowingly create content that is not truthful and authentic. Their solution: have the filmmaker make it clear, visually, when something is using GenAI, or note it at the beginning and end of the program.

This APA's best practices guide underscores that GenAI is a continuation of way documentary and non-fiction media have always grappled with ethics in general: for fair, accurate, and authentic storytelling through the lens of a documentarian's perspective. This applies whether it is GenAI, a reproduction, recreations, voiceover, or material from social media. All of these have been debated within documentary circles, with many best practice guidelines but no standards or regulatory control other than the opinion of peer filmmakers and audiences. Films that profoundly misrepresent their protagonist or even told outright lies could be subject to cease-and-desist orders or libel lawsuits. But GenAI sets up a new challenge: who will sue to stop a film's release if an outright lie is told, but it does not involve an actual human? What is there to stop less than ethical productions? This question will land square in the lap of the editor and post-production team, who are the ones who might be asked to create scenes using GenAI.

Alternatively, filmmakers have always grappled with how to ensure truthful, accurate storytelling. A filmmaker might make a truthful point using a fictionalized scene that focuses on the story's essence. Or they bring a moment from history to life through a re-enactment in lieu of an interview. In extreme examples, filmmakers who did not disclose to real people that they were being filmed for fictional, scripted productions resulted in people believing a scripted film was real when it was not, and resulted in national and international controversies, lawsuits, and accusations of hoaxes. (For example, the 2006 mockumentary "Borat," resulted in dozens of lawsuits for misrepresenting the film's intent to people who ended up in the final production.)

Filming people under false pretenses and misrepresentation has always been illegal and counter to the purpose of most documentaries, with the enforcement of these standards through a combination of public opinion and lawsuits. Creating false content or misrepresentations with GenAI presents a unique situation of having content but fewer people to enforce it.

Other fields are also grappling with the impact of GenAI. The strike by the Writer's Guild of America in 2023 was due, in part, to the need to establish when scripts can use GenAI, how they can use it, if at all, to still be credited as a scriptwriter, and to prevent studios from replacing human writers with GenAI script-o-bots. While they resolved that dispute, there likelihood that GenAI will rear its head again is very strong.

The APA guide and other examples of AI best practice guides:

- Archival Producers Alliance (APA) "Best Practices for Use of Generative AI in Documentaries" – https://www.archivalproducersalliance.com/apa-genai-initiative
- User manual – University of Michigan, Institute for Data and AI in Society–https://midas.umich.edu/research/research-resources/generative-ai-hub/users-guide/ – as opposed to a best practice guide, this research hub published a detailed user guide that includes the mandate of manually validating the results from GenAI.
- The *Columbia Journalism Review* discusses how to use GenAI in journalism: https://www.cjr.org/business_of_news/writing-ai-rulebook-artificial-intelligence-journalism.php

# Additional Sections

# i. Citations

Archival Producers of America GenAI Best Practices. (2024, September). Google Docs. https://drive.google.com/file/d/1WS4iZ2Wi_wft5x54RG-hYb45sf10W8nV/view

Attanasio, P. (1993, January 31). "Homicide: Life on the Streets" (Series, 122 episodes). NBC Studios.

Barr, M. (2015, June 24). "Mr. Robot": Creator Sam Esmail on Transitioning the Show From Feature Film to Pilot and More. *Forbes*. www.forbes.com/sites/merrillbarr/2015/06/24/mr-robot-usa-2/

Blaché, R., Blaché, S., & Blaché, A. G. (1996). *The Memoirs of Alice Guy Blaché* (2nd ed.). Scarecrow Press.

Black British Post Prod Collective [@blackbritishpostprodcollec4809]. (n.d.). An Interview With Freelance TV/Film Editor Zeb Achonu. YouTube. Retrieved August 31, 2024, from www.youtube.com/watch?v=8AdIf6Jr2LI

Chapman, W. (2023, June 28). Everyone Watches TV with Subtitles Now. How'd That Happen? *IndieWire*. www.indiewire.com/features/general/why-more-people-use-subtitles-1234875864/

Cizek, K. (2008). "Highrise." Https://Katerinacizek.com/Portfolio/Highrise-The-Collection/; National Film Board of Canada.

Color Of Change Hollywood. (2023, February 6). Retrieved April 2, 2023, from https://hollywood.colorofchange.org/roadmap/

Directors Guild of America. Television Director Development Programs. (n.d.). Retrieved April 2, 2023, from www.dga.org/The-Guild/Diversity/TV-Studio-Directors-Development-Programs.aspx

EditFest Global. https://editfestglobal.com. American Cinema Editors (ACE). Accessed 1 November 2024.

Editors Guild Staff. (2021, June 28). MPEG Survey Offers Inside Look At Industry Discrimination, Diversity, Pay and More. *CineMontage*. Retrieved April 2, 2023, from https://cinemontage.org/mpeg-diversity/ and https://cinemontage.org/mpeg-diversity/

Editors Guild Staff. (n.d.). Committees. Editors Guild – IATSE Local 700 > Utility Menu > About > Committees. Retrieved April 2, 2023, from www.editorsguild.com/Committees

Fainaru, S., & Fainaru-Wada, M. (2013). League of Denial: The NFL's Concussion Crisis. *Frontline*. www.pbs.org/wgbh/frontline/documentary/league-of-denial/

Ford, Y., & Barnes, J. (2017, January 23). "Strong Island." www.strongislandfilm.com/

French, K. (2021, January 28). Zeb Achonu – Editor. EDIT GIRLS. https://editgirls.com/careerstories/zebachonu

Fuster, J. (2021, November 12). Why Approval of IATSE's New Contract May Not Be a Sure Thing. *TheWrap*. Retrieved April 2, 2023, from www.thewrap.com/iatse-editors-guild-amptp-contract-vote/

Gaines, J., Vatsal, R., & Dall'Astra, M. (n.d.). *Women Film Pioneers Project*. New York, NY. Retrieved 2023.

Gordon, D. (2023, June 6). Why Is Everyone Watching TV With the Subtitles On? *The Atlantic*. www.theatlantic.com/ideas/archive/2023/06/watching-movies-tv-with-subtitles/674301/

Gutierrez, C. (2024, January 20). "FRIDA." www.imdb.com/Title/Tt30319555/; Amazon Prime.

Hammer Museum [@HammerMuseumLosAngeles]. (2024, July 24). Carla Gutiérrez Discusses "FRIDA." YouTube. www.youtube.com/watch?v=aOdzwOmEoQs

Hannah-Jones, N. (2019, August 14). The 1619 Project. *The New York Times*. www.nytimes.com/interactive/2019/08/14/magazine/1619-america-slavery.html

Harness, W. (2022, April 26). Dear Hollywood. Retrieved April 2, 2023, from https://iwillharness.com/program/dear-hollywood/

Hilton, E. (2020, July 13). Race-Equity Consultants in demand in Hollywood: "Never Once Have We Been So Busy." *The Hollywood Reporter*. Retrieved April 2, 2023, from www.hollywoodreporter.com/movies/movie-news/race-equity-consultants-demand-hollywood-never-once-have-we-been-busy-1302117/ https://borisfx.com/blog/aotc/art-of-the-cut-beef/

Huang, J. (2022, February 3). The After Effects of IATSE's Strike Authorization. *OnLabor*. Retrieved April 2, 2023, from https://onlabor.org/the-aftereffects-of-iatses-strike-authorization/

Hullfish, S. (2008-2024). *Art of the Cut: With Steve Hullfish*. Apple Podcasts. https://podcasts.apple.com/za/podcast/art-of-the-cut/id276157864

Hullfish, S. (n.d.). *Art of The Cut* (Episode: Beef. May 18, 2023) [Podcast, series]. BorixFX.

Hunt, K. (2019, October 3). How Oscar Micheaux Challenged the Racism of early Hollywood. *Jstor Daily*. Retrieved April 3, 2023, from https://daily.jstor.org/how-oscar-micheaux-challenged-the-racism-of-early-hollywood/

King, V. (2022, October 11). The Necessity of Diversity Editors in Hollywood. Blog. Retrieved April 2, 2023, from https://blog.finaldraft.com/the-necessity-of-diversity-editors-in-hollywood

Kumar, A. (2021). Body, Home, World – South Asian American LGBTQ+ Journeys. www.bodyhomeworld.com/

Kwan, D., & Scheinert, D. (2022, March 25). "Everything Everywhere All At Once." IMDb. www.imdb.com/title/tt6710474/

Landesman, P., & Jeanne Marie Laskas. (2015, December 25). "Concussion." Distributed by: Columbia Pictures, Sony Pictures Releasing. www.imdb.com/title/tt3322364/

Lee, S. (2024, September 16). Darth Vader's Voice: Navigating the Legal Frontier of AI in Hollywood. *Jhu.edu*. https://carey.jhu.edu/articles/navigating-legal-frontier-ai-hollywood

London South Bank University [@Londonsouthbankuni]. (n.d.). Female Editors – A New Frontier: A Trailblazing Women On and Off Screen Event. YouTube. Retrieved August 31, 2024, from www.youtube.com/watch?v=god5jtNICYs

Manhattan Edit Workshop [@mewshop]. (2017, May 15). Legendary Editor Anne V. Coates, ACE, on Combining Scenes in "Out of Sight." YouTube. www.youtube.com/watch?v=8m1TsOaNkKc

McGilligan, Patrick. (2009). *Oscar Micheaux: The Great and Only: The Life of America's First Black Filmmaker*. HarperCollins.
Mundy-Castle, A. (2023, June 15). "White Nanny, Black Child." www.imdb.com/Title/Tt29666745/; Doc Hearts, Tigerlily Productions. (Edited by Zeb Achonu.) www.imdb.com/title/tt29666745/
Mykhalevych, N. (2024, August 30). Survey: Why America Is Obsessed with Subtitles. *Preply.com*. https://preply.com/en/blog/americas-subtitles-use/
National Association of the Deaf. (2018, September 17). When is Captioning Required? *NAD*. www.nad.org/resources/technology/captioning-for-access/when-is-captioning-required/
Normanstudios.org. n.d. Oscar Micheaux. *Norman Studios Online Museum*, http://Normanstudios.org/nsdrc/project/oscar-micheaux
PBS Short Film Festival 2024 (2024, July 18). "Everything Everywhere All At Once": Editor on Career: Paul Rogers. YouTube. https://youtu.be/Z6BPnNMkH2w?si=viuw-VBppgF1_A3D
Pennington, A. (2024, February 7). Why Captions Are Now (Almost) Essential in Video Content Consumption. *NAB Amplify*. https://amplify.nabshow.com/articles/connect-captions-content-creation/
Rafferty, K., Loader, J., & Rafferty, P. (1982, March 17). "The Atomic Café" [Documentary]. The Archives Project.
Rajani, R. & Waithe, L. (n.d.). "Indeed Presents Rising Voices." 271 Films and Hillman Grad. www.hillmangrad.com/foundation/rising-voices
Ramón, A.-C., Tran, M., & Hunt, D. (n.d.). Hollywood Diversity Report 2022. *Socialsciences.ucla.edu*. Retrieved April 3, 2023, from https://socialsciences.ucla.edu/wp-content/uploads/2022/10/UCLA-Hollywood-Diversity-Report-2022-Television-10-27-2022.pdf
Robb, D. (2021, June 3). Three in Four Editors Guild Members Say They Believe Workplace Discrimination Occurs "Often" or "Sometimes." *Deadline*. Retrieved April 2, 2023, from https://deadline.com/2021/06/three-in-four-editors-guild-members-say-they-believe-workplace-discrimination-occurs-often-or-sometimes-1234768776/
Salazar, S. (2022, July 8). Wet Writhing, Eldritch Gurgling: A Chat with the Stranger Things Subtitles Team. *Vulture*. www.vulture.com/2022/07/stranger-things-subtitles-captions-team-interview.html
Siomopoulos, A. (2006). The Birth of a Black Cinema: Race, Reception, and Oscar Micheaux's within our gates. *The Moving Image*, 6(2), 111–118. https://doi.org/10.1353/mov.2007.0017
Staff. (n.d.). The Rough Assembly. Retrieved March 2, 2023, from www.theroughassembly.com/
Sultan, A. (2022). "Incognita's Infamous Adventure." www.imdb.com/title/tt9820580/fullcredits/?ref_=tt_cst_sm
Szalai, G. (2021, October 28). 79 Percent Say More On-Screen Diversity Is Needed in Film/TV, Viacomcbs Study finds. *The Hollywood Reporter*. Retrieved April 2, 2023, from www.hollywoodreporter.com/business/business-news/diversity-representation-study-viacomcbs-film-tv-1235037655/
Tabahriti, S. (2022, September 24). Subtitles Can Be Terrible: Netflix's Head of Accessibility Explains How Growing Up With Deaf Parents Impacts Her Work. *Yahoo Entertainment*. www.yahoo.com/entertainment/netflixs-head-accessibility-grew-deaf-082306828.html
The Berkeley Forum. (2024, March 10). Paul Rogers, Academy-Award Winner for "Everything Everywhere All At Once." *The Berkeley Forum*. www.youtube.com/watch?v=LwpMWMpqMYg

Trinidad+Tobago Film Festival [@ttfilmfest]. (n.d.). Emmy Nominee Carla Gutiérrez's #1 Editing Rule and More | ttff talk | ttff/21. YouTube. Retrieved August 31, 2024, from www.youtube.com/watch?v=WwMNFHK3Yxg

USC Annenberg. (n.d.). Annenberg Inclusion Initiative. *Annenberg Inclusion Initiative*. Retrieved April 2, 2023, from https://annenberg.usc.edu/research/aii

Waters, C. (2019, January 27). The Aussie Tech Company Behind the Oscar Nominees. *The Sydney Morning Herald*. www.smh.com.au/business/small-business/the-aussie-tech-company-behind-the-oscar-nominees-20190124-p50tg1.html

# ii. Image Credits

Figure 3.1 A screenshot of "A Better File Rename." Image by author.

Figure 5.1 Carla Gutiérrez editing with senior associate producer Laura Pilloni and producer Katia Maguire. Image credit: Paula Ospina.

Figure 5.2 The crew and stars of "Incognita's Infamous Adventure" prepping a shot on set. Image credit: Sarah Michele Bailey and Allie Sultan.

Figure 5.3 Sarah Michele Bailey and Christopher Bailey face off as Incognita and Baddio – VFX shots like this take enormous amounts of pre-planning and collaboration. Image credit: Chris Hollo and Ryan Rehnborg.

Figure 6.1 An Adobe Premiere timeline with six tracks sorted by dialog, SFX, ambience, and music. Image by author.

Figure 7.1 Víctor Hernández Stumpfhauser, composer for "FRIDA," and cellist Alexa Ramírez recording the score. Image credit: Víctor Hernández Stumpfhauser.

Figure 9.1 An excerpt of a transcript. Image by the author.

Figure 9.2 An excerpt of a caption file. Image by the author.

Figure 10.1 A standardized chart showing a common naming convention for DCPs, based on the InterSociety/ISDCF approach. Image by author.

Figure 11.1 "Body, Home, World" home page. Image credit: Aashish Kumar.

Figure 11.2 The mandala that became a metaphor for the navigation in "Body, Home, World." Image credit: Aashish Kumar.

Figure 11.3 The menu that allows viewers to travel into different parts of the "Body, Home, World" story. Image credit: Aashish Kumar.

Figure 11.4 Once a viewer chose a story, they were able to screen a short documentary segment of the "Body, Home, World" story. Image credit: Aashish Kumar.

Figure 12.1 Final composited still featuring Sarah Michele Bailey as Incognita, Darci Wantiez as Connie, and Tyler Evick as Buddy. Image credit: Chris Hollo and Ryan Rehnborg.

Figure 12.2 Final composited still featuring Sarah Michele Bailey as Incognita and Christopher Bailey as Baddio. Image credit: Chris Hollo and Ryan Rehnborg.

Figure 12.3 Green screen production still, before compositing, featuring Sarah Michele Bailey as Incognita. Image credit: Chris Hollo and Ryan Rehnborg.

Figure 12.4 Green-screen production still, after compositing, featuring Sarah Michele Bailey as Incognita. Image credit: Chris Hollo and Ryan Rehnborg.

Figure 12.5 Rotoscope frame, featuring Christopher Bailey as Baddio. Image credit: Chris Hollo and Ryan Rehnborg.

Figure 12.6 Still from Instagram @Incognitaseries. Image features Sarah Michele Bailey as Incognita. Image credit: Chris Hollo, Ryan Rehnborg, and Sarah Michele Bailey.

Figure 13.1 Carla Gutiérrez directing an actor in voice recording. Image credit: Adrián Gutiérrez.

Figure 13.2 Carla Gutiérrez and team sorting out the story in "FRIDA." Image credit: Paula Ospina.

Figure 13.3 Carla Gutiérrez editing "FRIDA." Image credit: Paula Ospina.

Figure 13.4 Art director and animator Renata Galindo, working on "FRIDA." Image credit: Paula Ospina.

Figure 13.5 Final matchback in the DaVinci studio on "FRIDA." Image credit: Paula Ospina.

Figure 14.1 Title image from "White Nanny, Black Child." Image credit: Courtesy of Doc Hearts.

Figure 14.2 Group session with participants in "White Nanny Black Child." Image credit: Courtesy of Doc Hearts.

Figure 14.3 Overhead shot of a sound bath session with participants in "White Nanny, Black Child." Image credit: Courtesy of Doc Hearts.

Figure 15.1 Alice Guy-Blaché portrait. Image credit: Public domain.

Figure 15.2 Women editing film at the Philadelphia studio of the Lubin Company, called "assembling and joining." 1914. Image credit: Public domain.

Figure 15.3 The title graphic from "A Fool and His Money." 1912. Image credit: Public domain.

Figure 15.4 Portait, Oscar Micheaux. Image credit: Public domain.

# iii. Additional Resources

**Website for Full Audio Interviews with Editors and Transcripts**

- www.melanielarosa.com/contemporarypost, www.contemporarypostbook.com, and at the publisher's webpage for this book.

**The Professional Software and Tools Mentioned in This Book**

- Adobe After Effects
- A Better File Rename
- Adobe Audition
- Adobe Premiere Pro
- Avid Media Composer
- Avid | Media Composer
- DaVinci Resolve
- Davinci Resolve Collaboration
- Frame.io
- LucidLink
- Premiere Team Projects
- ProTools
- Unreal Engine
- Virtual production stages
- Volumetric stages

**For Ongoing Learning About Editors and Editing**

- *Art of the Cut* – a podcast, YouTube channel, and book created by Steve Hullfish. www.aotc.borisfx.com or on podcasting apps and YouTube.
- *Cinemontage* – the website and magazine of the Motion Picture Editors Guide, with many interviews and technical developments: https://cinemontage.org/

- *Edited by* – a digital resource created by filmmaker and professor Su Friedrich to chronicle and compile women editors from throughout film history to contemporary women editors: https://womenfilmeditors.princeton.edu/
- *Editors on Editing* – a podcast and YouTube channel hosted on the site of EditFest, the conference of the American Cinema Editors (ACE) with interviews about many contemporary films: https://editfestglobal.com/editors-on-editing/
- *Manhattan Edit Workshop* – a podcast, YouTube channel, and book created by the New York City-based training institution. www.mewshop.com or on podcasting apps and YouTube.
- *The Rough Cut* – a podcast created by Matt Feury. www.theroughcutpod.com or on podcasting apps and YouTube.
- *Women Film Pioneers Project* – a resource compiling articles, films, photos, and more on hundreds of early women in film from around the world: https://wfpp.columbia.edu/
- Timeline on the technical history of editing, *The Evolution of Video Editing: From the Moviola to Machine Learning* – https://massive.io/filmmaking/the-evolution-of-video-editing/

## Sites for Ongoing Learning and Deeper Technical Dives

- Articles about building your computer, great editing jobs, creating portfolios and other issues: https://editstock.com/blogs/all
- Articles and white papers on the rapidly evolving world of media technologies and standards: https://www.smpte.org/discover
- Articles on evolving standards in digital video: https://www.isdcf.com/
- Aspect ratio cheat sheet: https://www.wearethefirehouse.com/aspect-ratio-cheat-sheet
- Knowledge base for cloud storage and team projects: https://help.frame.io/en/

## Sites to Learn About DCP Creation

- https://dcpmaker.com/docs/what-is-a-distribution-kdm/
- https://www.isdcf.com/
- https://registry-page.isdcf.com/illustratedguide/
- https://service.autodcp.com/long-take-make-dcp/
- https://www.cinematiq.com/posts/what-is-a-dcp

**Sites to Purchase Footage Packs for Use in College Editing Classes**

- Editstock.com provides unedited raw footage packs of independent films, with scripts, vfx, and scores, for editing and practicing. License allows students to use the footage on their reels.
- LinkedIn Learning editing courses: Many courses on LinkedIn Learning come with sample footage packs for students to use.

# Index

For Product Safety Concerns and Information please contact our EU representative GPSR@taylorandfrancis.com
Taylor & Francis Verlag GmbH, Kaufingerstraße 24, 80331 München, Germany

www.ingramcontent.com/pod-product-compliance
Lightning Source LLC
Chambersburg PA
CBHW071118020725
29050CB00015B/69
*9781032640037*